Studies in English and American Literature,
Linguistics, and Culture:
Literary Criticism in Perspective

Editorial Board
Literary Criticism in Perspective

James Hardin (*South Carolina*), General Editor

Stephen D. Dowden (*Brandeis*), German Literature

Books in the series *Literary Criticism in Perspective* trace literary scholarship and criticism on major and neglected writers alike, or on a single major work, a group of writers, a literary school or movement. In so doing the authors — authorities on the topic in question who are also well-versed in the principles and history of literary criticism — address a readership consisting of scholars, students of literature at the graduate and undergraduate level, and the general reader. One of the primary purposes of the series is to illuminate the nature of literary criticism itself, to gauge the influence of social and historic currents on aesthetic judgments once thought objective and normative.

The Critical Reception of Emerson

Since the 1820s, Ralph Waldo Emerson has provoked an unsettled response from his readers, resulting in a highly contentious critical debate. As we approach the bicentenary of Emerson's birth in 2003, opposition remains the defining element: Was he poet or philosopher? Did he liberate American literature or narrow it to a one-dimensional idea? Is his signature concept of self-reliance the most profound contribution to democratic individualism or the epitome of capitalism's impoverished thought? By the mid-twentieth century, the swing between condemnation and celebration of Emerson had given way to the familiar story of his bisected career, which provided a neat structure for viewing his life and work. Now that story is being challenged by the unlikely combination of poststructuralism and textual editing, and with the publication of an amazing repertoire of editions, the Emerson canon is changing. The result is that Emerson criticism now faces a far more complex group of writings than before. One hundred and fifty years after Emerson styled himself an "experimenter" who would "unsettle all things," this new critical history illustrates the continuing, thought-provoking success of that experiment.

Sarah Ann Wider is associate professor of English at Colgate University in Hamilton, New York.

SARAH ANN WIDER

THE CRITICAL RECEPTION OF EMERSON
UNSETTLING ALL THINGS

CAMDEN HOUSE

First published 2000
by Camden House

Camden House is an imprint of Boydell & Brewer Inc.
PO Box 41026, Rochester, NY 14604–4126 USA
and of Boydell & Brewer Limited
PO Box 9, Woodbridge, Suffolk IP12 3DF, UK

ISBN: 1–57113–166–3

Library of Congress Cataloging-in-Publication Data

Wider, Sarah Ann.
    The critical reception of Emerson: unsettling all things / Sarah Ann Wider.
        p. cm. – (Studies in English and American literature, linguistics, and culture.
    Literary criticism in perspective)
    Includes bibliographical references and index.
    ISBN 1–57113–166–3 (acid-free paper)
    1. Emerson, Ralph Waldo, 1803–1882—Criticism and interpretation—
History. 2. Criticism—United States—History. I. Title. II. Studies in English
and American literature, linguistics, and culture (Unnumbered). Literary criticism
in perspective.

PS1637.3 .W54 2000
814'.3—dc21

                                                                00–042929

A catalogue record for this title is available from the British Library.

This publication is printed on acid-free paper.
Printed in the United States of America

For Gail Baker and Paul Schmidt

Splendid moments of conversation
and always, a new Emerson

Contents

Acknowledgments

This volume chronicles the often contentious history of Emerson criticism. For such a book, acknowledgment becomes no simple matter of naming names, especially for one not temperamentally inclined to contention. There are too many people to thank, twenty years worth of conversations — in person and on paper — and so I give up that impossible task. You know who you are. You will see your parts in this project. At this moment, I trust to one of Emerson's fundamental observations. There is reward in work done and done so well. With you, and with the rising voices in Emerson criticism I look forward to thought-provoking years of "glad and conspiring reception."

S. A. W.
March 2000

Introduction: Emerson and His Audiences

REPORTING THE BIRTH of Emerson's first son, Anna Tilden Gannett, former student and vocal member of Boston's most prominent Unitarian Church, used an image by then familiar to Boston. "Mrs. Waldo Emerson has a son," she wrote, "Some ask the question was he born with *wings?*" At the time, the comic question seemed wittily apt. Entering the world the same year as his father's first book, the child was greeted with language reminiscent of the recent reviews of *Nature*. By 1836, reference to the fledgling author was already couched in the language of reputation. The barely-published writer was preceded by his image.

For later generations, 1836 was *the* beginning, and yet as Anna Tilden Gannett's comment suggests, that beginning had a long foreground. By the time she reported Waldo Emerson's birth, she had experienced a good decade of the Emerson image. Early in her journals, as she was contemplating Emerson's move into the ministry, and remembering her own enjoyment of his short-lived time as a teacher, she described him as the "best of this world," a phrase she reserved for the very few individuals to whom she could look for inspiration. Little did she realize that many writers of the next generation would use such "inspiration" as a convenient way to dismiss Emerson. By the century's end, Emerson's image was of a beneficent personality whose writings would not withstand the demands of the new "scientific" system of study. When it came to Emerson's ideas, they were, in Henry Adams' words, "naive."

The early-twentieth-century judgment rang uneasy changes against the comments from Emerson's first public appearances. Hearing Emerson preach, Anna Tilden Gannett, then Anna Tilden, measured the sermons according to the strength of their ideas. Registering her disappointment over one sermon, she noted, "there did not seem as much mind displayed." Debates have raged over the power and quality of that mind; and the reader was as often as much the target as the writer. She was judged by what meaning she took from Emerson's ideas.

While the last sentence could apply equally well to the early nineteenth as to the late twentieth century, it is the latter community of readers for whom this formulation most aptly applies. Since the late 1980s, critics focus their main attention on Emerson's ideas. Philosophy reclaims him. He is heralded as a founding force in American pragmatism and celebrated for his keen-eyed vision of power. His knowledgeable engagement in the sciences of his day is only now coming to light. Political philosophers return to his thought, not as a point of attack but one of origin. The long-debated meaning of self-reliance opens into a revitalized discussion, and Emerson stands on the cutting edge of thought about individualism within democracy. What the turn from the nineteenth to the twentieth century found unimaginable, the turn into the twenty-first century finds incontrovertible. Emerson is an accomplished philosopher and a brilliant writer whose work speaks presciently to an amazing array of academic fields. Rejected as a philosopher at the centenary of his birth in 1903, Emerson approaches his bicentenary with philosophical honors conferred.

This book itself suggests the ever closer affiliation between the disciplines the twentieth century so valiantly attempted to divide. As the calendar year turns from one millennium to the next, Emerson's philosophies — of science, of expression, of political systems, of history, of the individual — are embraced within the variety that now defines literary study.

Part of the Camden House series, *Literary Criticism in Perspective*, this book takes its marching orders directly from the series prospectus. These volumes are designed to "illuminate the nature of literary criticism itself." In the case of Emerson studies the nature of the criticism is decidedly contentious and frequently built on a troubling denigration of other positions. Thus, the temporal inclusiveness of this volume asks its readers to move beyond the ready dismissals that so often characterize the criticism. The denigration of a past audience or a particular group of readers serves no one well. The earliest comments on Emerson, written long before the establishment of "academic" criticism, remain interesting not simply as period pieces but as provocations to future study. But their voices need to be heard. Similarly, the decision to structure this reception history as a study of Emerson's works, rather than of a particular work, counters the narrowing impulse prevalent since the rise of New Criticism. Even with the late century alterations, Emerson criticism privileged a few essays. It is time to expand the Emerson canon beyond *Nature*, "Self-Reliance," "Experience," "Fate," and the wild card fourth essay of either "Circles" or "The Method of Nature" or "The Poet."

Much to its savvy chagrin, this book acknowledges and rebelliously replicates a peculiar pattern within Emerson studies. The critical reception of Emerson, indeed the critical reception of any well-known author, is a study in exclusion. The reasons are both innocuous and troubling.

Sheer volume demands limitation. For this study to become a book that is both affordable and accessible, length is a powerful consideration. At the same time, the necessity of exclusion raises other questions. Whose voices have not been heard? How would those voices change the nature of criticism were they included within the conversation. The opening of this chapter takes one small step in that direction. Before the second wave of feminism and the advent of feminist criticism, who would have thought to begin a book on the critical reception of Emerson with the voice of a Boston woman whose world was not the published word?

There are other voices to be heard, and this book can be considered a point of departure as well as conclusion. The story in this book often is the old story of Emerson criticism with its relatively few questions, its unbending approach and highly exclusive results. This narrative has been undeniably powerful and thus its potent representation in this book. A contentious construct from the late nineteenth and early twentieth centuries, its cumulative force shaped the nature of Emerson criticism even into the renaissance of the 1980s and 1990s. Behind that apparently unified narrative are many others, narratives that were excluded because the definitions of the time did not value them as critical or sophisticated. They are the voices of men and women pioneering adult education, instituting educational reform through experimental schools, creating their own version of a pragmatic self-reliance in the social programs they developed within their communities. These are the voices criticism will pay increasing attention to in the early twenty-first century.

Another group of voices also demands attention. Criticism in the United States is often insular, and Emerson criticism is no exception. For critics within the United States, Emerson's reception in other reading communities is not well known. The critical reception beyond the United States is a complicated set of stories. A clear indication of their importance appears in the late-twentieth-century work on Emerson and Nietzsche. Whether the nineteenth-century reception in France or the late twentieth-century reception in Japan, whether a question of influence or a matter of critical reception, we lack an integrative approach. The challenge for the twentieth-first century is that integration. To bring Emerson's voice to the future of Emerson studies, "There is much to say on all sides" (*Collected Works* 4, 89).

Nearly fifty years separate this volume from the last attempt to assess the whole of Emerson criticism. A quick glance at Frederic Ives Carpenter's *Emerson Handbook* (1953) is a startling reminder of what those years accomplished. Stephen Whicher, Jonathan Bishop, Joel Porte, Lawrence Buell, Barbara Packer, Stanley Cavell, David Robinson, Joel

Myerson: the names we associate with the pivotal studies in Emerson criticism had not yet appeared in print when Carpenter surveyed the state of Emerson criticism in 1953. While review essays and essay collections recently speak to the present and immediate past, no volume brings together the full range of Emerson criticism.

That range illustrates the peculiar difficulty readers have long faced in their interpretation of Emerson. Emerson's words raise unsettling possibilities as he himself acknowledged. In his 1841 essay "Circles" — an essay frequently quoted by critics of both the late nineteenth and late twentieth centuries — Emerson adopts the identity of "experimenter." He writes, "let me remind the reader that I am only an experimenter. Do not set the least value on what I do, or the least discredit on what I do not, as if I pretended to settle any thing as true or false. I unsettle all things" (*Collected Works* 2: 188). Written interpretation, however, rarely rests comfortably with such instruction. Its time-honored purpose has been to settle the meaning of a text, and even late-twentieth-century innovation in literary criticism has done little to change the penchant for settled meaning.

In the case of Emerson studies, criticism meets Emerson's unsettling words with a curious proliferation of myth-making oppositions. There are numerous "Emersons" who have appeared in the criticism, and they generally occur as a dualistic pairing: he is poet or philosopher; he liberates American literature or constrains it; he models a powerful self-reliance or an impoverished self-absorption. As in 1836, Emerson's reputation precedes him and now, as then, the image is not of Emerson's own making. Before we can turn to the works themselves, we must first examine the Emerson myths and their makers.

They are legion. In 1848 James Russell Lowell spoke of Emerson as a "Plotinus-Montaigne." He was idealist and skeptic in one, a kind of living oxymoron who was valued according to the reader's persuasion. Bliss Perry maintained that the division could be seen in Emerson's very face: "Seen from one side, it was the face of a Yankee of the old school, shrewd, serious, practical. . . . Seen from the other side, it was the face of a dreamer, a seer, a soul brooding on things to come, things as yet very far away" (*Emerson Today*, 1931: 1). Nowhere has the divide been greater than in the question of reform. Emerson's still inadequately understood involvement in the reform movements of his day has long been the target of one of the bitterest divisions within Emerson criticism. Was this eloquent advocate for self-reliance finally complicitous in the support of a very suspect status quo? Anti-materialist or faithful bourgeois; freedom affirming speaker or slavery upholding citizen — these dyads show how Emerson's image readily turns ugly in even the politest criticism. And criticism has not always felt a need for such politeness. The oppositions in Emerson criticism frequently take the form of attack. This vitriolic element marks a still unsatisfactorily explained phenomenon in Emerson criticism. What prompts these unrelenting attacks? What kind of reading provokes them?

Each age creates its own duality: infidel or prophet; philosopher or poet; adjourned hope or hopeless burden. Our most recent figuration is only one among the many that Emerson's several audiences have carefully crafted for their own peculiar needs. In the 1990s we asked, was Emerson a profoundly ethical thinker, a pragmatist with his eye on the actual, or did he remain the idealist for whom other people were primarily interesting as metaphysical problems? Our emphasis clearly reflects the decade in which we stood: our concern for ethical thought and action arose at a time when "small" wars weighed heavily upon individual and collective consciences, when the consequences of scientific and technological developments were and are still poorly imagined, when the divisions within the United States began to make Emerson's America look like a strangely unified landscape. We inflect our reading with our own concerns, and yet those very concerns are clearly connected to our predecessors.

No little ink has been spilt in the process of observing, reporting and analyzing such connections. The penchant for self-study in Emerson criticism appears in both the history of the bibliographies and in the narrative assessments of Emerson commentary. Even though the initial bibliographies are now superseded by Robert Burkholder's and Joel Myerson's monumental *Emerson: An Annotated Secondary Bibliography, 1816–1979* (1985, with supplement for 1980–91 published in 1994, and second supplement scheduled for 2003), the bibliographical proclivity appeared early. George Willis Cooke appended a bibliography to the 1892 edition of *Ralph Waldo Emerson: His Life, Writings, and Philosophy* (first published 1881). Cooke expanded this bibliography into a book-length work in 1908, but then for almost forty years as Emerson's academic standing fell, little bibliographical work was published. The mid-1940s updated the bibliography from 1908 to 1945, and in 1953 the most comprehensive modern bibliography appeared in Frederic Ives Carpenter's *Emerson Handbook*. From there, still struggling for a credible place within the academy, Emerson studies assembled its bibliography piecemeal with various checklists appearing at irregular intervals. The resurgence of interest in Emerson created a new demand for a central source. Burkholder and Myerson's became the standard bibliography in 1985; the yearly checklist in the fall issue of *Emerson Society Papers* fills the gap between supplements and Kenneth Walter

Cameron's *The Emerson Tertiary Bibliography* (1986) reminds its audience that even a seemingly exhaustive work like the 1985 volume with its more then 5600 items is incomplete. Cameron concentrates on the areas Burkholder-Myerson omitted or underrepresented: works published outside the United States, American journalism of the nineteenth century and work in "non-literary fields" (4–5).

In the world of narrative interpretation, writers as early as 1850 began to take a retrospective view of the criticism. In his essay for the *Massachusetts Quarterly Review*, Theodore Parker assessed the state of commentary on Ralph Waldo Emerson and found it sorely wanting. He urged his readers to continue their study of Emerson so that a truly valuable criticism could one day be written. Parker's call echoes in the persistently self-reflexive quality of the subsequent criticism. Self-examination became integral: to write about Emerson meant some form of engagement with the past.

So prevalent is this self-reflexive quality that the next two chapters of this book examine the particular genres (biography, essay collections, and review essays) used specifically for guiding the reader's reception of Emerson. These two chapters serve an additional function. Given the massive amount of material written about Emerson, they provide a suggestive microcosm for the critical history as a whole.

No moment defines that history more clearly than Matthew Arnold's 1883 Boston address on Emerson (published in *Discourses in America* in 1885). According to Arnold's verdict, Emerson was neither poet nor philosopher but an inspirational force. While twenty-first-century readers might initially doubt the staying power of those remarks, the seventy years between Arnold's words and Stephen Whicher's enormously influential *Freedom and Fate* betray their active presence. Chapters Three and Four look alternately at their effect on Emerson's reception as artist and as thinker. Even Chapter Five carries the curious echo of the 1880s in the rise of New Criticism and the particular difficulties faced by this approach when it turned its attention to Emerson.

The hold of New Criticism weakened with the sea changes of literary criticism in the 1960s and 1970s, but in Emerson studies the theory wars yielded new interpretations only through the advent of another force. Often assumed to be the drudge work of literary study, editing was anything but dull. It proved to be the most revolutionary force in the criticism, without which the "new" Emersons would be virtually unimaginable.

The final forty years of the twentieth century witnessed the publication of more words by Emerson than were published during his lifetime. At the center of this newly published Emerson stood the sixteen large volumes of his *Journals and Miscellaneous Notebooks, 1960–82*. In

addition, there was a modern edition of the Carlyle-Emerson correspondence, four additional volumes of letters, three of Topical Notebooks, one of poetry notebooks, four of sermons, one of antislavery
writings, three volumes of early lectures and a forthcoming volume of
later lectures. Also to be considered is the reediting — in some cases
substantial — of Emerson's works for the *Collected Works of Ralph
Waldo Emerson* (Harvard, vol. 1–5, 1971–) and the various editions of
the public and private writings of Emerson's friends and family. Chapters Six and Seven chart the effect of these publications — whether the
focus is on Emerson's style, his political stance, his contribution to
philosophy, his use of his reading, or his engagement with science.

While this book studies the critical reception of Emerson, that
phrase itself requires constant scrutiny. As the subsequent chapters will
show, the contentious divisions within Emerson commentary arise from
bitter disputes over audience. Who were the "best" readers of Emerson?
Who claimed the "real" Emerson as their own? Disparagement readily
entered the criticism with a variety of pejorative remarks aimed against
certain audiences. An examination of that disparagement causes the unsavory charges of racism or sexism or classism to redound against the
critic. Here we see the most troubling aspect of literary criticism in its
twentieth-century development. Product of and heir to the mixed
blessing of specialization, it often forwarded interpretation at the expense of understanding. Rather than perpetuating a divide that to some
may seem both necessary and desirable, this book chooses to reevaluate
the division that governed our criticism. If there is a future for Emerson's writing — and most would agree there decidedly is — who would
care to envision its reading occurring only within a closed circle? We
need to consider the various audiences of the past in order to imagine
their future counterparts. In the same way that the theory wars of the
late twentieth century resulted in a novel blend of theoretical and contextual approaches within Emerson criticism, so we need to encourage
a similar reassessment of the unexamined divide between critical and
appreciative, scholarly and amateur.

Were one to ask critics why they have returned time and again to
Emerson as the subject of their work, the answer might well suggest an
unnerving unity across time and reading communities. Responding
within a discussion of how, in the late twentieth century, we teach Emerson, Barbara Packer reminded that particular scholarly audience of a
single image (panel on "The Teaching of Emerson" at the American
Literature Association conference, San Diego 1998). There is, she told
them, something in the language that keeps us coming back. Not a
certain set of ideas but a particular feeling, not a kind of intellectual

duty but an unabashed pleasure. What nobody had yet mentioned, she remarked and implied that most were then thinking, was the unmistakable high we experience when we read Emerson.

I end this introduction by reflecting on that moment and the light it sheds on the genre you are about to read. What this reception history need not do is simply retell the story that is already told in the cumulative volumes of American literary scholarship, in the number of review essays on Emerson, in the opening chapters of book-length studies where the writer lays out with elegance the past that shapes his or her argument. What this particular work can offer is a chance to evaluate a variety of interpretive approaches. We have made meaning from Emerson since his first words were delivered from the pulpit in 1826. The ways in which we have constructed that meaning are several, and they merit close scrutiny. What company are we keeping when we choose a particular method for our work? While we look to the past and hear these critics and the audiences they imagined or addressed, we are equally invited to turn the question on ourselves. What is the function of our criticism at this present time and what response does my allusion yield in you, the particular reader now reading this book?

In working on an author around whom so many words have been centered, it is all too easy to forget the reader. There are, however, many ways of thinking about audience, and I would hope that this reception history could model at least one. In a field marked by division, what does it mean to break down the categories that separate readers? While we are wise to remember differences, we gain nothing by forgetting similarities. The late-twentieth-century scholar is not the late-1930s high school student is not the early-twentieth-century common reader. These individualities matter; interpretation is a product of the reader's role and those roles change with time and shift in affinity. That mid-1930s high school student may well have more in common with the late-twentieth-century professor than she did with the New Critics of her day. As I imagine the real readers of this book — undergraduates in an upper level seminar on Emerson, graduates familiarizing themselves with a field, professors wondering whether this will be a useful book for their students — I wonder what they will learn from these pages. Which readers will they privilege? Which voices will they find most persuasive? The criticism will tell — at least part of the story.

Works Cited

Arnold, Matthew. "Emerson" in *Discourses in America*. London: Macmillan, 1885: 138–207.

Bishop, Jonathan. *Emerson on the Soul*. Cambridge, MA: Harvard University Press, 1964.

Burkholder, Robert E., and Joel Myerson, editors. *Emerson : An Annotated Secondary Bibliography*. Pittsburgh: University of Pittsburgh Press, 1985.

———, editors. *Ralph Waldo Emerson: An Annotated Bibliography of Criticism, 1980–1991*. Westport, CT: Greenwood, 1994.

Cameron, Kenneth Walter. *The Emerson Tertiary Bibliography*. Hartford, CT: Transcendental Books, 1986.

Carpenter, Frederic Ives. *Emerson Handbook*. New York: Hendricks House, 1953.

Cooke, George Willis. *Ralph Waldo Emerson: His Life, His Writings, and Philosophy*. Boston: Houghton, Mifflin and Company, 1881. Expanded edition, 1892.

Lowell, James Russell. *A Fable for Critics*. New York: G. P. Putnam, 1848.

Myerson, Joel. *Emerson and Thoreau: The Contemporary Reviews*. New York: Cambridge University Press, 1992.

Parker, Theodore. "The Writings of Ralph Waldo Emerson." *Massachusetts Quarterly Review* 3 (March 1850): 200–255.

Perry, Bliss. *Emerson Today*. Princeton: Princeton University Press, 1931.

Whicher, Stephen. *Freedom and Fate: An Inner Life of Ralph Waldo Emerson*. Philadelphia: University of Pennsylvania Press, 1953.

1: "Only Biography": Emerson's Peculiar Life

"THERE IS PROPERLY no history, only biography": Emerson's negating affirmation rings with clear meaning for the history of Emerson studies. As Robert Burkholder noted in 1992, there was an overdetermined quality throughout the criticism. Part and parcel of the long-lived contentious element, Emerson's biography exerted a strange and strained influence over the criticism: strange because until recently most biographies agreed that Emerson's life was relatively uneventful; strained because the life without incident collapses upon examination. There were more than enough incidents to render material for a different kind of biography, as Robert Richardson's 1995 biography makes elegantly clear. The biographer's governing assumption determined the relevance of such incidents, and in most cases, that assumption was singular. Whether George Willis Cooke writing before Emerson's death or George Woodberry around the centenary of Emerson's birth or Stephen Whicher at the nadir of Emerson's reputation, Emerson's life was said to be in his works. In 1881 Cooke commented, "The life of Mr. Emerson has been in his thoughts, and these are in his books" (v). In 1959 Whicher echoed, "few men, few writers even, have lived more entirely in the mind than he" (vii).

Numerous biographers chronicled this life of the mind. This chapter can survey only a few. George Willis Cooke's *Ralph Waldo Emerson: His Life, Writings, and Philosophy* (1881) was the first book-length work to situate the study of the writings against the backdrop of the life. First published a year before Emerson's death, it eschewed a connection with biography as such. Cooke's purpose was the study of Emerson's writings, and to that end, the events of the life were used only to comment upon the writing. Similarly, the biographies that appeared shortly after Emerson's death and those prompted by the centenary celebration in 1903 followed this clear subordination. Most notable are the books by Oliver Wendell Holmes, James Elliot Cabot and Richard Garnett in the 1880s and George Woodberry in 1907.

While Cooke articulated the common equation of life and work, his biography stands apart from the other versions of this model. He often suspended chronology to discuss ideas and affiliations. Long extracts from Emerson's writings form the basis of the "biographical" chapters, and yet, Cooke retains a clear emphasis on certain lived (as opposed to written) aspects of Emerson's life. His chapter on Emerson's antislavery activities addresses the question that continues to trouble readers of Emerson: was Emerson soon enough and actively enough involved in the work to rid the country of slavery? Cooke gives the answer that would become common and yet remain unsatisfying for later readers. Citing Emerson's temperament, he notes that "Emerson was neither a zealous agitator nor an enthusiastic worker . . . for he was unfitted for it" (142). Later examinations of Emerson's antislavery activity would tell a markedly different story, particularly about his work in the 1850s, which suggests a powerful form of agitation and enthusiasm that still deserves to be taken more seriously than it has been. Although Cooke holds to the image of the meditative literary figure, he nonetheless refuses to back away from the real support Emerson provided and the real work accomplished through his antislavery addresses. Emerson's next biographer would not claim the same importance for those words.

Following Cooke's organization, Oliver Wendell Holmes added the imprimatur of his own name to the careful commentary on Emerson's life. Part of the popular "Men of Letters" series, Holmes' 1884 biography of Emerson remained the standard model of interpretation well into the twentieth century. To the late-twentieth-century reader, it is sobering to see the social darwinist twist Holmes gives to his obligatory chapter on Emerson's ancestry. In contrast to the late-twentieth-century's psychological interpretation of what it meant for there to be seven generations of ministers in Emerson's genealogical past, Holmes' version plays dangerously and flippantly with the "academic race" from which Emerson descends. While he critiques this social darwinist interpretation — pointing out the selective memory in a family's version of natural selection ("A genealogical table is very apt to illustrate the 'survival of the fittest,' — in the estimate of the descendants," 3), he nonetheless uses the same mythic notions of inheritance, especially in his discussion of Emerson's brother Charles and his early death.

Even before Holmes reaches the chronological point of Emerson's first major publication, he relies heavily on the literary work to shape the discussion. He mentions the lecture topics of the early 1830s and uses them to ground his general comments on Emerson. He writes, "Emerson had the same lofty aim as Milton. . . . In elevation, purity, nobility of nature, he is worthy to stand with the great poet and patriot, who began like him as a school-master, and ended as the teacher in a school-house which had for its walls the horizons of every region where English is spoken. The similarity of their characters might be followed by the curious into their fortunes" (76). As the list of virtues suggests, Holmes' biography is firmly grounded in the nineteenth-century tradition of the exemplary life. In Holmes' version, Emerson counts Milton as a contemporary. The turmoil of the 1840s and 1850s receives scant attention as does the Civil War. Emerson's antislavery activities are barely mentioned, and then only to connect them with an idealist's implausible scheme (Emerson's recommendation that the government buy the slaves out of slavery — an idea recent generations look at with greater interest). In marked contrast to Cooke, Holmes quickly passes over Emerson's support for John Brown. Where Cooke called attention to Emerson's 18 November 1859 and 6 January 1860 addresses, Holmes makes no mention of them. The whole matter of John Brown is dispensed with in a single sentence that makes Emerson a decidedly passive figure: "he took part in the meeting at Concord expressive of sympathy with John Brown" (211). No date is given, and the reader is left to conjecture whether this meeting occurred during the Bleeding Kansas years of the mid-1850s or the Harper's Ferry Raid of 1859.

Assessing the effect of Holmes' biography on the critics' perception of Emerson's antislavery activities, Len Gougeon describes Holmes' Emerson as a distinctly sanitized figure ("Holmes's Emerson and the Conservative Critique of Reform," 1994). The Emerson Holmes created to fit within the "American Men of Letters" was an admirable, slightly antiquated version. "He was a model of patience and good temper" (367). He was a writer designed for the needs of the young: "This was his power, — to inspire others, to make life purer, loftier, calmer, brighter" (373). Ever the idealist in Holmes' biography, Emerson is the isolated figure who gradually disappears into his biographer's apotheosis of him.

Holmes concludes his biography with a reversal that would become the common form of Emerson's supposed life. Announcing the centrality of Emerson's thought, quoting the works at length, examining them primarily from a thematic point of view, the biographer nonetheless ends his study by dismissing the importance of Emerson's works and the thoughts they express. In the end, it is the life after all that matters — not just any life but a highly abstracted version in which neither Emerson's lived experience nor his actual words hold central importance. In Holmes' estimation Emerson's words fall to a lower rank: "His writings, whether in prose or verse, are worthy of admiration, but his manhood was the underlying quality which gave them their true value" (420).

This subordination of life to writing and writing to idealized life continued for the next two decades, and it arguably persisted so far into the twentieth century that its influence on Emerson studies remains palpably present today. For all the biographies of Emerson, there is a persistently static figure in their midst. A strangely monolithic Emerson emerges from the long-standing dualism of "inner" and "outer" lives. This dualism is repeated in the structure of individual biographies and in the relationship between two biographies from the same period. The differing availability of Emerson's texts (what was published, what was still in manuscript) undeniably meant different inflections for this figure, but until Robert Richardson's 1995 biography, there was a haunting continuity among the writers of several generations.

In 1887, James Elliot Cabot provided readers with an extensive amount of new material for their assessment of Emerson. As Emerson's literary executor, he had access to the unpublished papers — sermons, lectures, letters, journals. He knew the material well, having worked with Emerson's daughter Ellen to edit many of the lectures and essays compiled in the 1870s. He entitled the work a "memoir" and defined his position as a simple purveyor of another individual's words: "My aim has been . . . to furnish materials for an estimate of [Emerson], without undertaking any estimate or interposing any comments beyond what seemed necessary for the better understanding of the facts presented" (v–vi). Cabot's concluding clause suggests just how impossible was his imagined task, for "the better understanding" was a decidedly contested area. While Cabot frequently avoids the editorial voice altogether, barely placing any of his own prose between the lengthy extracts from Emerson's writing, he nonetheless speaks directly on several occasions. The telling perception of reform appears here in familiar form. Cabot prefaces his chapter-long discussion of reform with these remarks: "When Emerson said in his letter to Margaret Fuller that he wished the *Dial* might lead the opinion of the day and declare the law on every great interest, he was unconsciously borrowing a tone that did not belong to him. He had no disposition to play the oracle, or to declare the law upon any subject" (2: 39). Akin to Cooke's and Holmes' argument from temperament, Cabot allies Emerson with the by-then familiar image of the solitary thinker.

Polite dissatisfaction greeted Cabot's work. While reviewers dutifully welcomed the inclusion of unpublished writings, they nonetheless lamented a prominent absence. There seemed to be no life in this work. Cabot's Emerson was as "corpse-cold" as the Unitarianism he once criticized. Richard Garnett, who wrote one of the first British biographies of Emerson (1888), found virtue in apparent limitation. He readily put the life in service of the works: Emerson's life was "devoid of incident," and was marked by "nearly untroubled happiness, and . . .

absolute conformity to the moral law" (9). His biography might not rate a mention at all, so similar in form to the other examples in the "life-work" model, except for its anticipation of later interests. Refusing to accept the increasingly isolated figure apparent in Cabot's and Holmes' books, he reminds his readers that Emerson's individualism carried forceful political implications. He also answered the complaints against Emerson's literary style by pointing to the centrality of change in Emerson's work: "This fluid, living, fluctuating beauty . . . makes amends for the want of linked continuity of thought" (196). He praised Emerson's involvement in science: "This is an age of science, and science has found no such literary interpreter as Emerson" (199). His claim would soon be disputed, and Emerson's connection with science would all but disappear for the next ninety years.

Garnett's observations ring closest to the late twentieth century's perspective. Even his choice for an opening scene resonates with later psychological readings. He begins with the day of Emerson's birth, told through the critical perspective of the father's absence. William Emerson enjoys the intellectual pleasures of Election Day while his wife Ruth literally labors at home. His description offers the Freudian twentieth century enticing material.

Every biography met with reviewer dissatisfaction. The assertion that Emerson's life was in his works became the governing truism, but readers wanted a different truth. There must be a dynamic vitality in the life itself. To that end, several works were published that, while not strictly biography, functioned as a kind of biographical genre. Best known is *Emerson in Concord* (1889). Written by Emerson's son and later editor Edward Waldo Emerson, it joins itself with Cabot's work by way of contrast. Praising Cabot's project, Edward Emerson acknowledges its limitations. A "story" written for "the world," it focused by definition on the public life. He, in contrast, would provide the private equivalent: "the citizen and villager and householder, the friend and neighbor" (1).

Other individuals also offered a communal understanding of Emerson's life. Moncure Conway published *Emerson At Home and Abroad* in 1882. Alexander Ireland's *Ralph Waldo Emerson: His Life, Genius and Writings* also appeared in that year. Edward Everett Hale's *Ralph Waldo Emerson* was published in 1893; Frank Sanborn's *The Personality of Emerson* in 1903. A decidedly mixed genre, these works mingle reminiscence with sweeping generalizations with the precisest of detail. They serve as a kind of literary ancestor to the 1980s reappraisal of the "great men" version of biography. Questioning the accuracy of the "spotlight" approach (the subject dominant, while other people are relegated to the background), several writers take the older notion of

Emerson and his Circle as the new way for writing a life. John McAleer's *Days of Encounter* (1984) and Carlos Baker's *Emerson Among the Eccentrics* (published posthumously in 1996, nine years after Baker's death) brought the individuals surrounding Emerson into the foreground. The value of Emerson's work could best be seen through the intellectual exchanges of the time.

For late nineteenth- and early-twentieth-century audiences, the question of value was strangely circumscribed. Cooke offers his study as a means of continuing Emerson's influence in the next generation. Holmes comments that Emerson's influence had always been among the young and suggests that the attraction lay in a certain immaturity of thought, namely idealism. Individuals would move beyond Emerson, but during a certain phase in their lives, Emerson provides a desirable ideal. Writing in 1907, George Woodberry questioned the assumption that Emerson was beneficial for everyone. He reminds his readers that "Emerson's limitations are fundamentally important" and identifies the primary of those limiting elements as Emerson's "doctrine of individuality" (188–89). He argues that "society achieves something which the individual alone cannot accomplish" and links this accomplishment to "civilization." In contrast, Emerson's emphasis on the individual curtails the importance of "institutional life." In consequence, the guarantors of moral life are taken for granted. Woodberry reminds his readers that such an assumption does not work well for "the life of humanity in the race." Emerson's ideas belong only to those with the same "moral ascendancy." For Woodberry, Emerson is no universal source of inspiration but a closely guarded figure whose influence should be limited to its "proper sphere" (188–89).

The social darwinism of Woodberry's "spheres" is as apparent to a late-twentieth-century audience as the discussion of "race" is in Holmes' biography. Interestingly, it is Woodberry's and Holmes' Emerson who became the accepted version for the twentieth century. Woodberry gives the most succinct description of this monolithic figure. In Woodberry's description, Emerson is the "extreme individualist" (32) who lived in a world of his own making. Impervious to circumstances, he survived the deaths of wife, brothers, and son precisely because his primary interest was the formation of the "private soul" (45). Emerson was a "self-isolated thinker" (157), and that isolation took its toll on his human involvement with others. "In the presence of the great miseries of the world he was dumb" (71). Finally, he was a man of the past. He belonged to the age of miracle, not science. For all the attempt to connect Emerson with evolutionary thinking, he was patently a thinker at odds with the Darwinian definition: "In setting up the doctrine of the sovereignty of the individual . . . he put himself in contradiction to the evolutionary conception of humanity at every point" (189–90).

Woodberry's image rang true for several generations of Emerson readers. The isolated thinker set apart from his society became the governing model, and with the development of New Criticism in the 1920s the focus on the text itself continued to overshadow the number of contexts in which Emerson's work might be read. The publication of the *Journals* (1909–14) opened up yet another possibility for reevaluation, but it largely went unexplored. With the exception of O. W. Firkins' *Ralph Waldo Emerson* (1915), Van Wyck Brooks' *Emerson and Others* (1927), and Bliss Perry's *Emerson Today* (1931), few critics undertook a considered reading of the new volumes of Emerson's writing.

Firkins plays well to a later audience. The importance he saw in "ecstasy" and "metamorphosis" established his work as a kind of literary critical forebear to critics of the 1980s and 1990s. Van Wyck Brooks fares less well. Seen as a modernist gone soft, his work now looks unusable to a later audience. To resolve the long-standing complaint that there was never any life in an Emerson biography, Brooks includes the *Journals* in a markedly different manner than did Firkins. Where Firkins quoted passages directly from the journals, respecting their status as independent texts and treating them as the equivalent of any other quoted passage, Brooks freely paraphrases them. He creates dialogue from the fragments of conversation Emerson reports. He asks his readers to imagine themselves in the middle of Emerson's thought. The Emerson who emerges from his pages — whether from the early *Emerson and Others* (1927) or the later *Life of Emerson* (1932) — is a curiously apologetic, self-effacing figure. While Brooks uses the journals to portray experience as if it were only just occurring, his Emerson remains the decidedly "self-isolated thinker." He is an observer, always looking in, never experiencing from within. Reviewing Brooks' *Life* for *American Literature*, Ralph Rusk termed the book "a very interesting experiment in the new biography" but found that its "effort to dramatize the life" of Emerson was a troubling success. Eminently readable, it might engage a popular audience and perhaps even induce the "youthful reader" to think of Emerson as something other than "merely a literary tradition, to be met with only in the pages of a text-book or an anthology" (71). For those already well-acquainted with Emerson's thought, however, the book offered little. Rusk writes, "This book is useless as an aid to an understanding of that part of Emerson's intellectual history which he himself did not make plain" (70–71).

Rusk would become the next major biographer of Emerson, the first modern biographer and the first to emphasize the multi-dimensioned nature of Emerson's life. Editor of the six volumes of Emerson letters (1939), Rusk knew from that textual experience the dynamic shape of Emerson's relationships. He sought to provide the first carefully detailed account of Emerson's life while at the same time reproducing the rich texture of the years through which Emerson lived. His final statement best conveys the Emerson he hoped to render through the five hundred pages of his biography. Commenting on Emerson's grave he writes, "The rough-hewn quartz of the gravestone that was erected within a few years and its inscribed lines on the passive master from 'The Problem' were fitting symbols of only two of the many discordant elements which, as this book has tried to show, were harmonized in Emerson" (*Life*, 508). Clearly writing against the time-honored dualism that structured most representations of Emerson, Rusk reminded his readers that Emerson embodied many elements and not just two. In keeping with the long-standing view of "contradiction," Rusk calls these elements "discordant." Part of the mid-twentieth-century attempt to find "unity" in a writer's work and life, he offers his own version of Emerson's unifying force. Where others would speak of Emerson as "reconciler," Rusk speaks in terms of harmony. His sentence also bespeaks the effect of the biography as a whole. "Were harmonized in Emerson": the passive voice connects Rusk's Emerson with his predecessors'. Despite the intricate detail, Emerson remains the isolated thinker within the world of Rusk's construction.

Rusk's biography received marked praise. In his *Emerson Handbook*, Frederic Ives Carpenter distinguishes Rusk's work from his predecessors'. Quoting Perry Miller's book review for the New York Times, he comments, "Professor Rusk's *Life* realizes for the first time 'the tangible density of Emerson's career'. . . . Emerson the man rather than Emerson the bloodless idealist comes to life in these pages" (41–42). There was still, however, dissatisfaction. For all his words of praise, Carpenter nonetheless began his section on Rusk's biography with caution. Terming it "the most important biography of Emerson," "the most realistic, the most complete, the most scholarly, and the most impartial," his estimation begins to fray through his protestation of "most." While the work "nearly fills the specifications for a 'definitive' biography," he leaves the door open for plenty of future studies. "As criticism, it suffers from the author's primary concern with fact and event, and (possibly) from his too-scrupulous objectivity. The briefer biographies and studies still interpret more clearly and explicitly Emerson's life in its relation to his writings and ideas" (41).

Carpenter gives detailed note to Cabot, Woodberry, Firkins and Perry and honorable mention to Holmes (for his vivid description of Emerson's "ancestral and social background"), Edward Waldo Emerson (like Cabot, "remains valuable as a source book"), Marie Dugard (like Woodberry published in 1907; "best" biography by a European) and Brooks ("using Emerson's own words as far as possible, described the man with unusual insight, and inspired several other scholars of Emerson . . . to employ the same method," 44). Carpenter's assessment, of course, could not include the one volume that would become the most influential work in Emerson studies for at least two decades. Published in 1953, Stephen Whicher's *Freedom and Fate* proved to be a powerfully definitive interpretation for both Emerson's life and work.

Its importance and influence cannot be underestimated, and as such will receive its own place of discussion later in the book. For now, its role in the biographical tradition is foregrounded. Writing at the height of New Criticism's influence, Whicher claimed Emerson even for that tradition. The long-standing complaint against Emerson's contradictory statements, the ongoing criticism of his apparently loose form made him no friends in New Critical circles. Whicher, however, found the way into the vocabulary of his era. Turning to the works themselves, and to the speakers within those works, he represented Emerson's essays as a great tragedy, a compelling drama of ideas. By studying that drama, he argued, the reader discovered "a new dimension of interest to [Emerson's] thought." In contrast to the static idealism of previous works, Whicher offered a different interpretation. He comments, "This book is intended to 'produce' that drama. It traces Emerson's surprisingly eventful voyage in the world of the mind" (vii). Well aware of the commonplace comments about Emerson's uneventful life, he challenges the reader to view events differently. They occur in the mind. He does not, however, challenge the old assumption that distanced Emerson from his lived experience. Placing his work in relation to Rusk's biography, he cites the detail-filled life of that work. It is, he says, "the best portrait we can hope to have of the life Emerson's contemporaries witnessed" (vii). This "best" still falls short of the implied readers' expectations. For all the context Rusk reproduces, "it does not attempt, however, to take us very far into the life of [Emerson's] mind" (vii). Whicher defines that as his project and presents his work as a "complementary sketch of the inner life of Ralph Waldo Emerson, the life — so much more real to him — of which the only record is his works" (vii).

In keeping with the old assumption about the "real" life of Emerson, Whicher expands this old ground to include the journals (just then beginning to be published in the modern edition of the *Journals and Miscellaneous Notebooks*, familiarly abbreviated as JMN). He also transforms the thematic exploration of earlier works into the "drama" he promised in his prefatory remarks. Emerson passes from the "unlimited claim" (26) of a strident self-reliance through a "growing naturalism" to an "ethics of vocation" (171). "His final optimism took him to a wise and balanced empiricism, a detached report on the human condition, and a genuinely humanist ethics. Yet it meant a defeat of his first unworldly protest against the world, a defeat that laid a shadow of promise unfulfilled across his later serenity" (172).

That drama came to define Emerson criticism. Whicher kept the old Emerson largely intact ("self-isolated thinker," revolutionary idealist grown serene in the acquiescence of old age) but offered new life within the old model. Still privileging the life of thought, he argued its difference. It was not, "as it has generally been represented, an eventless and static thing, to be defined and assessed, like merchandise, by a process of random sampling. Apart from the question of their validity, his ideas have an intrinsic interest in their dynamic relations to each other" (173).

It would take another forty years to bring Emerson's ideas out of their long-conditioned state of the invalid (both connotations applicable), but in the mean time Emerson biographical studies followed Whicher's drama, elaborating both the inner life and continuing his concept of "complementary" lives. The late 1970s and early 1980s saw a pairing similar to the Rusk-Whicher match, this time in reverse order: Joel Porte's *Representative Man: Ralph Waldo Emerson in His Time* (1979) and Gay Wilson Allen's *Waldo Emerson* (1981). Porte offered readers a new life of the mind. Twenty-five years after Whicher's account, he shifted the focus to the dynamism Whicher had noted. This nontraditional biography presented the mind in a new fashion, not as drama but as thought itself in process. Porte comments, "the emphasis here is in the right place for a student of Emerson — namely, on the *process* of self-creation and self-discovery. We shall keep our eyes not so much on Emerson the finished thinker as on Emerson in the act of thinking, working his way indefatigably to that land's end which was always just disappearing over the horizon of his thought" (xiii).

Porte's work tells an interesting story in its own process. As Porte himself noted, his book on Emerson was designed to make amends for his earlier comments about Emerson in *Emerson and Thoreau: Transcendentalists in Conflict* (1966). In that book, Emerson came in a poor second to Thoreau. Thoreau lived Emerson's revolutionary ideas while Emerson backed away from the force of his own thoughts. In keeping with Whicher's version, Porte described Emerson as a "prudential thinker" who finally altered his style to meet public taste. The perceived invalidity of Emerson's ideas played heavily into Porte's 1960s argument. Assuming the mid-twentieth century's position on nineteenth-century moral law, he finds Emerson's basis for thought and art "imaginatively insufficient" (191).

The next decade, however, worked a revolution in Porte's thought. Returning to Emerson with JMN in full swing, with Jonathan Bishop's *Emerson on the Soul* (1964) fully integrated into the criticism, and with an emerging new interest in Emerson's style (represented by Lawrence Buell's *Literary Transcendentalism*, 1973) Porte sees a different Emerson. He also acknowledges that he sees Emerson differently. Admitting his growing "sympathy" for Emerson, he strikes a kinship with his nineteenth-century counterparts and places himself in problematic relation to his contemporaries. In 1881 George Willis Cooke asserted that a writer must adopt an "ardent sympathy" with Emerson's ideas were he to write well on Emerson (vi). Porte grounds that approach in Emerson's own aesthetic of interpretation: "'We do not like to hear our authors censured,' as Emerson writes, quoting his friend Elizabeth Hoar, 'for we love them by sympathy as well as for cause'" (xxii). Porte's sentence describes both his own recasting of "sympathy" and defines yet another "new" approach that would become prominent in Emerson studies. He signals the increasing interest in Emerson's contemporaries. The approach traces its origins to the late nineteenth century. It lost currency during the era of New Criticism, and returned in new theoretical and textual dress with the "group portraits" of Carlos Baker and John McAleer. The phrase is Baker's and his book *Emerson Among the Eccentrics*, substantially completed at the time of his death in 1987, exemplifies the growing conviction that Emerson is best represented in the context of his many human relationships.

While Gay Wilson Allen's *Waldo Emerson* (1981) firmly participated in this emerging relational approach to biography, Allen kept the focus, as his title states, firmly on the individual subject. Answering the question "why another biography of Emerson," he cites the profoundly different "intellectual climate" that separates Rusk's world from his. Allen comments, "it is possible to see Emerson today in ways not possible when Rusk wrote his biography" (viii). Identifying both "social and intellectual background" as elements missing from an earlier period, he combines this contextualization with a psychological reading of the work (an approach that would be used more directly in Eric Cheyfitz's *The Trans-Parent: Sexual Politics in the Language of Emerson*, 1981 and Evelyn Barish's *Emerson: The Roots of Prophecy*, 1989) but also as an example of the emerging field of psychology. In Allen's words, Emerson merits the attention of the 1980s because of his ongoing interest in science, a point he argued six years earlier in his "A New Look at Emerson and Science" (1975). Woodberry's dismissal had not yet been successfully challenged. Imagining naysayers, Allen asserts, "the important point is that Emerson was pioneering in psychology" (xi).

In his biography, Allen sought to balance the old dualisms in Emerson studies. He would incorporate both the outer and inner lives, presenting the richness of experience as it was iterated in the events of Emerson's works and days. Assessing the strengths of Rusk's biography against its perceived weakness, Allen suggests he will succeed where Rusk failed. He comments, "Ralph L. Rusk's *Life of Ralph Waldo Emerson* has served well for three decades as the standard reference for the facts of Emerson's life, but it is weak on the intimate, personal life and in literary interpretation, which Rusk deliberately kept to a minimum" (viii). Partaking in the rediscovery of Emerson's poetry, Allen offers his contribution to that often maligned area of Emerson studies. With Holmes he called his readers' attention to Emerson's interest in Persian poetry. But on the issue of reform he parts company with Holmes, offering a much more active Emerson than Holmes displayed. Allen's Emerson turns anarchist at moments during the 1850s.

Allen's great hope was to sustain his three-pronged approach (facts, literary interpretation, inner life) throughout his account of Emerson's life. His title signaled his ambition. "Waldo Emerson": he argues that Emerson's renaming of himself sketched the best portrait of the man. "Waldo" was not simply the necessary adoption for a family with too many "Ralphs." It placed its owner in an ongoing tradition of independent thinking. Like the seventeenth-century Waldensians, he would pursue his own form of Protestantism. Its adoption, as Allen argues, also marks a decided change in Emerson's prose style.

Allen's work met with the divided response typical for Emerson biographies. Reviewers praised its attempt to bring Emerson into the paradigms understood by the twentieth century but noted that like its predecessors it oddly left out the figure at its center. Despite its variety of newness, it maintained the old picture of Emerson as "self-isolated thinker," calmly observing the world that he so provokingly critiqued.

That isolation finally broke with Robert Richardson's 1995 *Emerson: The Mind on Fire*. Well deserving the designation "definitive," it participates in many of the tropes of Emerson criticism while carefully evaluating and revising them. As Richardson tells his readers, the book was originally intended as an "intellectual biography, a companion piece to *Henry Thoreau: A Life of the Mind* (1986). Planning to follow the lead of Whicher and Porte, Richardson thought to study Emerson's intellectual development. His focus was the relation between Emerson's reading and Emerson's writing. That relation could only be told, he discovered, within the context of Emerson's "personal and social life" (xi). In short, he found "Emerson's intellectual odyssey . . . incomprehensible" in their absence. He terms his work "an intellectual biography as well as a portrait of the whole man" (xi), and it is Richardson's success that his work transforms the simple connection "and" into a causal one. The life of the mind emerges through and within the life of the man. In contrast to the earlier models of biography that followed a distinctly spotlight approach, Richardson creates a verbal world in which Emerson's words form only one part. He seamlessly weaves together the household details with Emerson's ongoing reading projects with his various conversations and their continuation across various genres.

Any number of examples could be used to typify Richardson's careful integration of the pieces we have known about Emerson's life and thought: Ellen's death and its relation to Emerson's contracting and expanding universe; Emerson's grueling lecturing trips, the fractured time Emerson experienced in the early 1850s. But no better example can be found than in the discussion of 1839 and the emergence of *Essays, First Series*. Encompassing a series of events that moves from daughter Ellen's birth imagined from Lidian's perspective through Emerson's ongoing work in poetry — his own and others — to the project he created for himself in his first publication of essays, Richardson cannily refuses to subordinate any one activity or event to another. For the reader, they unfold, tracing the process we might imagine Emerson followed as his work mediated between editing his and others' writing within the "spirited household" he and Lidian created. That we are allowed to see this household first, through Lidian's perspective, breaks the reader free of Emerson's supposed isolation. That such details introduce and in no way either compete with or subordinate themselves to the ideas of the essays illustrates how biography can alter the traditional assumption about what is important within a writer's life.

Richardson rapidly draws the biography to a close after the 1872 fire in the Emerson home. The last image of Emerson is of the resolute individual, five nights before his death, already ill with pneumonia, deliberately disassembling the fire in his study fireplace. The compelling figure of Richardson's Emerson is seen best through these carefully wrought vignettes. Neither harmonizer of discordant elements (Rusk) nor educated idealist accepting defeat (Whicher), Richardson's Emerson is the "prophet of individualism" whose prophecy meant a stunningly active engagement of the mind. The last substantive discussion of Emerson's life revolves around his changing engagement with science. In his prefatory remarks on Emerson, Richardson notes, "Emerson lived for ideas, but he did so with the reckless, headlong ardor of a lover. . . . He hated the passive notion of the mind as a blank slate. . . . His main image of the creative mind is of a volcano" (xi). The serene Emerson so popular with late-nineteenth-century biographers, so polemically useful to early-twentieth-century modernists is finally exorcised in Richardson's biography.

Richardson set out to free Emerson from his "vast unfortunate and self-perpetuating reputation" (xi). The various means toward freedom raise two issues well worth considering as we turn from the biographies to the other forms of Emerson criticism. As Richardson points out, his reenvisioning of Emerson's life was made possible by the availability of texts — in this case the letters and papers of Emerson's family and friends. With every expansion of available texts comes another revaluation, but while the increasing number of Emerson's words (the early lectures, JMN, the sermons) began to break down the time-honored model of isolation, only the full correspondence with others provided the evidence of how specious that image was.

Another image lingers and continues to structure Emerson criticism: an uneasy and unsettled divide between critical and appreciative studies. To term this divide unsettled at the turn of the millennium may surprise some readers, for we assume the division between general and scholarly readers took effect long ago. But such division is rapidly changing, as we continue to question the categories of our understanding. In his preface, Richardson distinguishes his biography from "its many worthy predecessors" (xii). A common move in Emerson biography, this remark does not end in the otherwise common conclusion. In contrast to the familiar question of inner versus outer, Emerson the man versus Emerson the bloodless idealist, Richardson marks his work with a difference. "Where this biography parts company with its many worthy predecessors is in its lack of interest in institutional Emersonianism — in Emerson's influence — and in its concentration instead on the man" (xii). Fostering another kind of separation, Richardson creates a provokingly double image through his phrase "institutional Emersonianism." Academic critics have long distinguished their work from Emersonianism — the popular reception of Emerson as a masterful source of inspiration. And yet, Richardson suggests, Emersonianism is not limited to the reader who takes Emerson to heart. There is an institutional version that claims Emerson for its own work and excludes the general reader from any possible understanding. Richardson questions such exclusivity but leaves unanswered the contentious dynamic between classes of readers and kinds of interpretation. This dynamic motivates the criticism, yet remains curiously unexplored. Its suppressed force will emerge in the next chapter where I trace the varied attempts to interpret the tradition of building up and tearing down Emerson's reputation.

Works Cited

Allen, Gay Wilson. "A New Look at Emerson and Science" in *Literature and Ideas in America: Essays in Memory of Harry Hayden Clark.* Robert Falk, editor. Athens: Ohio University Press, 1975: 58–78.

———. *Waldo Emerson.* New York: Penguin Books, 1981.

Baker, Carlos. *Emerson Among the Eccentrics: A Group Portrait.* New York: Viking Press, 1996.

Barish, Evelyn. "The Angel of Midnight: The Legacy of Mary Moody Emerson" in *Mothering the Mind: Twelve Studies of Writers and their Silent Partners.* New York: Holmes and Meier, 1984: 218–37.

———. *Emerson: The Roots of Prophecy.* Princeton: Princeton University Press, 1989.

Bishop, Jonathan. *Emerson on the Soul.* Cambridge, MA: Harvard University Press, 1964.

Brooks, Van Wyck. *Emerson and Others.* New York: E. P. Dutton and Company, 1927.

———. *The Life of Emerson.* New York: E. P. Dutton and Company, 1932.

Buell, Lawrence. *Literary Transcendentalism: Style and Vision in the American Renaissance.* Ithaca: Cornell University Press, 1973.

Burkholder, Robert. "History's Mad Pranks: Some Recent Emerson Studies." *ESQ: A Journal of the American Renaissance* 38 (1992): 231–63.

Cabot, James Elliot. *A Memoir of Ralph Waldo Emerson.* 2 vols. New York: Macmillan and Company, 1887.

Carpenter, Frederic Ives. *Emerson Handbook.* New York: Hendricks House, 1953.

Cheyfitz, Eric. *The Trans-Parent: Sexual Politics in the Language of Emerson.* Baltimore, Md.: The Johns Hopkins University Press, 1981.

Conway, Moncure Daniel. *Emerson At Home and Abroad.* Boston: Houghton, Mifflin and Company, 1882.

Cooke, George Willis. "Emerson's Literary Methods." Boston *Literary World* 11 (22 May 1880): 181.

Dugard, Marie. *Ralph Waldo Emerson, sa vie et son oeuvre.* Paris: A. Colin, 1907.

Emerson, Edward Waldo. *Emerson in Concord: A Memoir.* Boston: Houghton, Mifflin and Company, 1889.

Firkins, O. W. *Ralph Waldo Emerson.* Boston: Houghton, Mifflin and Company, 1915.

Garnett, Richard. *The Life of Ralph Waldo Emerson.* London: W. Scott, T. Whittaker, 1888.

Gougeon, Len. "Holmes's Emerson and the Conservative Critique of Reform." *Southern Atlantic Review* 59: 1 (1994): 107–25.

Hale, Edward Everett. *Ralph Waldo Emerson.* Boston: J. Stillman Smith, 1893.

Holmes, Oliver Wendell. *Ralph Waldo Emerson.* Boston: Houghton, Mifflin and Company, 1884.

Ireland, Alexander. *Ralph Waldo Emerson: His Life, His Genius, and Writings, a Biographical Sketch, to Which Are Added Personal Recollections of His Visits to England, Extracts from Unpublished Letters, and Miscellaneous Characteristic Records.* London: Simpkin, Marshall, 1882.

McAleer, John. *Ralph Waldo Emerson: Days of Encounter.* Boston: Little, Brown, 1984.

Perry, Bliss. *Emerson Today.* Princeton: Princeton University Press, 1931.

Porte, Joel. *Emerson and Thoreau: Transcendentalists in Conflict.* Middletown, CT: Wesleyan University Press, 1965.

———. *Representative Man: Ralph Waldo Emerson in His Time.* New York: Oxford University Press, 1979.

Richardson, Robert D. Jr. *Emerson: The Mind on Fire.* Berkeley: University of California Press, 1995.

———. *Henry Thoreau: A Life of the Mind.* Berkeley: University of California Press, 1986.

Rusk, Ralph. *The Life of Ralph Waldo Emerson.* New York: Scribners, 1949.

———. Review of *The Life of Emerson* by Van Wyck Brooks. *American Literature* 5:1 (March 1933): 70–72.

Sanborn, Franklin B. "Emerson among the Poets" in *The Genius and Character of Emerson: Lectures at the Concord School of Philosophy.* Frank Sanborn, editor. Boston: J. R. Osgood, 1885: 173–214.

Whicher, Stephen. *Freedom and Fate: An Inner Life of Ralph Waldo Emerson.* Philadelphia: University of Pennsylvania Press, 1953.

Woodberry, George Edward. *Ralph Waldo Emerson.* New York: Macmillan Company, 1907.

2: "Our Age is Retrospective": Genres of Reception

REVIEWING SEVERAL BOOKS on Emerson in 1992, Robert Burkholder asked a deceptively simple question: could readers finally accept multiplicity? There were many Emersons and not one. It was time to move beyond the old dualism so potently inscribed in the warhorse label of "Plotinus-Montaigne." Emerson was better understood when granted the multiplicitous interest he evoked. He was as multifaceted as the many faces of his numerous portraits. The word is apt. The portrayal of Emerson has been integral to the critical history. As Burkholder notes in his review essay, criticism was integrally bound to biography. When critics wrote about the work they invariably wrote about the life, using some element of the life to frame interpretation.

Nowhere is the biographical penchant more apparent than in its influence on the many forms of Emerson retrospective. Several genres emerge from this self-reflexive habit: the yearly review in *American Literary Scholarship*, two types of essay collections, and the various review essays in scholarly journals. Although reception history has only come into its own in the 1990s, the previous decades saw an increasing interest in how a field of literary study developed. Combining this general interest with the specific impetus in Emerson criticism to engage with or disengage from the current "Emerson reputation," the last four decades of the twentieth century have given Emerson scholars much pause to consider their work. This chapter explores that predilection for self-examination. Beginning early in the century with Bliss Perry's *Emerson Today* (1931), it measures the fall and rise of Emerson's reputation through the development of an influential form: the essay collection. Evaluation became an ostensibly collective project, and Emerson criticism increasingly paid lip service to multiplicity. The unanswered question remained: did a plurality of voices finally give voice to a plurality of Emersons?

In *Emerson Today*, Bliss Perry encouraged his readers to evaluate the various criticisms of Emerson, as well as their own assumptions about a writer they might not have known how to read well. Acknowledging and addressing the well-known weak spots in Emerson's writing, Perry unfailingly meets each difficulty. But he is no old-fashioned Emersonian. He will not defend what he sees as flawed, and when discussing Emerson's much debated optimism, he does not hesitate to call Emerson's understanding of evil "philosophically inadequate" (131). He does, however, remind the reader that what is inadequate in one arena may be "practically wise" in another. Emerson's refusal to accord evil a positive power is also the refusal of individual or political paralysis. Whether the metaphysical "problem of evil" or the specific question of political reform, Perry presents an Emerson whose eye was trained on probable action. As Perry notes, and as Thomas Wentworth Higginson claimed before him, Emerson's apparent diffidence toward the problems of his day was, in retrospect, a wise choice. By remaining so close to the abstract principle, Emerson guaranteed himself a later audience. Perry suggests that the very generalizations for which Emerson had been and was still blamed were in fact what enabled his writing to remain current. Citing the essay "Politics" as an example he says that the watermark on the page "read[s] unmistakably 1931" (108). As Perry builds his portrait of Emerson, he plays with various versions of double-sidedness. The two faces of Emerson shape his discussion and discussions to come, but in his case, the dualism works in several directions. It divides "the man of his time" from "the man for all time." It also depicts the power of Emerson's apparent contradictions. Perry calls him "this gentlest of iconoclasts" (126) and represents him as an unassuming, mild-mannered individual who quietly left Concord for lecture engagements and as quietly returned, but during the journey it was certain that he had dropped a bombshell somewhere.

For Perry, this strange combination of opposites demonstrates Emerson's power and his importance for the current day. Perry describes Emerson as a reconciler, the individual who brings and holds together particularly recalcitrant parts of human ideas and experience. He quotes James Rowland Angell, then President of Yale, to forward this point. Noting the increasing specialization of knowledge, Angell called for a counterbalancing "inclusive vision." He was not sanguine about its success, however. Although the need became greater with every year, its fulfillment was, in Angell's words, "utterly impossible." Perry agreed with Angell's assessment but not with his conclusion. He also felt the urgent need of a reconciling vision, but unlike Angell, he did not lament its "utter impossibility." Emerson set the precedent. The individual who both understood and shared in "the inclusive vision and the poise of an Emerson" could well create the wide-ranging coordination called for by the times (134).

In much of the book, Perry is clearly on the offensive, constructing his arguments to disarm the attackers. He carefully addresses the issues that plagued readers of Emerson, not only Emerson's views of evil, but also the question of the social irresponsibility of self-reliance, the still troubling question of Emerson's denial of a personal God, the reputed coldness of Emerson's personality, and the notorious inconsistencies found in Emerson's prose. He also offers his own counterweight to such pointed moments of defense. Focusing on Emerson's mysticism, he calls for a much more detailed consideration of what *mysticism* meant in Emerson's context. Pointing the way toward such work, he cites Emerson's varied reading as a clue to the complexity of his thought. Perry also reminds his reader of another aspect of complexity. Turning to the topic of Emerson's poetry, he argues for its reconsideration.

Even with his two-pronged presentation of Emerson as mystic and poet, Perry is still in the precarious position of the individual who answers those who have written before him. Given the nature of the book, an assessment of what had been and was being written about Emerson, such dependence may be inevitable. Noting that Emerson fared better in the critics' eyes than did many nineteenth-century authors, he reminds his readers that critics are not exempt from bias. He questions several of the assumptions governing the attacks on Emerson. Citing the tendency to see the past as a more innocent time, he economically deploys the telling details that prove the opposite. Taking the readers first to the seventeenth and eighteenth centuries, he asks them to think about "innocence" in the flesh. "To imagine John Smith and John Winthrop and William Bradford as novices in human society is amusing," he writes, "Neither were Franklin and Washington and Jefferson precisely babes in the woods" (105). His summation of the nineteenth century is blunt in its description of casualties. "It was," he said, "a turbulent, caustic, questioning, many-sided period." And so, he reminds the reader, was Emerson. He cites Emerson's willingness to let an antislavery speaker into his pulpit and notes his impassioned rhetoric two decades later after the Compromise of 1850. The myth of innocence, he maintains, serves neither the past nor the present well.

Cautioning against the ready acceptance of such myth-making, he also advises a hard look at what reappears over time. Noting the present pessimism, he suggests its occurrence is hardly unique or surprising. The attitude is all too similar to any post-war period, and the writers who claim their view as definitive would be well advised to remember what defines them. Calling up the familiar charges against Emerson, quoting Henry Adams on Emerson's naiveté and Barrett Wendell on his supposed inexperience and James Adams on the "shallow optimism" and the "fatally easy philosophy," he questions the direction of such criticism. These men, he says, are judged by their own words. Borrowing a story from Bret Harte, he suggests that the critics themselves, in their supposed open-eyed wisdom, have been fooled. Like the "pensive and inexperienced Chinaman" of Harte's story, Emerson, "the childlike and bland," wins the game every time (101–04).

At this point in his discussion, Perry steps back, ostensibly apologizing for perpetuating the very behavior he questions. In place of epithet exchange or a game of one-upmanship, he advocates the hard work of literary criticism. He sends his readers back to the texts and then to the contexts.

> The only way to discover the truth or falsity of Emerson's utterances is to read and re-read, with prosaic fidelity, everything that he wrote; to test its pertinence to American life by a thorough-going examination of the history of the United States during his lifetime and of the social, political and literary movements since his death; and finally to test the validity of his counsels to the individual by a dispassionate and unwearied comparison of them with other reports about human life that men have found significant. No such ambitious program has been attempted by any of Emerson's biographers and critics. It is not likely to be undertaken until a great deal of hitherto unprinted material has been published and assimilated. (104)

Perry's comment speaks the story of Emerson criticism in the last forty years. With the publication of the *Journals and Miscellaneous Notebooks*, the "ambitious program" recommended by Perry became reality. At the beginning of his book, he notes the powerful material made available with the 1909–14 publication of the journals. Such material, he let the reader know, was by no means exhausted. Not simply would the journals bear continued study, but the material in manuscript remained to be assessed. He commended that work to the rising students of Emerson, but the next generation would barely be able to begin the project.

The reason for such delay is not simple. In part, the sheer volume of material weighed heavily against quick production. Arthur McGiffert's selection of twenty-five sermons was published in 1938. Rusk's six volume edition of the letters appeared in 1939, but another decade and a half would lapse before any additional manuscripts were turned into print. World War II certainly explains some of the time lag, but other factors were also at work. They come sharply into focus in yet another retrospective work: Frederic Ives Carpenter's *Emerson Handbook*, published in 1953, quietly marked the sesquicentennial of Emerson's birth. In sharp contrast to the celebratory note of 1903, Carpenter's book is cautiously optimistic about the future of Emerson studies. Written as a survey of the existing criticism, it is divided into four sections: biography, prose and poetry, Emerson's ideas, sources and influences. Each section concluded with an annotated bibliography, still useful for what it reveals about the focus of criticism at the time. The books listed reflect both the relatively small amount of "critical" (as opposed to "appreciative") material that had been written on Emerson and also the emergent sense of the critic's necessary specialization. Carpenter includes the nineteenth-century critics such as Matthew Arnold and George Woodberry, but his comments make clear that the way of the future will be with recently published work. Books from the past still remain important or useful for what they reveal about the evolving image of Emerson, but unlike Perry, Carpenter will not claim an unshakable value for them.

Perry encouraged his readers to reconsider the evaluations of the past. What seemed outmoded was, if carefully examined, still current. He writes, "Fifty years in the history of science bring startling changes. Fifty years in the history of literature may mean very little in the way of revaluation. A great book is not a corner lot, whose value must be reassessed from year to year as the population shifts. Are we and our friends of the present decade any better judges of wisdom and beauty as revealed through words than were Charles Lamb and his friends a hundred years ago?" (99–100). Fifty years, however, could make a tremendous difference depending upon the half century in question. Perry's theoretical fifty years describes the distance from Emerson's death to the early 1930s. Fifty years stand between the centenary and the date of Carpenter's *Handbook*. The substantial shift occurred in the twenty years that Perry chose not to imagine. The two decades between Perry's and Carpenter's books witnessed a significant change within the university and beyond it. They represent a profound difference in the evaluation, or rather devaluation, of Emerson in the intellectual market. Part of that change reflected the increasing uncertainty about the relationship between "higher" learning and "general" education. Angell's prediction of an ever-widening gap between fields of knowledge was borne out in the increasingly sharp division between academic disciplines. With the G.I. Bill, the student population changed markedly, bringing individuals into the universities who a generation before would not have been in attendance. The G.I. Bill also brought in an older population whose focus was very much on the world beyond the classroom. At the same time, Carpenter was writing in the wake of not just one, but two wars. The "fashionable pessimism" Perry had limited to a few years became the tenor of the intellectual age. And the pressures of the moment offered little hope for optimism. As Carpenter's book went to press, the hearings run by Joseph McCarthy's House Committee on Un-American Activities were in full swing.

Acknowledging that Emerson's reputation may well have reached its nadir, Carpenter suggests a certain urgency in the need for reevaluation. The United States needed Emerson's words more than ever before. He allies Emerson's support of individual liberty and understanding of democracy with a desirable American dream and tells the reader that the nation is now in danger of abandoning the very ideals on which it was formed. He comments,

> The crucial question for our times is whether these ideals — which Emerson believed eternal — will continue to govern our American thought and practice or whether they were the temporal products of a century of peace and prosperity which a later century of war and depression may discredit and even destroy. . . . If, under the stress of recurrent wars, America should abandon in practice its constitutional liberty and democracy, Emerson's dream would be discredited. And if America should further abandon in theory its historic ideals of liberty and democracy, believing them to be the temporal products of nineteenth century security, rather than eternal truths, then Emerson's American dream would be destroyed utterly. (164)

Carpenter's small plea is buried in the middle of a book of analysis. It is a central point; yet Carpenter makes clear that the readers of his book cannot credibly become polemic champions of democratic freedom. The emergent methods of literary criticism require a different approach. Carpenter writes for an audience of professors and students. He does not imagine, as did Perry, that the general reader will take interest in the book, although he does make a claim both for Emerson's centrality to American culture and the scholar's responsibility to that culture.

That sense of responsibility may well explain Carpenter's clear emphasis on Emerson's ideas. In a book of 250 pages, one hundred of those are dedicated to an examination of the governing intellectual concerns. Another fifty pages can be added to that since the section on sources and influences centers on philosophical rather than literary influence. The question of "whose concerns" merits a double answer. Carpenter shapes his focus according to the criticism. While the issues he designates as central were indeed central to Emerson, his primary concern rests with the critics' interpretations and in particular with the most recent arguments. In his estimation the crux is dualism. Earlier in the book he draws upon Perry's extended discussion of the "two sides of Emerson's face." He returns to it here to explore the "logical paradoxes of his thought" (108). He gives the reader various terms for the division: the "unreconciled" two laws from Emerson's "Ode, Inscribed to W. H. Channing" ("Law for man, and law for thing"), the ideal as op-

posed to the real, Yankee realism as opposed to Transcendental idealism. There are certain predictable oppositions, however, that he pointedly refuses. He will not divide Emersonian mysticism/idealism from
American pragmatism, and in his careful conjoining of the two, he suggests the reconciliation for which scholars had long been searching.

Like Perry, Carpenter saw mysticism as a way around the difficulties
posed by aligning Emerson with idealism. Idealism in the 1950s fared
no better than it had in the 1930s or at the turn of the century. Unlike
Perry, however, Carpenter pursued precisely the kind of study Perry
himself advocated. Perry may have had Carpenter's *Emerson and Asia*
(1930) in mind when he called for continued, careful study in the area.
In both his early and later work, Carpenter is well aware that a focus on
mysticism could short-circuit his cause. Proclaiming its centrality to
American thought, he is nonetheless careful to say that it remains a
"vaguely-defined idea" (113). In the *Handbook*, he offers a range of
definitions as the first part of his specific discussion of "Emerson's
ideas." Surveying the varieties of mysticism with which Emerson was
familiar, he argues that Emerson's eclecticism worked to his advantage.
While he borrowed from many traditions, his whole was greater than
the sum of the parts. The difference, Carpenter maintains, rested in
Emerson's distinct blend of mysticism and pragmatism. Whatever the
"mystic experience" was, Emerson was certain it was governed by "the
pragmatic use of the experience as a means of knowledge" (114).

Distancing Emerson from Romanticism, Carpenter consistently
draws the readers' attention to the ways in which Emerson's concept of
intuition was firmly grounded in a particularly American context.
Looking back to H. D. Gray's 1917 study, he draws an unbroken line
between the first named practitioners of American pragmatism (Peirce
and James) and the "pragmatic mysticism" (Gray's phrase) shaped by
Emerson in his writings. Carpenter himself had published several articles on Emerson and pragmatism. Like mysticism, it was a tricky concept, and to avoid its vague definitions he included sections on both
Peirce and James as well as several introductory pages allying Emerson's
thought with one particular element within pragmatism. "Action" was
necessary for the "true understanding of 'ideas'" (167). Carpenter argues that critics perpetuated a mistaken understanding of Emerson's
idealism and, in consequence, imposed structures that finally did not fit
well with Emerson's words. In the wake of that misunderstanding, Emerson's pragmatism continued to be overlooked and was positively
misinterpreted.

In his connection of Emerson to American pragmatism and its pro-
ponents, Carpenter also sought to dissociate Emerson from other move-

ments and individuals. Chief among those were Romanticism (the site of Yvor Winters' attack) and Puritanism (a favorite term of twentieth-century obloquy as Perry reminded his readers and often seen as the first cause of the Genteel Tradition and as albatross around Emerson's neck). To use the word *Puritanism* in connection with Emerson may well seem a strange and strained combination to those who cut their scholarly teeth on Daniel Howe's, Lawrence Buell's, David Robinson's and Wesley Mott's work on Unitarianism, but in the absence of those studies, Emerson's past was seen as a very different thing. Unitarianism in the 1950s was connected primarily with eighteenth-century Rationalism, a short-lived aberration in the fervor of New England religion. Emerson was coupled with the earlier version of New England Protestantism, and even Perry Miller's work, which did much to wean readers away from the early twentieth-century stereotype of Puritan sterility, reinforced the legacy of Calvinism and continued to obscure the role of Unitarianism. While Carpenter gives perfunctory attention to the relationship between Unitarianism and Transcendentalism, he finds the debate over Emerson's Puritanism much more interesting. Praising Perry Miller's then-recent essay "From Edwards to Emerson" (1940), he connects Miller's work with his own emphasis on mysticism. Glossing a passage from Miller's essay, he writes, "Emerson developed the mystical *implications* of Edward's [sic] Puritan idealism and gave them full, *explicit* realization" (196). Here, as elsewhere, Carpenter's Emerson is the "practical idealist" (167).

There was one other connection. In the early 1950s, Nazism was seen as one form of idealism, and one writer was understood to be its main philosophical support. Friedrich Nietzsche was the figure in question, and as Carpenter was well aware, the connection between Nietzsche and Emerson was well known if not well understood. The urgency Carpenter felt in this area of discussion may well be specific to his time, but the importance of Nietzsche in recent Emerson studies warrants more than a cursory mention of Carpenter's inclusion.

Carpenter clearly saw the connection operating on a different plane than the connections with Romanticism or Puritanism. In each case, the damage by association was local. Yvor Winters might well have harmed Emerson's reputation when he used him to embody his distaste for Romanticism, but the damage though noticeable was not necessarily fatal. Similar to the association with Puritanism, it was an obstacle but one that could be readily overcome by closer study. From Carpenter's perspective, a far greater danger lay in the connection with Nietzsche. Nietzsche's affinity for Emerson, a topic that received some significant attention between 1900 and 1920, became an exceedingly troubling issue given the use of Nietzsche by the Third Reich and the popular identification between Nietzsche's writing and Hitler's action. Carpenter devoted a separate section to a discussion of Nietzsche and Emerson. He bluntly stated his purpose: "If Emerson's ideas, developed by Nietzsche resulted in Nazism, the conclusion is obvious and damning" (246). He notes the "impressive" list of parallels: Emerson's and Nietzsche's ideas of power, the "revolt against the ministry and against orthodox Christianity"; Emerson's self-reliant individual and Nietzsche's "Superman," both authors' treatment of the past; each writer's concept of the poet-philosopher whose language was aphorism.

Nietzsche's indebtedness to Emerson was clear. Carpenter maintained that such debt incurred no obligation on Emerson's part. He separated the two for reasons he deemed fundamental. He distinguished them as writers and he distinguished between their use of dualistic extremes: Nietzsche was the "tragic" writer; Emerson was the "mystic." In Nietzsche, Carpenter sees a thinker for whom the extremes were unrelenting and unameliorated. Emerson's ideas, on the other hand, "were always qualified by other equally important ideas, and balanced against them" (248). In Carpenter's interpretation, Emerson was the reconciler; Nietzsche, the nihilist and finally the more conservative of the two.

Perry had earlier used the image of "reconciler" to describe Emerson. It became the central trope of 1950s criticism. In Sherman Paul's *Emerson's Angle of Vision* (1952), it appeared in Emerson's predominant images: the trope of sight and the image of the circle enabled Emerson to create a union of opposing forces. Stephen Whicher gave a slightly different twist to its meaning. In *Freedom and Fate*, the tone is darker, presenting the reader with the irreconcilable losses encountered when death punctuates life. In his study of Emerson's intellectual development, Whicher divides Emerson's life in two, sharply distinguishing between the affirming vision of the 1830s (culminating in *Essays, First Series*) and the cynicism-bordering skepticism emerging in the 1840s and readily apparent in the essay "Experience," and confirmed by the essay "Fate." As drawn by Whicher, the intellectual life shows an unbalanced dualism. Eight years of "challenge"; forty years of acquiescence. The reconciliation Emerson found himself involved in was not the outwardly directed process emphasized by Perry and Paul and Carpenter but an inward struggle of acceptance and decline.

The Emerson of defeat proved a curiously useful figure in the 1950s and 1960s. Chapter Five will explore the power of Whicher's interpretation in greater detail, but for now, it echoes against the very different Emerson available through the criticism today. While many would argue that this Emerson is not singular — there are many Emersons, not one — acquiescence would not be the likely word for any of them. Today's Emerson is an Emerson of power, a sharp (not sad)-eyed skeptic who saw perpetual questioning as no defeat. He is a pragmatist, a brilliant expositor of life's fragmentary and fractured nature. For this generation, Emerson often becomes the ideal post-modernist, calling attention to language's own limitations, emphatically showing the human constructedness of knowledge. The immediate, if not long, foreground of this late-twentieth-century figure needs its own description. In many ways the development from Edwards to Emerson involved a much shorter critical journey than the forty years it took to move from Emerson the acquiescent, almost tragic writer to Emerson the philosopher of power.

With the increasing professionalization of literary criticism, the scholar's task of mastering his or her field becomes a golden impossibility. Exponential increase is a slight understatement to describe the number of articles and books that appear in any one year. *American Literary Scholarship* certainly rises to that challenge, summing up the year's publications in the various fields of American literature. In its inaugural volume for 1963, it announced its purpose: "The selective evaluation" of "the unmanageable quantity of current American literary scholarship." "Unmanageable" in 1963 meant 1500 items per year; today that number swells to more than 5000.

To understand the change in Emerson criticism at the end of the twentieth century, the student of Emerson criticism would be well advised to read consecutively through the Emerson section of these volumes. Compare, for example, entries from the first year, from the early 1980s and the mid-1990s.

1963:
Although only a few years ago scholars were universally acknowledging an apparent decline in interest in the life and writings of the Sage of Concord and he was being dismissed in some circles as an outdated Victorian, there has recently been a resurgence of interest that belies any supposed loss of vitality. (Walter Harding, 4)

1982:
This year was *Annus Mirabilis* for Emerson, the centenary of Emerson's death, and scholars rose with alacrity to the occasion with contributions appropriate to Emerson's influence on American literature and thought. The preeminent accomplishment, in a galaxy of contributions of high order, was the issuance by the Belknap Press of the two final volumes of *The Journals and Miscellaneous Notebooks of Ralph Waldo Emerson*. . . . The importance to scholars of the avail-

ability of this reservoir of original material cannot be overestimated. (Wendell Glick, 3)

1996:

The political implications of Transcendentalism continue to be a predominant concern for scholars in this field, expressed both in readings of Emerson's ethical and social thought and in reassessments of Thoreau's use of the pastoral mode. Emerson's association with pragmatism, broadly defined, and the intersections of Transcendentalism with pragmatism, rather than their divergences, also continue to be important issues. (David Robinson, 3)

Not only can one trace the development of a particular line of criticism (the focus on metamorphosis in the 1970s or the reemergence of Emerson as philosopher in the late 1980s and early 1990s), but the very categories defining the entry and the implicit assumptions of the year's reviewer offer a wealth of material in the unwieldy process that is literary criticism. The last phrase of that last sentence announces its own end-of-the-twentieth century assumptions. For most decades of the twentieth century, literary criticism was not an unwieldy process at all. For Perry, there were two schools — literary and biographical. The literary sought out the distinctive nature of the writer; the biographical turned the writer into a representative man. The "New" Critics, with their emphasis on the text itself, valued their approach precisely for its clarity. Even the late 1970s and early 1980s with their ongoing theory wars generally found the warring methods easily distinguishable: marxist, psycho-analytic, feminist, post-structuralist, new historicist. The late 1990s refused any such clarity, privileging the richness of interpretation made possible by the disintegration of boundaries.

Essay collections offer another window on the criticism of a particular period. Such collections can be divided into two different types: the topically centered collections (and here one could include special issues of scholarly journals as, for example, the 1997 *ESQ: A Journal of the American Renaissance* special issue on Emerson and Nietzsche), and the representative or historical collections, volumes that attempt to bring together the essays on Emerson deemed best or most influential. In this second category, time frames differ. A collection may cover both the nineteenth and twentieth centuries, as do Thomas Rountree's *Critics on Emerson* (1973) and Robert E. Burkholder and Joel Myerson's *Critical Essays on Ralph Waldo Emerson* (1983) or restrict themselves to a relatively short amount of time (the twenty-five year span covered by Harold Bloom's *Emerson*, 1985).

Milton Konvitz's and Stephen Whicher's *Emerson: A Collection of Critical Essays* (1962) rests on the cusp of these categories. Announcing itself as the first of its kind, it combines the topical with the representative overview. It includes William James's and George Santayana's turn-of-the-century essays on Emerson, as well as a 1903 essay by John Dewey. Most of the essays, however, are from the 1940s and early 1950s, chosen, in Whicher's words, to represent Emerson's "complex intelligence and sensibility" (vi). Whicher's introduction reminds the reader of the "pejorative tradition" in Emerson criticism (vi). He quotes Winters' charge that Emerson was a "fraud and sentimentalist," then distances this volume of essays from such polemical pieces. The naysayers are represented by Santayana (on Emerson's limitations as a social critic) and H. B. Parkes (his 1941 discussion of Emerson's troubling "vision of evil" — or lack thereof). The balance of the volume, however, is devoted to Emerson's "complex intelligence." Many of the essays are centered in a biographical approach as is Henry Nash Smith's "Emerson's Problem of Vocation," an essay that would meet with frequent reprintings for its use of the life (Emerson's own real-life dilemmas about settling into an occupation) to explain the development of a key concept in the Emerson repertoire (the scholar active through his thought). There are essays on Emerson as literary artist (F. O. Matthiessen's treatment of "Days" from *The American Renaissance*, Charles Feidelson's discussion of symbolism, Norman Foerster's essay on the "organic principle" in Emerson's writing), on Emerson as philosopher and social critic (a selection on Emerson as "reconciler" from Sherman Paul's *Emerson's Angle of Vision*, 1952), from Whicher on "Emerson's Tragic Sense," from Perry Miller and John Dewey on Emerson's understanding of American democracy, from Newton Arvin on the "intellectual and emotional discipline" behind Emerson's much maligned optimism (50). Emerson's profile here is less the two-sided idealist/realist than the honest thinker unwilling to confine difficult questions to one-dimensional answers. The key word is thinker: as with Carpenter's *Handbook*, this Emerson is studied more for the interest of his thought than for his writing itself. The emphasis is not surprising, given the "pejorative tradition's" attack against the so-called simplicity of Emerson's ideas and New Criticism's ill fit for discussion of both Emerson's poetry and prose.

While the power of that pejorative tradition was slowly being broken in the 1950s and 1960s, its hold clearly signaled the need for another type of study, one that would bring together within the cover of one volume a variety of commentators on Emerson. This type of collection arose with the initial work of reception history. As critics became increasingly interested in the various responses to the authors they were studying, the words of those audiences became increasingly important. The project was multi-faceted. In some cases (and Emerson is certainly one), a clear part of the project was recovery, or as one essay series entitled it: "recognition" (University of Michigan; Emerson volume edited by Milton Konvitz in 1972). Such collections offered readers a chance to see the author's continuing relevance for themselves. As Rountree notes in his 1973 collection, "the times seem to need critical clarification of Emerson the man and writer." Hoping to provide that clarification through his excerpted essays and books, Rountree offers the reader both "variety" of approach and a path through the "temporal development" of Emerson criticism (10).

In their volume *Critical Essays on Ralph Waldo Emerson* (1983) Burkholder and Myerson also emphasize clarity. The introduction to the volume outlines their purpose "to accurately reflect criticism on Emerson" from his first publication to the 1980s. They provide a useful reminder that certain essays may well be powerful but not representative. They give the example of Francis Bowen's negative response to *Nature*. Often reprinted (it is included in Sealts' and Ferguson's *Nature: Origin, Growth, Meaning*, in Rountree as well as Konvitz *The Recognition of Ralph Waldo Emerson*), its familiarity obscures the strong positive response to a book that the late twentieth century had been taught to think of as the recipient of mostly negative criticism. Seeking to correct the balance, they offer a volume filled with many then unfamiliar voices. If any editors were well positioned to create a representative selection, it was undoubtedly these two. Having edited the extensive, 700+ page *Emerson: An Annotated Secondary Bibliography* (1985), they knew the available material in ways that no other critics could. In part, they hoped to reclaim nineteenth-century commentary for serious consideration. As they comment, the materials from that period were not simply "puffs" or "attacks." Emerson met with "perceptive and judicious criticism" from his contemporaries, a reality that may well have been obscured by the early twentieth century's need to represent the past as a place of immature understanding.

Noticeably absent from the collection are the most vituperative of the 1920s and 1930s attacks against Emerson. Like Konvitz and Whicher, Burkholder and Myerson choose to represent the negative criticism of Emerson through more measured channels (Santayana, as with Konvitz and Whicher, and Henry Brann). Also absent is the essay Whicher termed the most influential for the first fifty years of the twentieth century. Matthew Arnold does not appear, though Frederic Huntington's similarly minded criticism does ("Ralph Waldo Emerson" originally published in the *Independent*, 1882). Burkholder and Myerson presuppose some prior knowledge for readers of this volume. As they say, it "supplements" the standard works, which as of 1983 were the biographies by Cabot, Holmes and Rusk; Perry Miller's various essays, Stephen Whicher's *Freedom and Fate*, Newton Arvin's "The House of Pain and the Tragic Sense"; Henry Nash Smith's essay on "Emerson's Problem of Vocation" and Joel Porte's *Representative Man*. Through their nineteenth-century selections they hope to expand and complicate the reader's understanding of contemporary response to Emerson. With the selections from the twentieth century, they aim to take the reader beyond the Emerson of the 1830s, focusing on essays about Emerson "early" and (truly) "late" in his career and discussions of the ideas with which Emerson worked throughout his life.

Comprehensive in nature, Rountree's, Whicher-Konvitz's and Burkholder-Myerson's collections all take the whole history of Emerson's reception as their province. Lawrence Buell's 1993 *Ralph Waldo Emerson: A Collection of Critical Essays* limits the time frame to a tight but potent thirty years. Identifying the book as the successor to Konvitz-Whicher, Buell emphasizes the problematic nature of Emerson's representative status. While often evoked as a "key reference point" for the "nature of American distinctiveness" (1), the plurality of Emerson's legacies prevents any definitive account. Buell focuses on Emerson as a literary figure and places him first in his cultural context (the influence of Edwards and Franklin in essays by Perry Miller and William Hedges followed by Buell's discussion of "Unitarian liberalism" and its voracity for intellectual culture: "Persian and Indian . . . Judaeo-Christian, Greco-Roman and European" (49). In subsequent sections, Emerson is considered in light of the uneasy dynamic between the individual and society (essays by Whicher, Mary Cayton and Sacvan Bercovitch) and for his influence upon American literature (essays by Harold Bloom and Richard Poirier). Emerson's style forms the central part of this section on Emerson's "literary achievement" (essays by Jonathan Bishop, Julie Ellison and Glen Johnson). The final section (essays by Stanley Cavell and Merton Sealts) questions and redefines "the *practice* of scholarship" (11). The essays chosen for this section represent widely different approaches, thus reminding the reader of Emerson's long-standing identity as intellectual provocateur.

Other collections focus on a single text. Premier among these is Merton Sealts' and Alfred Ferguson's *Emerson's Nature: Origin, Growth, Meaning* (1969, enlarged 1979). Their book includes the text of *Nature* as well as the significant journal, lecture and letter passages behind its composition. The book itself and its publication are described, and the major changes between the 1836 and 1849 editions given. The second section includes a variety of responses to *Nature* targeting the initial comments, the late-nineteenth-century response, the mid-twentieth century, as well as essays from the 1970s included for the second edition. Other volumes followed suit, though in a more modest way and with a clear focus on the book as a teaching text (C. David Mead's *The American Scholar Today*, 1970).

In addition to this focus on individual texts were studies specific to a particular time or place. William Sowder focused on Great Britain and Canada in his *Emerson's Impact on the British Isles and Canada* (1966) and the bibliographical extension in *Emerson's Reviewers and Commentators* (1968). Useful in Sowder's bibliography are its annotations as well as its index.

The most extensive collection of contemporary reviews appeared in Joel Myerson's *Emerson and Thoreau: The Contemporary Reviews* (1992). Quoting the reviews in their entirety (with the exception of the long quotations from Emerson), the volume provides the fullest primary account of the nineteenth-century response. In his introduction, Myerson surveys the concerns that shaped nineteenth-century criticism: Emerson's unconventional style, the ongoing conversation about whether he was a poet or a philosopher, the fears voiced for his "irreligious views" or the praise offered for his return to a pure religious sentiment, and finally the lament in the later reviews of a power repeating itself.

Essay collections are now a staple of literary criticism. In one volume they provide, or hope to provide, a manageable view of the past and/or current criticism. But to create such manageability, the editors must follow their own well-defined selecting principles. These principles articulate the critical tenor of the times. For the student of recent Emerson reception history, the introductions to such collections are a good place to begin, and the best example will be taken out of order, reversing chronology for the present moment.

Harold Bloom's introduction to the volume of essays simply entitled *Ralph Waldo Emerson* (1985) makes no attempt to practice the "no interference" school of criticism. He uses the introduction to comment on the state of Emerson criticism as well as the State of the Nation. He gleefully enters the theory wars, mincing no words about what he thinks of the current affairs. Using Emerson's far from kind description of insipid individuals in a philanthropic meeting, he equates graduate student reading groups with simpering philanthropists. The French theorists fare worse, but it is not simply the university that comes under fire. In his general celebration of Emerson, Bloom finds the perfect moment to criticize the Reagan era and returns to a theme often sounded in Emerson criticism. Emerson, he comments, should not be held responsible for the various uses made of him, though the reader may well wonder about Bloom's choice of image. He writes, "True, Emerson meant by 'his class of persons' men such as Henry Thoreau and Jones Very and the Reverend William Ellery Channing which is not exactly . . . Ronald Reagan and the Reverend Jerry Falwell. . . . Shrewd Yankee that he was, Emerson would have shrugged off his various and dubious paternities" (9–10).

Much of Bloom's introduction is about Emerson refracted through the lens of the 1980s United States. Critical reception was once again merging with the popular, and while only scholarly views of Emerson appear in the selected essays, the opening announces a different book. "Emerson," Bloom writes, "is the mind of our climate," and he wants to make certain that the reader knows which way the wind is blowing. He has no patience with those who ally Emerson with Transcendentalism. Continuing the dissociation from idealism, Bloom calls him "an experiential critic and essayist" (1). He is "the inescapable theorist of all American writing," seen best in the journals, though not in the journals excerpted. As daunting as this may seem, the individual must read them whole, in order to experience "the influx of insight followed by the perpetual falling back into skepticism. They move endlessly . . . knowing always that neither daemonic intensity nor worldly irony by itself can constitute wisdom" (5). Here is the center of Bloom's Emerson, an individual who was the quintessential "American theoretician of power" and a "frightening theoretician" at that. Bloom wonders how Emerson was ever seen as a "sentimentalist," given his commitment to the risky venture of "exalting transition for its own sake" (4). Toward the end of the introduction, he raises the question he considers seminal for Emerson studies. Repeating the importance of Emerson's influence on American literature, he asks the reader to think not about *how* Emerson influenced contemporary and later writers but *why*.

Bloom calls his question "scarcely explored," yet it could be argued that Emerson criticism has spent much of its energy trying to answer it. Carl Bode's rather idiosyncratic *Emerson: A Profile* (1968) takes Emerson's life, inner and outer, as the key to explaining the *why* of Emerson's influence. Bode introduces the essays in his collection by way of an introduction whose title rings the note of an earlier time: "Emerson: Enough of His Life to Suggest his Character." The selections take the reader back to the nineteenth century. Bode includes a section from Edwin Percy Whipple's "Recollections" of Emerson, Holmes' biography, Annie Fields' comments on Emerson as lecturer (first published in *The Atlantic Monthly* in 1883), Charles Eliot Norton's centenary address, as well as excerpts from both Van Wyck Brooks' and Rusk's biographies. The collection concludes with a then recent piece but its province is also the past: H. L. Kleinfield's study of Emerson commentary between his death and the centenary celebrations. Two other recent pieces are included: Jay Hubbell's discussion of the antebellum South's response (or resistance) to Emerson and Daniel Aaron's 1951 discussion of Emerson's complicated stance on democracy (also included in Konvitz and Whicher).

The biographical bent of Bode's choices are apparent, but from the introductory notes for each selection it is clear that the "profile" of the title is double. Not in this case the two sides of Emerson's face, but the criticism, he suggests, draws the portrait of both Emerson the writer *and* of the audience that created such portraits. Thus the selection from Brooks is included in part to show what it was that made Brooks such an effective "popularizer of nineteenth-century American literature" (66). The reprint of Norton's centenary address also serves multiple purposes. Bode clearly enjoys the irony of Andrews Norton's son paying tribute to the individual his father condemned. But Norton's inclusion also serves to distance Emerson from the Genteel Tradition: where Emerson remains interesting in his own right, Norton is no more than a period piece. Perhaps the most revealing comment appears in his introduction to the selections from Annie Fields. Writing well before feminist criticism had given us new interpretive approaches, Bode is clearly uneasy and as clearly radical with his claim that Fields' pieces are "pivotal" to his book. They provide a first hand account from a seasoned member of Emerson's audience. She attended his lectures, read his books and discussed both with him in the literary salon she created in her Boston home. Bode readily imagines the critical comments from his readers. Wouldn't his project be better served by including selections from the recent critics? If he wants to explore the relation between the "character" and the "writer," there was a rich source closer at hand. Bode mentions Matthiessen's "brilliant study of Emerson's mind and art" as well as Paul's and Whicher's work on "Emerson the writer" (77). Granting their excellence, he also sees in their inclusion a dangerous limitation. They were "too coherent for my purpose," he writes, "they gave *their* order to Emerson" (78). In contrast, Annie Fields reportorial style returns the reader to the primary material, in this case the voice of someone who was in one of Emerson's initial audiences.

While Bode's purpose might well strike the later reader as dated ("What I wanted was the feel of Emerson's writing"), his comments on Whicher, et al. and his inclusion of nineteenth-century voices were prescient. Essays and books emergent in the age of New Criticism undeniably sought to give "order" and "coherence" to their subjects (and, some would argue, this is precisely what the critic does whether his methods arise from New Criticism or Marxism or post-structuralism). But as Bode suggests, the order created by the scholar's argument may lose something, may lose much, of the author's writing. With the publication of the hitherto unpublished Emerson as well as the publication of writings by those in the Emerson circle, the old order slowly collapsed. As Bliss Perry predicted in 1931, a thoroughgoing reevaluation of Emerson awaited such availability of the unpublished material. Carpenter echoed this idea with his emphasis on additional unpublished material: writings by not only Emerson but by the other Emersons, Charles and Edward. Trapped by the limitations of his own era's assumptions, Carpenter does not mention the figure whom the 1990s sees as the most important of the "other" Emersons: Mary Moody Emerson.

The late twentieth century defined this extensive process of reevaluation as its work and claimed the absolute importance of these "new" texts of Emerson. A survey of the various essay collections from the last quarter of the twentieth century reveals that the volume bound most tightly to the past and its "pejorative tradition" is the one with least emphasis on JMN. In David Levin's introduction to *Emerson: Prophecy, Metamorphosis, and Influence* (1975), the tone remains apologetic. Levin agrees that Emerson's contradictions solve nothing, and he turns to what he sees as the harder question: "What pernicious effect did his most seductive ideas and attitudes have on the lives and works of his successors"? (vi). Levin hopes to step around this issue by refocusing attention on "Emerson the writer." He terms this concern "central," an assertion borne out by the late 1970s and early 1980s (Porter, Neufeldt, Ellison, and Packer). At the same time, he cannot overlook the ongoing concern with the implications of Emerson's ideas. Many of the papers themselves are response pieces to the recently published and highly influential *Imperial Self* (Quentin Anderson, 1971). Anderson argued that Emerson was a central force in the creation of a conquering United States individualism. Self-reliance writ large became Teddy Roosevelt riding up San Juan Hill.

The tone of the essays in this collection is thus defined by the concept and necessity of response. The critics are clearly responding to the renewed attack on Emerson's concept of self-reliance, but in each case, response suggests a possibility for reinterpretation. The key word for these essays is found in the title: *metamorphosis*. In each essay, Emerson is represented as a figure highly responsive to the issues of his time. This response is in turn characterized by Emerson's ability to transform those issues, reshaping response into creation. As another word in the

title suggests, this book is also about *prophecy*. Not only does it pave
the way for the increased focus on "Emerson the writer," it also signals
what would become the featured essays of Emerson criticism in the
next ten years ("Experience" and "Fate") as well as providing the governing metaphor for Emerson criticism in the early 1980s. *Metamorphosis* would indeed become the most thought-provoking concept for
critics such as Neufeldt and Packer. Not coincidentally, these critics
would also provide the way out of the aging model of the two-part career.

That model died hard, as Robert Burkholder reminds his readers in
his 1992 review essay of several books from the late 1980s. Critics continued to divide Emerson's writing into a dualistic development generally tied into a "pivotal" moment in the life. The pivotal moments
changed: was it the moment in the "Jardin des Plantes" in 1834, high-
lighted as early as Bliss Perry and featured by Matthiessen and Whicher;
or the resignation from the Second Church with its ensuing "problem
of vocation" or the death of Waldo and its subsequent disillusion or an
early crisis of health and faith in St. Augustine? Whatever the moment,
as Burkholder suggests, the effect on the discussion of Emerson's writing was the same: a very few essays came to represent the whole.

While the "small" Emerson canon continues to prevail (and much
could be said about the selections in American literature anthologies as
well as collections specific to Emerson), there has been a gradual
broadening of that canon due to the sheer volume of newly published
Emerson. In his introduction to a collection of essays published for the
centenary of Emerson's death, Joel Myerson succinctly gives the reason
(and implies the need) for a "fresh starting point for studies of Emerson"
(vii). While 1982 offered a convenient time for such reassessment, the
real rationale rested in a more solid foundation than the magic of num-
bers. He writes, "We are now in an excellent position to do this [assess
Emerson's life and writings] because of the quantity and quality of previously unpublished manuscript material made available in the last
twenty years" (vii). The volume of essays lives up to Myerson's promise,
including essays on the lesser known, in some cases then unpublished
or understudied works (Wes Mott's essay on Sermon V; Robert Burkholder's on the contemporary reception of *English Traits* and Ronald
Sudol on the poem "The Adirondacs") as well as demonstrating just
how essential the journals are to the study of Emerson's essays. In each
of the essays, the writer draws upon the journals to illustrate the creation of a text (as in David Hill's discussion of "Experience" and David
Robinson's essay on "The Method of Nature") or uses the journals to

illuminate a part of the life (Evelyn Barish on Emerson's "Crisis of Health"; Glen Johnson on the problem of vocation).

In a review essay published two years later that gives an overview of the 1982 publications, Myerson again emphasizes the importance of editions in Emerson criticism. He maintains that the criticism itself has been shaped first and foremost by the texts available at any given time. Myerson presents four different "stages" of Emerson criticism, each ushered in by the appearance of a new edition of Emerson's works. The first is marked by James Elliot Cabot's *A Memoir of Ralph Waldo Emerson* (1887), adding as it did various lengthy quotations from Emerson's letters and other unpublished writing; the second began with the publication of the ten-volume edition of the Journals (1909–14), offering the most extensive and uninterrupted selection from Emerson's "savings bank." Myerson notes O. W. Firkins' use of this material in his double study of the life and the works in *Ralph Waldo Emerson* (1915), a book still interesting for its emphasis on experience (both the concept and the essay) and experimentation as the central aspects of Emerson's thinking and writing. Other than Firkins, however, Myerson sees a blank twenty years of mostly "appreciative" essays followed by the effect of Ralph Rusk's six-volume edition of the *Letters*. From there followed Rusk's biography and Stephen Whicher's "enormously influential" *Freedom and Fate*. The fourth period coincides with the primary (and still ongoing) phase of publishing previously unpublished manuscript material, in this case the *Early Lectures* and the *Journals and Miscellaneous Notebooks*, a project that appropriately enough concluded its sixteenth and final volume in the centenary year of Emerson's death.

The early 1980s produced their own "annus mirabilis" in Emerson criticism: not only the editions, but also Gay Wilson Allen's biography (*Waldo Emerson*); critical studies by David Robinson, Leonard Neufeldt, Barbara Packer and Julie Ellison; the massive primary and secondary bibliographies (Myerson; Burkholder and Myerson) and four volumes of essay collections. Little wonder that in a review essay in *ESQ: A Journal of the American Renaissance* in 1984, Lawrence Buell called Emerson scholarship a veritable "industry," and contrasted it sharply with the still recent, but increasingly "old days," when the "field was clearly on the move, but [with] its contours . . . reassuringly clear" (117). Buell takes his readers back to the late 1960s, a time when Emerson was still in the process of "being restored to a place of intellectual primacy." The "debunkings of T. S. Eliot and Yvor Winters" were losing their hold, but there was still steady work to be done in that line of recovery. Major studies had been published: Rusk's biography of the "outer" and Whicher's biography of the "inner" lives,

Vivian Hopkins' study of Emerson's aesthetic, Charles Feidelson's work on symbolism, Sherman Paul's on the intellectual background, Jonathan Bishop's "unprecedentedly sensitive account of how Emerson was to be read." The critical studies were good, but not too many. Buell's comment that the key reading of both primary and secondary texts could be accomplished in a single semester would be the envy of any of today's graduate students. Less envious, from the latter's perspective, however, would be the sharply-defined focus of Emerson studies, which would now be seen as exceedingly narrow. In the late 1960s the interest remained with Whicher's Emerson, the Emerson of the 1830s.

While Buell, like Myerson, gives primacy of place to the editions, he also speculates on the role of theory in producing the variety of new studies. He credits Harold Bloom's various discussions of the "anxiety of influence" as the source of the theory interest. By drawing closer attention to the "intertextuality" that emerges from Emerson's much discussed place in American literature, Bloom opened the way to further discussion of language and its discontents. Buell allies the deconstructionist interest in the "fractured" nature of discourse with the heightened and positive attention paid to Emerson's "fragmentary style" and "the elements of indeterminacy and discontinuousness in Emersonian rhetoric" (133). The long-standing liability in Emerson commentary turned out to be an asset after all.

Buell ends his essay by looking to the future. He maintains that a mutual course of learning needs to take place between those who work on a theory-based model and those who work on a text-based model of scholarship. He advises each side to learn from the other. Theory needs to take a fuller account of the actual physical reality of the texts and what they tell us about the compositional process of a particular individual (there is not only a text in Buell's class, there is also an author). In return, those who center their discussions on textual concerns stand to benefit from the theory relevant to "textual evidence."

A decade later, in the publication of *Emersonian Circles* (Wesley T. Mott and Robert E. Burkholder, editors, 1997), that question of "mutual learning" was still in flux. But as Emerson — and the Emerson criticism of the 1980s — had taught us, in flux is power. Describing the then current state of Emerson criticism, Mott and Burkholder noted the impact of both the explosion of Emerson texts and the proliferation of literary theories. They comment, "given the richly pluralistic state of contemporary literary history and criticism, no single methodological approach can hope to establish for our generation a fixed definition of Transcendentalism, the shape of our nation's literary canon, or even the significance of Emerson" (ix). Celebrating a virtue in this indeterminacy, they bring together a variety of approaches on a variety of topics. Far different from the isolated and solitary figure of Whicher's book, the Emerson of these essays is an individual deeply involved in the intellectual issues of his day and with the individuals articulating those issues — whether Henry Thoreau, Mary Moody Emerson or Theodore Parker. One element draws the essays in *Emersonian Circles* together. All are based firmly in what the editors term "empirical research" (x). The focal point involves another center to this particular circle, for the essays themselves honor Joel Myerson, the individual who undoubtedly accomplished the most for textual scholarship in the late twentieth century. Not simply for Emerson but for all the figures in the Transcendentalist group, Myerson has supported and forwarded numerous publications including excellent bibliographies, collections of critical essays, editions of journals and letters, and *Studies in the American Renaissance.*

Essay collections remain an active genre within Emerson criticism. As this volume goes to press, a volume on Emerson's letters was in the planning stages, a Norton Critical edition of Emerson is scheduled to appear in 2000 (Saundra Morris and Joel Porte, editors), and two complementary volumes have just been published within months of each other. Featuring the word *guide* or *companion* in their titles, both illustrate the range of late-twentieth-century interests. Each adopts a different approach to illustrate that range. Oxford's *A Historical Guide to Ralph Waldo Emerson* (Joel Myerson, editor) was in production as this volume went to press. Designed to represent Emerson as a "product of his time," the guide focuses on the various contexts from which Emerson's writings emerged. With essays on individualism (Wesley Mott), religion (David Robinson), science (William Rossi), the antislavery and the women's rights movements (Gary Collison, Armida Gilbert), the volume places Emerson squarely within his time and yet as decidedly locates him within the concerns most interesting to contemporary scholars. The collection also reflects and responds to the longstanding influence of Emerson's biography on the interpretation of his works. Considerations of biography frame the volume. The book opens with a two-fold look at Emerson's life and concludes with an essay on Emerson and his biographers (Ron Bosco).

In the preface to The *Cambridge Companion to Ralph Waldo Emerson* (1999), editors Joel Porte and Saundra Morris announce an unconventional definition for an apparently conventional concept. Their "critical introduction to Emerson's work" is "not intended . . . to provide conventional instruction" (xv). As did Bloom in his 1985 edition of essays, Porte and Morris identify Emersonian provocation as their goal. They foreground the importance of domestic life in the development of Emerson's ideas (essays by Phyllis Cole on Mary Moody Emerson and by Julie Ellison on Waldo's death). In an overview by Saundra Morris, readers are invited to return to the poems, an area that had fallen out of interest since the 1970s. Catharine Tufariello reconsiders the Whitman and Dickinson connections, once thought to be dead-ended through the number of studies prompted by Bloom's anxiety-of-influence model. Familiar ground is revisited: there is an essay on Emerson's theory of nature by Robert Richardson; by Jeffrey Steele on Emerson's, Fuller's, and Thoreau's concepts of friendship; and by David Robinson on the intellectual background of Transcendentalism.

Unlike the 1982 *Emerson Centenary Essays* (Myerson, editor), there was no perceived need for a "fresh starting point" (*Emerson Centenary Essays*, vii). Certain of Emerson's position in the academy, these essays need not so much argue for their interpretations as connect the reader with Emerson's relevance. In essays by R. Jackson Wilson, Michael Lopez, Albert von Frank and Robert Weisbuch, Emerson is a markedly contemporary figure. Describing the 1841 audience for *Essays, First Series*, von Frank turns the mirror toward his readers: "*Essays* is a book for a world in which history is arid, men are washed-out images of deferred or absent authority, virtue is held to be disadvantageous, laws are disbelieved and dishonored, love is personal aggrandizement" (113). Lopez argues the public nature of power as Emerson represented it in *The Conduct of Life*, a book often seen as a private guide for the individual reader. Weisbuch examines Emerson's response to Europe as the "determined resistance" of the individual whose land bore the legacy of colonization (193). Wilson and von Frank explore the role Emerson created for himself as lecturer and essayist. Noting his penchant for words that would shock the listeners, Wilson studies the balance Emerson created between the offensive and decorous statements in the lectures. With Robert Milder he adds a cautionary note, reminding the reader how difficult our retrospective evaluations are. This is largely Milder's point in his essay "The Radical Emerson?" as he attempts to flesh out the lived history of Emerson's engagement in the political world of his day. Von Frank suggests the limits of such caution. While "our" interpretation of the past will never be their experience of the present, his view on Emerson's provocative nature is unwavering: Emerson's writings firmly oppose the way meaning has traditionally been made within Western cultures. In contrast to the processes of defining and enclosing, Emerson was forcefully experimental and expansive. Von Frank comments, "Few such books are as deliberate or as self-conscious as Emerson's *Essays* in setting all that is familiar in the world of the reader against the vision of the author" (107). As Porte reminds the reader in his overview of Emerson's reputation, that confrontation has often been avoided by turning Emerson into "a straw man conveniently set up and knocked down for polemical purposes" (12). Eschewing the polemical, this volume suggests a different model, one in which analysis does not mean attack. Porte and Morris conclude their preface with a set of directions for the reader. "Recent literary theory encourages readers to appreciate texts for their lack of closure and to explore in them whatever is most suggestive, inconclusive, and evolving. Emerson's work seems to thrive in this critical and analytical environment, inviting, as it always does, our active engagement" (xv).

By the late 1990s, the empirical and theoretical forms of scholarship assumed the proportions of an Emersonian dualism greatly in need of the twenty-first century's "active engagement." Unanswered is their relationship to each other. As Philip Gura's concluding essay in *Emersonian Circles* makes clear, the "textual" and the "theoretical" still do not always sit well with one another. Calling for a full scale cultural history of American Transcendentalism (a call that dates back to the 1960s), he cautions the potential authors that they must let theory "inform," not "prejudice" their work (268).

The uneasy alliance is registered in many works of the late twentieth century, suggesting an unresolved problem for the twenty-first. At the same time, the text-based research forms a clear path for immediate scholarship. Nancy Simmons' edition of Mary Moody Emerson's letters and Phyllis Cole's biography of her pave the way for future work on women within the Transcendentalist movement. Len Gougeon's, Linck Johnson's and Albert von Frank's work on Emerson's antislavery involvement opens up a growing field of studies on Emerson's social thought. And Emerson's return to respect within philosophical circles suggests that the once dead question of Emerson as philosopher returns to active and vital life. The next chapters will take up these concerns, but for now this preview of the story concludes with three epigraphs from recent observers of Emerson criticism:

> What each of these new editions promises is that the debate over the most effective means of interpreting Emerson will continue and that new Emersons will inevitably emerge as more primary material is made generally available to scholars.
>
> — Robert Burkholder, *ESQ* 38: 1992, 239

Emerson and his influence, if its nuances and skepticisms were deeply enough explored, would prove disturbing, even disruptive of the critical-interpretive enterprise as most people practice it.

— Richard Poirier, *The Renewal of Literature*, 26

Attempting to write the order of the variable winds in the Emersonian climate is a hopeless task, and the best critics of Emerson, from John Jay Chapman and O. W. Firkins through Stephen Whicher to Barbara Packer and Richard Poirier, wisely decline to list his ideas of order. You track him best, as writer and as person, by learning the principle proclaimed everywhere in him: that which you can get from another is never instruction, but always provocation.

— Harold Bloom in *Emerson*, 8

Works Cited

American Literary Scholarship. Durham, North Carolina: Duke University Press, 1963–.

Bloom, Harold, editor. *Ralph Waldo Emerson*. New York: Chelsea House, 1985.

Bode, Carl. *Ralph Waldo Emerson: A Profile*. New York: Hill and Wang, 1968.

Buell, Lawrence. "The Emerson Industry in the 1980s: A Survey of Trends and Achievements." *ESQ: A Journal of the American Renaissance* 30 (1984): 117–36.

———. *Literary Transcendentalism: Style and Vision in the American Renaissance*. Ithaca: Cornell University Press, 1973.

———, editor. *Ralph Waldo Emerson: A Collection of Critical Essays*. Englewood Cliffs, NJ: Prentice Hall, 1993.

Burkholder, Robert. "History's Mad Pranks: Some Recent Emerson Studies." *ESQ: A Journal of the American Renaissance* 38 (1992): 231–63.

Burkholder, Robert E. and Joel Myerson, editors. *Critical Essays on Ralph Waldo Emerson*. Boston: G. K. Hall, 1983.

———, editors. *Emerson : An Annotated Secondary Bibliography* Pittsburgh: University of Pittsburgh Press, 1985.

Carpenter, Frederic Ives. *Emerson and Asia*. Cambridge: Harvard University Press, 1930.

———. *Emerson Handbook*. New York: Hendricks House, 1953.

Feidelson, Charles, Jr. *Symbolism in American Literature*. Chicago: University of Chicago Press, 1953.

Firkins, O. W. *Ralph Waldo Emerson*. Boston: Houghton, Mifflin and Company, 1915

Gray, Henry David. *Emerson: A Statement of New England Transcendentalism as Expressed in the Philosophy of Its Chief Exponent*. Stanford: Stanford University Press, 1917.

Howe, Daniel Walker. *The Unitarian Conscience: Harvard Moral Philosophy, 1805–1861*. Cambridge, MA: Harvard University Press, 1970.

Konvitz, Milton R. *The Recognition of Ralph Waldo Emerson: Selected Criticism Since 1837*. Ann Arbor: University of Michigan Press, 1972.

Konvitz, Milton R., and Whicher, Stephen E., editors. *Emerson: A Collection of Critical Essays*. Englewood Cliffs, NJ: Prentice Hall, 1962.

Levin, David, editor. *Emerson: Prophecy, Metamorphosis, and Influence*. New York: Columbia University Press, 1975.

Matthiessen, F. O. *American Renaissance: Art and Expression in the Age of Emerson and Whitman*. New York: Oxford University Press, 1941.

Mead, David, ed. *The American Scholar Today: Emerson's Essay and Some Critical Views*. New York: Dodd, Mead, 1970.

Miller, Perry. "From Edwards to Emerson." *New England Quarterly* 13 (1940): 589–617.

Mott, Wesley T. *"The Strains of Eloquence": Emerson and His Sermons*. University Park: Pennsylvania State University Press, 1989.

Mott, Wesley T. and Robert E. Burkholder, editors. *Emersonian Circles: Essays in Honor of Joel Myerson*. Rochester: University of Rochester Press, 1997.

Myerson, Joel, editor. "An Emerson Celebration." *New England Quarterly* 56 (1983): 275–83.

———, editor. *Emerson Centenary Essays*. Carbondale: Southern Illinois University Press, 1982.

———, editor. *Emerson and Thoreau: The Contemporary Reviews*. New York: Cambridge University Press, 1992.

———, editor. *A Historical Guide to Ralph Waldo Emerson*. New York: Oxford University Press, 2000.

Paul, Sherman. *Emerson's Angle of Vision: Man and Nature in the American Experience*. Cambridge, MA: Harvard University Press, 1952.

Perry, Bliss. *Emerson Today*. Princeton: Princeton University Press, 1931.

Porte, Joel and Saundra Morris, editors. *The Cambridge Companion to Ralph Waldo Emerson*. New York: Cambridge University Press, 1999.

Robinson, David. *Apostle of Culture: Emerson as Preacher and Lecturer*. Philadelphia: University of Pennsylvania Press, 1982.

Rountree, Thomas, editor. *Critics on Emerson*. Coral Gables, FL: University of Miami Press, 1973.

Sealts, Merton M. Jr. and Alfred R. Ferguson. *Emerson's Nature: Origin, Growth, Meaning*. Enlarged edition. Carbondale: Southern Illinois University Press, 1979.

Sowder, William J. *Emerson's Impact on the British Isles and Canada*. Charlottesville: University of Virginia Press, 1966.

———. *Emerson's Reviewers and Commentaries*. Hartford, CT: Transcendental Books, 1968.

Whicher, Stephen. *Freedom and Fate: An Inner Life of Ralph Waldo Emerson*. Philadelphia: University of Pennsylvania Press, 1953.

Winters, Yvor. "Jones Very and R. W. Emerson: Aspects of New England Mysticism" in *In Defense of Reason*. Chicago: The Swallow Press, 1937: 262–82.

———. "The Significance of *The Bridge*, by Hart Crane Or What Are We to Think of Professor X?" in *In Defense of Reason*. Chicago: The Swallow Press, 1937: 577–603.

3: Contesting the Poet: Emerson in the Nineteenth Century

ONE NINETY-FIVE PAGE BOOK, two addresses, one public letter, one broadside poem: the publishing record was remarkably short when reviewers began assuming their readers' prior knowledge of Emerson. Writing in 1838, in the wake of the Harvard Divinity School controversy, James Freeman Clarke found only one way to describe Emerson's style. It was, in a word, "Emersonian." For those who kept current in the commentary on American literature, no other explanation was necessary. The writer who had published so few of his words nonetheless established himself (at least in some quarters) as an incomparable essence. Other reviewers were quick to consolidate the particular characteristics that defined this signature style. The assessments were not complimentary. No system could be discerned either in the local structure of an Emerson essay or the large structure of an Emerson volume. In the absence of system, there was an overabundance of contradiction. A decided penchant for paradox appeared in the sentences as did a taste for the epigrammatic. The analogies were "subtle," the associations, "curious" and his illustrations extravagant. Reviewers termed his writing "peculiar."

The assessment stuck, and as quickly as many twentieth-century critics distanced their interpretation from the past, the complicated legacy of the first commentators invariably informed their work. This chapter addresses that complexity by teasing apart the various strands of contention among nineteenth-century audiences. What emerges is the longstanding and still operating uncertainty over Emerson's place: is he poet? philosopher? both? neither? That uncertainty took shape in a particular approach. The earliest commentators on Emerson vigorously engaged in a dualistic process of definition. Evaluation proceeded by comparison, and comparison in this case meant contrast. The comparative method established a number of divisions within the criticism. The present chapter considers three of the most influential debates. It begins with the vexed question of Transcendentalism and Emerson's relation to it. For the nineteenth century, the question as often as not turned into an argument over originality: was Emerson simply an imitation of Carlyle who in turn was an imitation of German idealism?

The comparative approach included audience as well as author, and the middle section of this chapter studies the reviewers' potent characterization of Emerson's readers. From the mid-1830s well into the late century, these readers were invariably represented as young. The opposing side of the equation was either direct or implied: the imagined youth of Emerson's audience contrasted starkly against the maturity or stodginess (depending upon the reviewer's persuasion) of those to whom Emerson did not speak. By late century, the terms began to change. What once had been youth was now merely appreciation. The critical reader of Emerson had entered maturity and by implication left Emerson behind with the once youthful but now supposedly uncritical, appreciative audience.

Nowhere was the comparative approach more influential than in the ongoing debate over Emerson's poetry. While Matthew Arnold's 1883 address in Boston became the most memorable moment in the argument, his words form simply one part of an unsettling dynamic. In an age of categorization, Emerson did not fit comfortably into any designation. The nineteenth-century debates over Emerson's place as a poet offer a particularly vivid example of readers' attempts to make sense of Emerson's highly experimental style.

Style was invariably the question, and the question was not unlike a many-headed monster. Dispatch with one issue and two more appeared in its place. The quickest solution was a deft substitution of language. Were you writing in England, the word for Emerson was "Carlyle." Were you writing in the United States, the word for Emerson was "transcendental." In his frequently reprinted review of *Nature*, Francis Bowen attacked this "revival of the Old Platonic school" for the havoc it wrote (*Contemporary Reviews*, 8. Given the ease of access and the excellence of selection, Joel Myerson's 1992 *Emerson and Thoreau: The Contemporary Reviews* serves as the source for this discussion of the contemporary reception). The American Transcendentalists, he commented, were distinguished by a "*mirage* of meaning" created by a highly affected "poetical vocabulary" (Bowen's emphasis, 8). The consequence was "obscurity of language," rendered in "loose and rambling speculations, mystical forms of expression" and so-called "utterance of truths" that appeared to be no more than "a number of random casts to obtain at last the desired combination" (10).

Many another critic played the Transcendentalist card to the same effect, and the effect was lasting. Frederic Ives Carpenter was still trying to undo the apparent damage in his 1953 *Emerson Handbook*. In 1985, Harold Bloom introduced his edited collection of essays with the following disclaimer: "Emerson is an experiential critic and essayist, and not a Transcendental philosopher. This obvious truth always needs restating, perhaps now more than ever, when literary criticism is so over-influenced by contemporary French heirs of the German tradition of Idealist or Transcendental philosophy" (*Emerson*, 1). Many would take issue with Bloom's genealogy of literary criticism, but in Emerson studies the vexed connection between Emerson and Transcendentalism remains just that. In the mid-1980s Lawrence Buell coined the phrase "the de-transcendentalization of the Emerson image," a phrase that played directly into a longstanding image of Emerson as the inveterate idealist whose individualism produced a highly suspect optimism.

This image is indeed the question. Whose Transcendentalism does it reflect and whose version of Emerson? In the 1997 volume of essays *Emersonian Circles*, editors Wesley Mott and Robert Burkholder remind their readers that the old question had still not been satisfactorily answered: what was Emerson's "influence on New England Transcendentalism" (ix)? For many, Transcendentalism perpetually suffered under its negative reputation. What was needed was a thoroughgoing cultural history that would represent American Transcendentalism in all its complexity. The contributors to the 1984 reference volume *The Transcendentalists: A Review of Research and Criticism* (Myerson, editor) offered an avenue into that study, amply carried out by a number of 1990s publications. Foremost among them are Barbara Packer's entry in the *Cambridge History of American Literature, 1820–1865* (1995) and the two-volume *Biographical Dictionary of Transcendentalism* and *Encyclopedia of Transcendentalism* (Wesley Mott, editor of both, 1996).

While recent criticism devotes increasing energy to rethinking old interpretations of American Transcendentalism, it also turns its attention to the other half of the early reviewers' equation. Robert Burkholder's study of the contemporary reception of *English Traits* (1982) and Lee Rust Brown's study in *The Emerson Museum* (1997) of Emerson's adaptation of European romanticism to American needs take late twentieth-century readers back to England. Twenty years earlier, Kenneth Marc Harris pursued the Emerson-Carlyle connection in his book-length study (*Carlyle and Emerson*, 1978). Fourteen years earlier, Joseph Slater edited the Emerson-Carlyle correspondence in a modern edition (1964), including many more letters than in the 1883 volumes edited by Charles Eliot Norton and bringing the letters into accordance with twentieth-century editing practice. As Slater wrote in his introduction, "There are few works of fiction or fact which tell a fuller story of the life of the mind" (73). Part of the continued interest in intellectual history filtered through a prominent individual (in this case, two), Slater also was fully part of the editing process that would redefine Emerson studies in the last forty years of the twentieth century.

Harris connected the writers through his own definition of Transcendentalism: both Carlyle and Emerson relentlessly explored the illusions by which human beings effectively lived. For Harris, however, there was a key difference: Carlyle argued ceaselessly against human dependence upon illusion; Emerson accepted it as a necessary element in human behavior, and one that need not be combated. Harris in turn suggests reciprocal influence — that Carlyle learned as much from Emerson as Emerson from Carlyle.

The British nineteenth century would have found little merit to such interpretation. From their perspective, there was no doubt who was the teacher, who the pupil. From the first British publication of Emerson, the two were compared; both were generally found wanting but the American version was seen as a poor imitation of a flawed original. Nonetheless there were defenders like John Heraud who in 1841 championed Emerson by turning British reception against itself. Heraud paid the British reading public no compliments. "An English reader takes up a book to avoid the trouble of thinking; he expects to find in it some system to which he can refer as an authority for all his words and deeds" (105). Little wonder, then, over the readers who found Emerson's writing obscure. Down-playing the connection with Carlyle, he notes difference where others saw similarity. The key to that difference was style: where Carlyle "generally deals with recognizable persons and facts. . . . Emerson's thoughts and conceptions lack this sensual embodiment" (105). He praises Emerson's thoughts for their difficulty, allying them with both creation and revelation, and finally defends Emerson from the charges of obscurity by once again reminding his readers of their own limitations. Claiming truth as Emerson's province, Heraud speculates on the inevitable limitations of language. Determined by and bound to its human use, it cannot fully express the larger meaning toward which, under the guidance of an Emerson, it aspires. If his "utterances" are "broken," that is the necessary condition of their existence (106). Only mundane thoughts can be adequately expressed, and thus the charge of obscurity comes back to haunt the individual who cannot fathom Emerson's style.

Style was frequently the critics' concern but so were the ideas it expressed. The complaints against Emerson's religious views are well-known. What is worth repeating here is the duration of that criticism. The uneasiness with Emerson's position was not simply a phenomenon of the Divinity School Address (1838) and its aftermath. As late as *The Conduct of Life* (1860), *Knickerbocker*, in a relatively favorable review, complained to the author, "THOU HAST NO CHRISTIANITY" (297). While praising Emerson for this, his "most practical work," the reviewer reflected on the changes he saw in the twenty-five year "career." Attributing the early style to an immature thinker struggling for expression, the reviewer breathed a sigh of relief over the "comparatively clear and simple" style of the later prose. For all the apparent clarity, however, one thing was still missing. The reviewer comments, "[Emerson] dwells too much in the region of thought" and offers a single corrective to the perceived problem: "Mr. Emerson has still another 'plane' to reach; that of the living, breathing actual, about which he *writes* so well. He has yet to *become* a portion of it" (297).

Today, those who read the contemporary reviews might well come away with the impression that Emerson's excellence remained undiscovered until after his death. The negative criticism is both extensive and biting. The reviewers did not soften their language. When they took issue with Emerson's ideas, they often adopted the tone of attack. Andrews Norton's comments (1838) in the *Boston Daily Advertiser* after the delivery of the Divinity School Address are well-known but certainly not isolated. The reviewers' language was strident and often merciless. Writing for the *Southern Rose* in 1838, Samuel Gilman added his comments to the Divinity School Address controversy. Although he criticized the "bitterness" of the Boston commentary, his tone was hardly cordial. He refers to Emerson's paragraphs as "cloudy," characterized by inconsistency and "incomprehensibilities," a word he substitutes after he first tries out "absurdity" (57). Turning to the 1838 Dartmouth address "Literary Ethics," he has little good to say: "All is dogmatism, assumption, dictation. The writer, we are sorry to say, appears to consider himself the *infallible instructer* of his age" (58). And so the reviews proceed, through the "point-blank contradictions" found in *Essays, First Series*, the pages "disfigured" by the "tricks" Emerson plays with words. The reviewer for the ever-demanding *Athenaeum* asserts that on literary merit alone the essays are "absolutely below criticism" (99).

As Theodore Parker would remark in 1850, Emerson commentary was known for its antagonism. Surveying the written record in the fourteen years since Emerson published *Nature*, he did not hesitate to make swords out of words when the need arose. Buffooning the reviewers, he describes them as fawning public servants whose only method of evaluation was a small-minded measurement of minutiae. In their unctuous dim-wittedness, their criticism became nothing more than self-judgment or, in Parker's more colorful description, the critic practiced a form of legal suicide. His critical death came at his own hand. In contrast to Emerson's non-sectarian, non-partisan approach, the critics adopted a rigid bias. Parker writes, "few men in America have been visited with more hatred, — private personal hatred, which the authors poorly endeavored to conceal, and perhaps did hide from themselves. The spite we have heard expressed against him, by men of the common morality, would strike a stranger with amazement" (228). Pausing for the moment on the defining tone of the negative reviews, it is worth noting that the current reader of Emerson may still be no stranger to this spite.

Antagonism punctuates twentieth-century Emerson criticism. As the chronology unfolds in this chapter and the next, these contentious voices will be heard within their particular contexts, but for now one might easily imagine a genealogy that passed from Andrews Norton to William Maccall to Paul Elmer More to T. S. Eliot to Yvor Winters to Quentin Anderson and Bartlett Giamatti. In each case, commentary on Emerson merged with attack against him, his ideas, and his writings. The resultant situation was never simple. The attacks were launched by individuals who were and remained powerful cultural critics. Their influence lasted into the next generation, and the emerging writers inherited an unresolved antagonism. Given its uninterrupted presence, antagonism itself became part of the criticism, but more than that, Emerson continued to provoke later readers to their own repertoire of heated statements. Parker notes the "personal hatred" in the critics' comments. That tone has curiously been repeated by those for whom Emerson was never a "real" person.

For one relatively short span of time, the antagonism ceased, or rather, was diverted. As the late nineteenth century began increasingly to define itself by its self-advertised modern quality, Emerson became a curiously recalcitrant figure. He was deemed outdated by those for whom any form of idealism was untenable; he was considered dangerous by those who felt his ideas of individuality were appropriate for the select few, but not for the many. The public image of Emerson in the late nineteenth and early twentieth century was often a carefully sanitized one. Where the first half of the century used Emerson's "noble-mindedness" and "purity of character" to serve as a guarantor for the radical nature of his ideas, the late century substituted the character for the writings. Emerson's greatest contribution was, so this image said, not in the much maligned style or in the ideas about individualism or about society or about deity, but in the singular example of a life lived in accordance with principle.

The image was not without its cracks and not without its questioners, but before watching its appearance and questioning its hegemony, the contemporary response proves instructive on two other counts. Not only does it allow us to see how quickly Emerson developed a reputation among the reading public; it also raises the complexity of the many audiences involved in Emerson's work. There was the British audience and the American and a growing interest in nineteenth-century France. As quickly as that sentence is read, the necessity of the plural form becomes apparent. There was no single audience in Great Britain or France, no unified audience in America. There were the critics who condemned Emerson and the critics who praised him; those who found little of permanent value in his work and those who forecast a permanent place for him not solely in American but in world literature. The reviewers, however, were only one class of reader. Nina Baym's reminder in *Novel, Readers, and Reviewers* (1984) is instructive. The readers who were reviewers did not necessarily represent the private individuals who read for quite different reasons.

In the case of Emerson criticism, the complexity of audience is doubly striking. The reviewers readily painted the portrait of the reader they imagined for Emerson's works. The likeness depended upon the critics' taste: for those who found Emerson a writer well worth dismissing, the audience was readily portrayed as "silly" or effectively powerless. Those who heard Emerson's voice as the voice for the future offered a different identity: their reader was young, ready to assume power and potentially well-equipped by Emerson's words. In both cases, the reader was a construct built as part of the reviewer's appraisal. The actual readers were of course different, but their implied counterparts shared a single feature across an ideological divide. Whether Emerson was anathema or aspiration, the reviewers unfailingly characterized Emerson's audience as "young."

The characterization lasted well into the twentieth century and underwent a revealing development in the published record. The early reviewers often used the youth of the audience as a double-edged weapon. For those who saw little worth in Emerson's writing, his attractiveness to a young audience was yet another form of criticism. Commenting on the likely effect of the Divinity School Address, G. T. Davis of the *Boston Morning Post* assumes a short duration for Emerson's ideas, noting their particular and limited appeal. He writes, "We cannot, however, believe that the peculiar views set forth with so much confidence and fascination by Mr. Emerson are likely to take a very deep root in the American heart. They are too dreamy, too misty, too vague to have much effect except on young misses just from boarding school or young lads, who begin to fancy themselves in love" (40). He contrasts these two populations with the "sturdy" American, who will never substitute "instinct" for well-argued "reason." In the same year, Samuel Gilman likewise assured his audience that Emerson's influence would not last. Contrasting the indiscriminate adulation of the young with the balanced assessment of society, he foresaw a short reign of popularity for Emerson: "The young may be dazzled and delighted for a while . . . but society will at length rigidly demand some solid and tangible platform for its belief" (58). Reviewing the *Poems* nearly a decade later, Francis Bowen similarly used the youthful audience as a way of diminishing Emerson. He comments, "At the head of the list stands Mr. Emerson, whose mystical effusions have been for some years the delight of a large and increasing circle of young people, and the despair of the critics" (165).

The critics' despair knew no party lines. As Orestes Brownson noted in his review of *Essays, First Series*, Emerson did not write for the convenience of the reviewers, and those who were largely supportive of Emerson's writing also found that they assigned themselves an exceedingly difficult task. Calling upon the youth of Emerson's audience was one way out of this difficulty. By focusing the attention there, they readily reminded their readers that Emerson could not be dismissed. While the negative criticism relegated Emerson to the young misses and lads, the supporters saw those same youths as the upcoming adult generation. Here, of course, we might expect the "young misses" to disappear, but they do not. The reviewers who lauded Emerson for the strength of his influence on young people were more likely than not to include women as well as men. Emerson's appeal was inclusive. Reviewing *Essays, Second Series*, Margaret Fuller notes the "deep-rooted, increasing" influence "over the younger portion of the community" (114). Writing in 1850, Theodore Parker finds that the influence has not waned: "we think no man who writes the English tongue has now so much influence in forming the opinions and character of young men and women" (227). And when the criticism fell back to the negative, one reviewer framed his comment entirely in reference to Emerson's role as parent to his reading children. Emerson betrayed his responsibility by creating such a dark view of life; from *The Athenaeum's* vantage point, "No father would give it [Emerson's book] to his son as a guide for his 'Conduct of life'" (288).

When later audiences questioned the relevance of Emerson and/or his writings, the subject was often youth. Reviewing *Letters and Social Aims* in 1876, George Lathrop wondered whether Emerson had finally written himself out of his youthful readers. Returning once again to Emerson's lack of system, he doubted that individuals raised on the scientific method would stomach Emerson's unlikely and highly imaginative combinations. Criticizing Emerson's penchant for unending streams of comparison, Lathrop maintained that the absence of critical discrimination could only hurt Emerson's reputation with the youth of 1876. He writes, "it seems to us that he weakens his hold on the younger generation, which is getting a distinctly scientific habit of comparing and contrasting and approximating, and will not allow too large a place to the unsupported intuition, especially if it proceed from a mind which in its several utterances directly conflicts with itself" (335). The public writers in the next generation would dissociate themselves from Emerson. He was increasingly represented as a writer for one's youth and equated with the immaturity one discarded in adulthood. In the published record, this view extended from the 1890s to the 1930s, with a savor of it lingering into the 1960s.

Even in the mid-nineteenth century, reviewers fought hard to keep the association with youth from becoming a liability. The connection with immaturity was always one step away. To accept a different interpretation, one had to be interested from the outset in valuing the new over the well-established. Those who found power in Emerson's writing often attributed it to that force. A reviewer for the *Literary World* blamed Emerson's "cold reception" on the United States' vexed worship of convention. The "new" world held tightly to old-world distinctions. The reviewer comments, "To be free of faults has been a safer passport to the welcome of reviews and drawing rooms than to be fertile of excellence" (170).

While this reviewer identifies reviewers and household readers as one and the same, other reviewers suggested a critical divide between them. The drawing room was likely to be much more hospitable to Emerson's writings because it ostensibly had less invested in the literary status quo. While it might claim authority as a defender of decorum (and here, of course, Emerson received sharp criticism from some quarters), it was not the governing body for faultless expression. As "L. W. B" wrote in a general essay on Emerson for the *Yale Literary Review*, "It is a matter of fact that Mr. Emerson has numerous readers and warm admirers, and with these the cry of Nonsense! Absurdity! Blasphemy! will be of little avail" (248). Written in 1850, the essay marks the publication of *Representative Men*. Although it says little about the book itself, it heralds the publication as a signal event and uses this celebration to chide the naysayers. Suggesting that those who criticize Emerson the most have read him the least the reviewer comments, "The appearance of a new book from the pen of Mr. Emerson is an event of no little interest and importance in the literary world. We say this with confidence, notwithstanding the sneers and deprecations of many excellent people who are ignorant of his productions, and of a few who are not." In contrast to that ignorance, the reviewer encourages readers to undertake a more considered examination of Emerson's writing. "Would it not be more just and philosophical to search for the elements of this power, than to decry and ridicule its effects" (248).

While this review spends relatively little time in that search, using most of the essay to criticize the critics, it does suggest that Emerson's strength resides in his ability to make the old new. The reviewer writes, "by the introduction of new items and new facts, unknown to the commonplace book of the poet, he re-creates old scenes of which the eye was tired, and restores to them more than their primitive interest" (248). Other reviewers agreed with this observation and played their own themes upon the question of originality. Whether Elizabeth Peabody revisiting *Nature* two years after its publication or William Henry Channing praising "The American Scholar," these "warm admirers," celebrated Emerson's "imaginative power" (23) and its contribution to an emerging American literature. Channing bluntly commented, "The public are tired of parrots" (30).

For many readers, Emerson's was a new voice whose excellence was best judged by its effects. He was a catalyst of individual thought; he prompted others to examine and express their own ideas. In the words of one British reviewer (*The Critic*, 1847), "The very controversies occasioned by such a philosophy are beneficial, and therefore we forgive even the most eccentric dreams of Mr. Emerson for the sake of the agitation they make in the stagnant waters of our intellectual kingdom" (191). Those who valued Emerson's words for their provocative power made no secret of their opinion: criticism against Emerson betrayed its stagnant source.

Stagnation appeared in many forms, and reviewers saw Emerson unsettling them all. In the mid-1840s, with the publication of *Essays, Second Series*, a number of reviews cited particular areas most in need of Emerson's force. In Emerson, Margaret Fuller found the necessary corrective to American materialism. A reviewer for *The United States Magazine and Democratic Review* who signed himself "A Disciple" termed Emersonian compensation a clear improvement on the flawed "duty" of Kantian ethics (134). Frederic Henry Hedge maintained that Emerson's power as a philosopher was only beginning to be understood. Singling out the essay "Experience" as his key text, Hedge writes, "What pleases us best in this chapter, is the strong emphasis which it gives to the present momentary life. This is not an article peculiar to the Emersonian philosophy. It is one, perhaps the only one, in which all philosophies unite" (120). Surveying the great names of philosophy's varied schools, Hedge gives Emerson pride of place: "we have met with no statement of this doctrine so adequate to our conception of it" (120).

The favorable reviews also claim power for Emerson's style, though here the challenge was greater. The reviewer for the *United States Magazine and Democratic Review* counters the charge of flawed form by drawing upon Emerson's own aesthetic. Flaws were in fact strengths. "Genuine" thought required "spontaneous and unpremeditated enunciation" (135). Turning criticism into praise, he writes, "The Essays are said to resemble 'a string of mosaics, or a house built of medals.' It may be so; [yet] . . . a single aphorism often suggests the whole economy of being. . . . They are faithful transcripts of thought . . . fragmentary only in so far as the view which every man takes of life must be fragmentary" (135–36). Seven years earlier, during the contention over the Divinity School Address, Theophilus Parsons spoke yet more boldly on behalf of Emerson's prose. "His extraordinary brilliancy of language, his frequent beauty of imagery, and the originality of his style . . . have won for him decided success" (363–7). And yet, the argument from style was the hardest to win. Even the favorable reviewers found that the common literary conventions were mercilessly binding. Few would praise Emerson's writing itself; some would defend it and others would apologize for it, but almost without exception, the favorable reviews knew as little what to make of the style as did those who attacked it out of hand. Theodore Parker allied the self-sufficient sentences with Emerson's own emphasis on individuality. He writes, "It is remarkable to what an extent this individualization is carried. The essays in his books are separate and stand apart from one another, only mechanically bound by the lids of the volume; his paragraphs in each essay are distinct and disconnected, or but loosely bound to one another; it is so with sentences in the paragraph, and propositions in the sentence" (241).

Parker was one of the few who would celebrate Emerson's writing on its own terms. He called the style "one of the rarest beauty; there is no affectation, no conceit, no effort at effect" (241). He was in the minority. Even Margaret Fuller conceded "This writer has never written one good work," though the other half of her sentence is essential to the whole of her meaning. She significantly adds a suggestive qualification. The work is not good, *if* the standard of judgment relies on valuing the whole over the part (115). Late-twentieth-century critics would take this "if" as a signal point of departure, changing the standard for evaluation and in the process changing the way we value Emerson's style. Between Fuller and post-structuralism stands a long history of attempts to comprehend Emerson's writing. The organic principle was called up for active duty; unifying elements were sought in the imagery, in the illustrations, in the essays' speakers. The late twentieth century might well say with the mid-nineteenth: "They cannot analyze it — they cannot appropriate it" (131). We are still looking for ways to write well about Emerson's style.

The nineteenth-century reviewers are instructive in their emphasis. They repeatedly note the spoken origin of Emerson's written work. Mentioning the popularity of Emerson's lectures, they speculate about the effect of an aural form on a written essay. Reviewers also spend a considerable amount of thought on what gives Emerson's statements their force. They repeatedly point to the role of assertion in Emerson's essays. Well worth consulting in these discussions are Parker's essay, Frederic Henry Hedge's piece for *The Christian Examiner* (1845) and the review of *Essays, Second Series* in the *United States Magazine, and Democratic Review*.

As Emerson the man entered old age the lasting effect of his writings was increasingly in question. Reviewers sounded a note of doom. The novelty of the 1840s had worn off long ago. What then was new, was now old. Remarking once more on the "obscurity" of Emerson's writing, a reviewer for the *Athenaeum* returned to the all too apparently disjointed nature of Emerson's sentences. The "infinitely repellant particles" lost their force. They were "completely isolated." Commenting on *Letters and Social Aims* (1876), the reviewer writes, "[Emerson's] influence is on the wane. He wants that last and most useful gift of genius, the power to keep young in society, and to advance with advancing years. Modern work and modern speculation scarcely reach him. . . . He begins to stand, accordingly, among the men of today, a figure of the past, not yet remote enough to be venerable, but unserviceable for present needs" (329).

Others were not so quick to pronounce him "unserviceable." Throughout the 1880s — both before and after his death — writers returned to the prospect of a youthful audience in need of Emerson's voice. The process of revivification began even before Emerson's death with *The Literary World's* celebratory issue in May 1880. Appearing the week of Emerson's birthday, the issue featured a range of materials: critical essays, tributes, poems, excerpts, bibliography. Thomas Wentworth Higginson contributed a piece on "Emerson as the Founder of a Literature." Frederic Henry Hedge claimed Emerson both as philosopher and poet; Walt Whitman disputed the claim to poet or philosopher but granted him the title "Critic, or Diagnoser" (177). George Willis Cooke excerpted a short piece on "Emerson's Literary Methods" from his forthcoming *Ralph Waldo Emerson*. Even with critical comments by

Whitman and measured statements from Higginson, the dominant tone was the superlative. Emerson displayed, "the white splendor of God's grace" (181). His was "a name which this country will cherish as worth more than any crown-jewel or Koh-i-noor diamond" (174); he was "high as the highest, as grand as the grandest" (183).

Over the next two decades, Emerson became that highly venerable figure, rendered eminently serviceable for a society's particular needs. Those needs were rapidly changing and highly contested. From the 1880s through the centenary in 1903, Emerson was reclaimed, disclaimed, heralded for a new audience, restricted to an old. In these years, Emerson decidedly wore two faces. As vigorous a revolutionary as ever, he was lauded for his experimental ventures. As vague an idealist as ever, he was turned into an inspirational friend whose life meant more than his words.

As the reviews of both *Poems* (1847) and *May-Day* (1867) make clear, Emerson's abandonment of traditional form rendered his place among poets uncertain. The mid-nineteenth century judged Emerson to be too "philosophical" in his poetry. The *Athenaeum* saluted the "strong mind" behind the poems but found the poems themselves wanting in "art." They were "effusions" rather than "compositions" and while the pieces were often striking, the whole sounded more like "philosophical memoranda" than poetry (151–52). The *Critic* held to a similar position: "there are in this volume [*Poems*] unmistakable evidences of genius," but the evidence does not add up to poetry. The reviewer's explanation speaks clearly for a mid-nineteenth-century assessment. He faults the poems for being too difficult to remember. Most of Emerson would never pass muster for recitation. Balancing between a criticism of the audience and a criticism of the writer, the reviewer reveals his own ambivalence about the current definitions. Uncomfortable with the philosophical element within the poetry, he nonetheless finds a flaw in the readers' expectations as well. The poet's province is not mathematical proof but an appeal to the heart. Poems should be "memorable" (read "memorizable"). The rhyme and meter should carry the work "into the hearts of men, to mould their thoughts, and be a part of their language." Emerson's irregular rhyme and erratic meter clearly did not accomplish this end, and yet the reviewer was not content to leave the criticism with Emerson. Although he loses patience with the "unintelligible" character of the poems, he nonetheless belittles the readers in the process. Emerson's poetry would never be "popular" nor would it find its way into the numerous poetry "collections of 'Beauties of the Poets,'" volumes which "everybody deems it a duty to possess, even if they never read them" (148–49).

By this estimate Emerson's difference was hardly a liability after all. American reviewers took a similar approach, adopting their own tone of bemusement when trying to comment on the poetry. The reviewer for the New York *Daily Tribune* showed no sympathy for the traditional definitions of poetry and their "martinets in metre." Yet the reviewer himself favored those martinets when it came to Emerson's metric variations. He termed Bryant and Longfellow clearly superior and yet claimed "there is no living man whose writings could so illy be spared from our Literature" (150). Though he could not say why, he nevertheless asserted Emerson's importance, pointing to "the writings themselves" as their own best evidence.

Even at the time of *May-Day's* publication (1867), reviewers were beginning cautiously to praise the prospects Emerson opened through his poetry. In his comparison of the poetry and the prose, David Wasson noted the divergence between the styles. While the prose became ever more dense with ideas, the poetry illustrated a fluency and "richness of color" lacking in the essays. William Dean Howells championed the "irregularity" of the poems and suggested that it would prove a defining characteristic for American poetry in the future. Observing that Emerson had become far more popular than earlier critics ever predicted, he allied that growing popularity to the very change wrought by Emerson's writing. The standards of literary evaluation were no longer what they had been, and while the revolution was not yet accomplished, Howells foresaw Emerson emerging triumphant: "he enjoys a far greater popularity than criticism would have augured for one so unflattering to the impulses that have heretofore and elsewhere made readers of poetry; and it is not hard to believe, if we believe in ourselves for the future, that he is destined to an ever-growing regard and fame" (317).

The revolution was farther from completion than Howells envisioned. It could be argued that such completion came only after the break-up of New Criticism and the reevaluation of aesthetic and literary critical standards that defined the 1970s and 1980s. The established aesthetic for poetry retained its strong hold on popular and critical audiences alike, and while a growing number of voices were championing the new aesthetic, their progress was fitful at best. This can best be seen in the first "critical studies." Blending life and work, such books were largely biographical but included substantial sections devoted to discussion of the works themselves. George Willis Cooke's *Ralph Waldo Emerson* (1881) is illustrative. Written while Emerson was still alive, it announced a two-fold purpose: to instruct and to honor. While the combination might well sound the ominous note of character at the expense of writing, Cooke made clear that such opposition was unnecessary. His book would enable the reader to pursue a "study of the writings of Mr. Emerson" (v). It would also offer the younger generation of readers a clear insight into Emerson's influence.

Cooke defines his work as "interpretation," not "defense or criticism" (v). The categories are his, and the distinction aptly represents the growing divide within Emerson commentary at the end of the century. While later readers might well construe Cooke's "interpretation" as "defense," he thought differently of his approach. He sought to read the writings by the standard Emerson devised. For example, his chapter on poetry begins with the disparaging remarks made about Emerson's poetry when it was first published and suggests that Emerson's poetic interest was closer to the Metaphysical poets than to his nineteenth-century contemporaries. He notes Emerson's so-called inconsistency of form as simply one choice among many and one in keeping with Emerson's ideas about poetry. The approach is cumulative. He singles out "The Sphinx" as the example to demonstrate the successful crafting of idea into poem. Its success outshines the work of the prose: "The Sphinx" "deals with some of the questions discussed in his best essays, and gives a solution even better stated than any he has furnished in prose" (251).

Joel Benton's *Emerson as a Poet* (1883) parts company with the "life and works" model, focusing solely on the poetry. It might well be called the first monograph on Emerson. It took a single premise as its rationale: Emerson's poetry had been unduly neglected and deserved close and critical examination. Benton's concern was as much to diminish the importance of the poetry Emerson did not write as to heighten the credibility of the poetry that he did. Working against the assumptions of what constitutes poetry, Benton suggests that those who do not see poetry in Emerson's poems expose their own narrow standard. He calls this "delinquency of perception" "unhelpable" and looks instead to the "candid and broader view [that] will not believe that beauty exhausts itself in a single type" (48).

The bulk of Benton's discussion is devoted to describing the "type" that Emerson's poetry embodies. He ranges from explication of specific poems to generalizing statements about the poetry itself. He emphasizes the expansive nature of the poetry: it is known through its "constant relation to the breadth of some endless horizon" (49). It offers "one broad synthesis after another in close succession" (85). He confers the key word of nineteenth-century praise: the poems are "suggestive." Their excellence lies in Emerson's ability to "overload his words with the most urgent stress of beauty and meaning" (50). Benton unapologetically gives the greatest importance to the part, not the whole, and draws his reader's attention to the various devices Emerson used to create that "most urgent stress." Elsewhere he calls that "stress" a "polarized vitality" (85). He cites the deliberate disruption of meter (as seen in "The Amulet") and comments on the power Emerson creates through brevity of line or phrase. He argues for the careful composition of the poems, citing the precision of Emerson's diction. He notes the importance of the speaker's perspective within the poems (25) and agrees with his contemporary William Torrey Harris that Emerson pioneered the structural device of thought rhyme.

Benton's work, however, did not carry the imprimatur of the established critic. His book appeared in the same year as another influential pronouncement on Emerson's poetry. Central in this late-century debate over Emerson's writing was a particularly potent arbiter. Little more than a year after Emerson's death, Boston newspapers again chronicled a war of words over Emerson's significance. Fifty years earlier, Andrews Norton used Emerson's Divinity School Address to condemn the "latest form of infidelity," and its embodiment in the Unitarian ministers of Transcendental persuasion. In the 1880s, however, the infidel was no erstwhile minister but a well established British critic, and the faith that was under attack was none other than the works of a man who repeatedly urged his audiences to avoid institutionalizing ideas.

When Matthew Arnold delivered his Boston address on Emerson in December 1883, he may well have been practicing his own firm commitment to a particular style of criticism. But to the American audience he was little better than a grave robber. His commentary on Emerson bluntly demoted Emerson from the heights of literary or philosophical accomplishment and offered a consolation prize in return. The next several generations of Emerson critics would attempt to turn down that particular offer, but Arnold's prize was difficult to refuse. Like it or not, readers lived under the image Arnold created for Emerson.

Those who have read the long history of Emerson criticism know the power of Arnold's remarks. As Whicher comments in the preface to his and Milton Konvitz's 1962 *Emerson, A Collection of Critical Essays*, "The most influential single essay on Emerson is still by far Matthew Arnold's lecture" (v). While the same cannot be said today, Arnold's influence lingers as critics continue to reclaim Emerson for philosophy, argue his literary merit (though this battle has largely been won) and dissociate him from the category of the "inspirational." Even those who have never read the Arnold lecture in part or in whole, find themselves responding within the structure it codified.

Arnold's criticism was by no means new. Agreeing with those who had spoken before him, Arnold noted that Emerson's writing was flawed by obscurity. The absence of carefully crafted connections broke each work into pieces and showed no development or movement. The parts might well be brilliant but the whole was never as good as the pieces of which it was made. The same could be said of Emerson's ideas. Arnold comments, "He cannot build; his arrangement of philosophical ideas has no progress in it, no evolution" (169). While Arnold echoed what had often been said, his words became far more than another nineteenth-century complaint against Emerson's refusal of convention. In part the power lay in the source. Arnold was not simply one more reviewer but the foremost cultural critic of his day. Timing was also a problem. To many, the attack seemed mean spirited, aimed as it was against a figure whose recent death had just been profusely mourned.

Arnold did not simply restate the common criticisms. He ventured a definitive assessment of Emerson's place and did not hesitate to bar Emerson from the status Americans most desired. Arnold told his audiences, "I do not, then, place Emerson among the great poets. But I go further, and say that I do not place him among the great writers, the great men of letters" (159). Wherever Arnold looked in Emerson's writings, he saw fragments: "passages of noble and pathetic eloquence . . . passages of shrewd and felicitous wit . . . passages of exquisitely touched observation of nature," but "the requisite wholeness" never emerged from its parts (162). Arnold repeats his triple negative: "We have not in Emerson a great poet, a great writer, a great philosophy-maker" (178). What remains, Arnold assured his listeners, was a "relation" of "superior importance," but despite a few attempts to meet Arnold on his own terms, most critics heard only a second-best in this so-called "superior importance." Likening Emerson to Marcus Aurelius, Arnold termed him "the friend and aider of those who would live in the spirit" (179). Excellence was defined by a combination of inspiration, aspiration and consolation. Arnold made large claims for this limited excellence: Emerson's essays were the most important prose work of the nineteenth century. While they could be called neither philosophy nor art, they were, all the same, a powerful force for individual readers. Arnold located this power not in the writing but in the life: "his insight is admirable; his truth is precious. Yet the secret of his effect is not even in these; it is in the hopeful, serene, beautiful temper wherewith these, in Emerson, are indissolubly joined" (193).

Response was fierce and swift. Not even Arnold's assertion of "superior importance" could assuage the American audience. His comments galvanized the discussion about Emerson generally and about Emerson as philosopher or poet in particular. The summer following Arnold's address, Franklin B. Sanborn defended Emerson's poetry at the yearly session of the Concord School of Philosophy. Part of the special session on the "Genius and Character of Emerson," Sanborn's "Emerson Among the Poets" faults Arnold for basing his judgment on the most minor element within poetry. Arnold valued the "accomplishment of verse" over the "clairvoyance of the imagination" (174). Sanborn suggests that Arnold would have judged more wisely had he adopted one of Emerson's own definitions for poetry. Borrowing a phrase from "Poetry and Imagination," Sanborn approvingly quotes a sentence on how poetry should be evaluated. It read, "The great poets are judged by the frame of mind they induce" (180). Sanborn continues the quotation, reminding his readers that Emerson invited the "severest criticism." In Sanborn's view, this was precisely where Arnold erred. He took surface for substance and rendered weak, rather than severe, criticism.

Sanborn's emphasis on the imagination would remain a standard in Emerson criticism for the next thirty years. With Benton, he locates the power of the poetry largely in Emerson's diction, and like Benton, though more directly, he sees deliberate choice in Emerson's irregular rhythms. Sanborn comments, "he purposely roughened his verse, and threw in superfluous lines and ill-matched rhymes, as a kind of protest against the smoothness and jingle of what he called 'poetry to put round frosted cake'" (211). Even more so than Benton, Sanborn is lavish of quotation. He includes thirteen poems in thirty pages, often quoting twenty to thirty lines at a time.

Writing in the wake of Matthew Arnold's commentary, E. C. Stedman begins his chapter on Emerson in *Poets of America* (1885) by acknowledging the quantity of material recently published on Emerson, but he makes no mention of Arnold's verdict. Instead, he raises the specter of repetition. Borrowing a question from James Russell Lowell, he asks "Can anything new be said of him" (133). That pronoun kept interesting company: here of course it refers to Emerson, but in Lowell's use the figure was Shakespeare. The thrust of Stedman's discussion, however, is not elevation by association. Stedman does not play the "Emerson as American Shakespeare" tune as had Melville for Hawthorne. He took other familiar ground. Entering the ongoing debate on Emerson as a poet, he sought to convince his readers that Emerson's genius lay in what was pronounced by some as an impossible combination. Emerson was the poet-philosopher, and in Stedman's view the two were not mutually exclusive. Stedman's comments are revealing, both of his time and of the ongoing uneasiness in the discussion of Emerson's poetry.

At the opening of the chapter, Stedman emphasizes difference in terms of method. Poets and philosophers do not work in the same way, and "as a poet, Emerson found himself in a state, not of distraction, but often of indecision, *between the methods of philosophy and art*" (134). Stedman maintains that the reader of Emerson is best-advised to keep this "indecision" of method in mind, and in fact, his emphasis on method and its value places Stedman's voice where the late-twentieth-century critic can hear it. He values Emerson, not for the individual poems, but for the process they represent and the process they effect. "Emerson has given us thought, the habit of thinking, the will to think for ourselves" (177).

Stedman cautions his reader to practice that habit deliberately and vigorously when the subject matter is Emerson's writing. He divides tributes into two categories: those that are pure adulation and those that are committed to "searching, studying, expounding" Emerson's "originating force" (137). He lumps certain "Emersonians" together with the "Browningites," taking aim at those who would defend their writers even in passages that fail. He is no "old-fashioned Emersonian . . . who makes it a point of faith to defend the very passages where the master nods" (168). Of course, one critic's sleep is another's waking moment, and the line Stedman uses to justify his complaint might well be praised by a critic of a different aesthetic persuasion.

From the mid-1880s until O. W. Firkins' 1915 *Ralph Waldo Emerson*, critics turned increasingly to Emerson's vision of the poet and to Emerson's poetry itself. Useful in the counterattack against Arnold, it offered critics the chance to define a new standard for poetry. Even E. C. Stedman and Oliver Wendell Holmes, two writers known for their otherwise conservative stance, lauded Emerson for the newness he built into his structures. Holmes' discussion is dominated by his own penchant for analogy (Emerson's poetry is algebra to his contemporaries' arithmetic; the poems themselves are introduced as the "fine dress" of a ballroom), but among his image-rich paragraphs are comments about the radical quality of the poems themselves. Emerson writes with the "brave nudity of the rhythmic confessional" (317). This is as daring as Holmes will be, and he is never far from reminding the reader of Emerson's flaws. He agrees with Arnold's point on the lack of "evolution" in Emerson's poetry. In opposition to Benton, he laments the number of excellent fragments and the lack of excellent wholes. He charges Emerson with carelessness in rhyme and meter and suggests that Emerson shied away from difficult metrical forms. Stedman championed the opposite position. With Sanborn, he saw deliberate intent in Emerson's rough meter: "Who sounds one perfect chord can sound again. His greater efforts in verse, as in prose, show that he chose to deprecate the constructive faculty lest it might limit his ease and freedom" (159–60).

Edmund Gosse's 1888 piece in the *Forum* responded in part to Stedman's praise in his *Poets of America* and threw down yet another gauntlet for the American readers. In an article entitled "Has America Produced a Poet," he answered with a firm "no." Looking over Bryant, Longfellow, Emerson and Poe, he found that only the latter two came close to England's master poets. Emerson fell short for the usual reasons. Although his "best lines and stanzas" were as good as the great poets, "Emerson, as a verse-writer, is so fragmentary and uncertain that we cannot place him among the great poets" (185). Gosse was joined by Charles Richardson ("Emerson as a Poet" in his 1889 *American Literature, 1607–1885*) and Coulson Kernahan ("A Half-Made Poet" in the *London Quarterly Review*, 1889) who both agreed that Emerson's formal experimentation largely failed. Responding to the older generation's assessment, a younger group of critics took the opportunity to question the existing definitions of poetry. While some continued to argue for the well-respected conventions of form, topic, rhyme and meter, others championed an Emersonian liberation from all such formal considerations. As Elisabeth Luther Cary noted in *Emerson: Poet and Thinker* (1904), her contemporaries responded "more readily" to the "certain harshness of measure" in Emerson's poems than did a previous generation (208).

The attention paid to Emerson's prosody in these years was itself the means to a new aesthetic. Cary noted the canny rhythmic variations in Emerson's poetry and argued that Emerson's attempts to break convention were doubly successful: they were thought provoking and beauty creating. Never novelty for its own sake or for the simple effect of shock, Emerson's unlikely figures of speech were balanced by an "integral idea . . . the curve and balance of inner harmony" (212). Writing for the *Unitarian Review* in 1891, Frank Stearns pointed to Emerson's short forms and seven-syllable line to define the modern element within the poetry. Harvey Whitfield Peck defended the much maligned "Brahma" in his article on the "poet philosopher" in *The Arena* (April 1905). In a series of explications in *The Coming Age* (January 1899–March 1900) and *The Arena* (February 1904–March 1905), Charles Malloy continued his project of revising the common perception of Emerson's poetry. His approach emphasized Emerson's use of metaphor. At the heart of the poetry was "the force of the figure." That force required special handling. It could well be misread, and Malloy sought to undo that misreading.

No single individual spent more time lecturing on and writing about Emerson's poems than did Charles Malloy. Akin to his contemporary Charles Ives, Malloy subsidized his study of Emerson through another profession. Where Ives sold insurance to support the experimental music he allied with the Transcendentalists' thought, Malloy operated a shoe business out of Waltham, Massachusetts. His true profession, however, was lecturing. He became a prominent presence in various summer schools as well as urban lecture series. Malloy emphasized Emerson's own reading — both what he read and literally how he read poetry aloud. In the very stresses of the spoken poem, Emerson enacted the central idea of his poetic principle. Malloy argued that Emerson combined the minister's work with the poetic vocation and that for both, success depended upon performance. He comments, "Mr. Emerson's poems needed that he should read them. He was the prince of all readers. He illustrated his own demand — that a minister should be able to read a good meaning into the poorest verse in the hymn book" (*A Study of Emerson's Major Poems*, 118).

Malloy's championing of Emerson's poetry is interesting in light of Emerson reception. Malloy himself was keenly aware of the earlier response to Emerson's poems and uses this response to frame his own. He cites the mid-century assessment, quoting Francis Bowen's disparaging remarks as well as Parker's humorous lament. He writes with full knowledge of the past, whether a quarter or a half century before. The ridicule that met "Brahma" upon its 1857 publication in *The Atlantic Monthly* is the stimulus behind one series of his turn-of-the-century explications. The judgments by Oliver Wendell Holmes and James Russell Lowell are others. Malloy is also firmly committed to creating a contemporary audience for Emerson — poetry and prose alike — though he trusts the prose will need fewer of his words.

Refusing to divide Emerson's audience, he writes a unity across the growing divide between critical and appreciative. He notes the member of the women's reading group who conveyed her despair over completing her essay on "Mithridates." He acknowledges that he too had faced similar uncertainty about the meaning. His discussion then provides enough context for the puzzled reader to place the poem in a metaphor of reform. For him, the reading club or summer school participant was as essential a reader as the emerging academic or cultural critic. He saw himself and writers like William Torrey Harris as partners with all readers of Emerson. He founded the Emerson club in Boston, conducted "Emerson-Browning devotional services" at summer schools, wrote detailed essays on the poems in which context and metaphor blend so that Emerson's poems might be read on their own terms.

Malloy's story does not end with the early twentieth century. His multi-dimensional presentation would itself come in for ridicule by modernists and humanists alike. He typified the "New Thought" that post-World War I writers would decry, but Malloy clearly meant substance where others saw ephemera. Malloy took Emerson's poems as an intellectual enterprise in which meaning was by definition inspirational. His version of inspiration depended upon study. For a reader to value Emerson's poetry, he or she needed to read voluminously in the sacred texts and myths of other cultures. They also needed a clear grasp of how metaphor works.

Almost seventy-five years later, Malloy's work returned and was published as a stated "dawn" to a new evaluation of Emerson. Kenneth Walter Cameron's firm commitment to expanding the reader's understanding of an Emerson canon is apparent yet again in his collection of Malloy's pieces into one volume. Entitled *A Study of Emerson's Major Poems* (1973), it asked the late-twentieth-century reader to suspend their reflex condescension toward late nineteenth-century criticism. Cameron dedicated his book to Carl Strauch, the individual who, like Malloy, devoted his critical career to a study of Emerson's poems. In his dedication, Cameron notes the "day about to dawn," an image borne out by the 1970s with its renewed interest in Emerson as poet, an interest that will receive its own discussion in Chapter Six.

Even with the growing experimentation in poetry at the nineteenth century's end, its value remained in question among the critical observers of philosophy and literature. As early as 1884 lectures at the Concord School of Philosophy (published in 1885 as *The Genius and Character of Emerson*; Sanborn's defense of Emerson's poetry was also part of the program), Julian Hawthorne acknowledged the problems facing those who would write or speak about Emerson. Hawthorne's concern was suggested by the very title of the session ("the genius and character of Emerson"). When twelve individuals are invited to speak within a framework that apparently announced an endless stream of praise, there might well be cause for silence. He warns his audience against "nerveless admiration" (91) of Emerson and presents an unnerving reminder that an apotheosized Emerson would readily turn from liberator into tyrant. It also represents a profound misinterpretation of Emerson's work. Turning Emerson's unsystematic thought into a virtue, Hawthorne argues that the fault lay with the system makers. Reminding his readers that all such systems are simplifications, selecting out the features that do not easily form a seamless whole, he maintains that the price of consistency is the price of truth. With a system, you hold the part not the whole.

While Hawthorne's comments may strike the late-twentieth-century reader as decidedly modern, his view was by no means unique. Twenty years later at the Emerson centenary celebration in Concord, Thomas Wentworth Higginson praised the "fragmentary" nature of Emerson's approach (*Centenary of the Birth*, 63). Criticizing those who used the oft-noted "lack of system" to disparage Emerson, Higginson redefined the perceived absence as clear proof of excellence. "System-makers are short-lived," he writes, "each makes his single contribution, and the world passes on" (63–64). The longer he looked at systems, the more wary he became. What they gained in clarity they forfeited in creativity. Turning preacher for the moment, he exhorts his listeners, "let us not lose faith in the greatness of the spontaneous or fragmentary life" (64).

Hawthorne told his 1884 listeners to value Emerson's "tendency" over his "actual results" (77). Higginson privileged series over system. Their comments anticipate work of late twentieth-century critics. In *Emerson and Literary Change* (1978), David Porter centers Emerson's poetics in a theory of process. Leonard Neufeldt reminds his readers how central the idea of metamorphosis is to Emerson's writing (*The House of Emerson*, 1982), and Richard Poirier celebrates Emerson's system-breaking language: "continuous acts of troping, syntactical shiftings, rhetorical fracturings"(*The Renewal of Literature*, 1987, 33).

While this celebration of fracturing, shifting and troping speaks clearly for its late-twentieth-century context, the late-nineteenth-century parallel is worth noting, especially because it has often been overlooked in the cult of worship surrounding Emerson after his death. Hawthorne ends his piece with a quotation from the essay that has been one of the feature pieces of late-twentieth-century criticism. Calling it a "characteristic" passage, he leaves his readers with these words from "Circles": "Let me remind you that I am only an experimenter. Do not set the least value on what I do, or the least discredit on what I do not, — as if I pretended to settle anything as true or false. I unsettle all things: no facts are to me sacred, none profane. I simply experiment, — an endless Seeker, with no Past at my back!" (*Genius and Character of Emerson*, 91).

The unsettling aspect of Emerson's thought was often on the minds of late-nineteenth-and early-twentieth-century readers. In the case of two singular artists of the twentieth century, Emerson's experimentation provides the aesthetic for their work. Charles Ives and Frank Lloyd Wright remain two of the most prominent interpreters of Emerson's ideas. In his writings they each heard a call to their own work. Wright praised Emerson's organicism, allying his own conceptualization of built space with Emerson's metre-making argument. Positioning himself as the Emerson of architecture, he commented, "architecture is itself whatever is organic. It is the organic pattern of all things. This remains the hidden mystery of creation until the architect has grasped and revealed it . . . now we say that architecture in a more philosophical sense is whatever significance structure itself possesses. It is the significant structure of all created things as the mind may know them. . . . It is at best that magic framework of reality that we sometimes touch upon when we use the word *order*. Architecture is the aura (or "oversoul" as Emerson might say) of structure" (*Architecture and Modern Life*, 1937; p. 219 in *Collected Writings*, vol. 3).

Ives likewise sought to translate Emerson's ideas into a different form. Seeking the musical equivalent of Emersonian expression, his Concord Sonata opens with a movement entitled "Emerson," a movement in which the conventions of sonata form are absent, replaced by Ives' experiments in self-reliant sound. Ives wrote his *Essays Before a Sonata* (1920) to articulate his musical vision in a verbal form. It serves as a companion piece to the musical work. In the opening paragraph of his Emerson essay, Ives asserts his own knowledge. Current in the Emerson debates, he readily offers his own interpretation: "It has seemed to the writer that Emerson is greater — his identity more complete, perhaps — in the realms of revelation — natural disclosure — than in those of poetry, philosophy, or prophecy. Though a great poet and prophet, he is greater, possibly, as an invader of the unknown" (11).

While Ives and Wright, like Whitman before them, championed ungoverned innovation in all forms of expression, others were keenly aware that experimentation easily went awry or unheard. The power associated with innovation was forceful, and yet it might as readily destroy worth as create excellence. John Jay Chapman epitomizes this ambivalence toward innovation. His long, thoughtful essay on Emerson was first published in 1897. Its original title suggests its own peculiar relation to the system of tradition. In the *Atlantic Monthly*, the essay appeared under the title, "Emerson, or Sixty Years After." The reference to the passage of time is curious. On the one hand, there is the obvious arithmetic. Writing the essay in 1896, Chapman notes the sixty-year anniversary of *Nature*. The date of publication also measures sixty years between Chapman's readers and the first audience for Emerson's version of the American scholar. Chapman singles out the address for special attention, asserting that "Emerson has left nothing behind him stronger than this address" (*Emerson, and Other Essays*, 17). From Chapman's point of view, it contains the substance of Emerson's belief.

The reader should turn to it if he turns to nothing else. While the "sixty years" of Chapman's title is thus an obvious reference to "The American Scholar," his late-nineteenth-century audience would not have missed his other allusion. Sir Walter Scott's most popular novel *Waverley* carried as its subtitle "'Tis Sixty Years Since." The phrase became a shorthand used to indicate a careful reverence for the past — careful because the users prided themselves on their own well-studied understanding of history and reverent because the present dutifully learned its lessons from the past. Its connection with Emerson is not what one would expect given an individual who complained about retrospective ages and styled himself "an experimenter with no past" at his back.

Chapman's application of the phrase to an essay on Emerson is thought provoking in light of his own ambivalence toward Emerson. On the one hand the phrase is bitingly critical. When Chapman describes the 1830s, he makes it clear that decade has little to teach the 1890s except in its ugly resemblance to the present. It was "the era of American brag," a "time of humiliation, when there was no free speech, no literature, little manliness, no reality, no simplicity, no accomplishment. . . . We were over-sensitive, insolent, and cringing." The effect on the individual was sobering. Chapman writes, "Such social conditions crush and maim the individual, and throughout New England, as throughout the whole North, the individual was crushed and maimed" (9–10). Chapman uses this representation to display the one "accomplishment" he most values in Emerson. Citing Emerson's commitment to the individual, he celebrates his protest against the "tyranny" of democracy (100–108). Chapman locates this "tyranny" in what he calls "moral cowardice" (29) and unifies Emerson's writing by presenting it as a consistent attack against such moral failing.

In so doing, however, Chapman sounds suspiciously similar to the argument from morality put forth by the voices for the Genteel Tradition. Chapman would not appreciate the alliance and indeed tried to distance his Emerson-as-moralist from theirs. He turned to Emerson's style as proof of his difference. Finding virtue in the lack of system, he asserts that Emerson escaped a complicitous status quo by his truly independent "stimulating pictures and suggestions" (29). His images and assertions were never governed by a single proposition. Where his genteel counterparts chide Emerson for failure of form, Chapman maintains that the experimental form was part of the project.

Emerson's poetry, however, fails on both counts. "The fault with Emerson is that he stops in the antechamber of poetry" (91). Unlike Benton or Sanborn, he could not be fed on the fragments produced by a dynamic and suggestive imagination. The only way to reclaim Emerson's poetry was by allying it with the tradition Emerson's writing created. Praising Emerson's poetry for its ability to evoke the landscape, he notes the particularly New England quality of the work and begins to think in terms of literary tradition. *New England* is stamped clearly on this poetry of place, a place both external and internal. Emerson's poems evoke their region by the placement of the individual reader. Imaginatively located within the New England landscape, he is at the same time distanced from any particular personal relations. This technique is not Emerson's alone. Chapman associates Emerson's poetry with the recently published and widely remarked Emily Dickinson. Even here he is uneasy. Though he accords Emerson a literary tradition, he doubts its excellence. He writes, Emerson "is the chief poet of that school of which Emily Dickinson is a minor poet" (84–85). "Minor" is apparently Chapman's major assessment of this kind of poetry: he faults it for "too much thought, too much argument" (94).

Published within a year of Chapman's words, but for a decidedly different audience, *Pleasant Hours with American Authors* (1898) faced the same dilemma of assessment. The headnote to the Emerson entry begins, "To classify Emerson is a matter of no small difficulty. He was a philosopher, he was an essayist, he was a poet" (71). Unlike Arnold, the editor refused to define the subject by exclusion and unlike Chapman, made no apologies for Emerson's style: "He was a prophet who, without argument, announced truths which, by intuition, he seems to have perceived; but the thought is often so shadowy that the ordinary reader fails to catch it" (71). The one echo of Arnold appears in the poems included in the volume. The editor assures the audience that these poems, unlike some others, are designed for the ordinary reader. Both are pieces Arnold praised; each now challenges a late-twentieth-century audience to find their excellence. In his lecture, Arnold selected two examples of exceptional excellence to prove the rule of Emerson's poetic failure. He cited the "Concord Hymn" and four lines from "Voluntaries." With Arnold's imprimatur, that quatrain would become ubiquitous: "So nigh is grandeur to our dust,/ So near is God to man,/ When Duty whispers low, '*Thou must*,'/ The youth replies '*I can.*'" If returned to their original context, these lines become exceedingly interesting. A stanza within "Voluntaries," they form part of Emerson's sustained argument with the slave-mongering United States. Arnold's praise, however, is devoid of such particular reference. Whether or not he assumed that his listeners would immediately recall the Civil War circumstances behind the quoted lines, the lines themselves took on a life of their own, appearing and reappearing well into the twentieth century as the touchstone of Emerson's worth.

The editor of *Pleasant Hours* quotes both the "Concord Hymn" and the stanza from "Voluntaries." Thought-provokingly different, however, is each writer's assessment. What Arnold termed "noble lines" with "commanding force," the editor of *Pleasant Hours* equates with popularity and ease of comprehension. For the reader of *Pleasant Hours*, Emerson's reputation remained untarnished. Emerson was "the liberator of American literature." Despite the difficulty of classifying Emerson, the editor's introduction would hazard a final claim: "Emerson was pre-eminently a poet" (71).

The editor was not alone in this thought. From 1880 until the early 1930s the single most consistent area of inquiry was Emerson's status as poet. The discussion took shape in several basic questions, questions that were clearly, to borrow William James' phrase, live questions for the day: was Emerson a poet? what were the distinguishing characteristics of Emerson's poetry? what was Emerson's contribution to American poetry? Essay-debates in periodicals, essays in the newly formed scholarly journals, book chapters in "larger" studies either of Emerson or of a more general topic, editor's introductions to Emerson anthologies — the answers appeared in various places. Their frequency bespoke another concern whose power shaped the discussion of Emerson in the first half of the twentieth century. Whatever the verdict on Emerson's poetry, there was no question about his place in philosophy. The doors of philosophy were closing on Emerson. Arnold's "friend and aider" might be argued back into an identity as poet, but it would take nearly another century to make the case for philosophy. The next chapter traces the power of this exclusion.

Works Cited

A Disciple. "Emerson's Essays." *United States Magazine, and Democratic Review* 16 (June 1845): 589–602.

Arnold, Matthew. "Emerson" in *Discourses in America*. London: Macmillan, 1885: 138–207.

B., L. W. "Ralph Waldo Emerson." *Yale Literary Magazine* 5 (March 1850): 203–06.

Baym, Nina. *Novels, Readers and Reviewers: Responses to Fiction in Antebellum America*. Ithaca: Cornell University Press, 1984.

Benton, Joel E. *Emerson as a Poet*. New York: M. F. Mansfield and A. Wessels, 1883.

Bloom, Harold, editor. *Ralph Waldo Emerson*. New York: Chelsea House, 1985.

Bowen, Francis. "Nine New Poets." *North American Review* 64 (April 1847): 402–34.

———. "Transcendentalism." *The Christian Examiner* 21 (January 1837): 371–85.

Brown, Lee Rust. *The Emerson Museum: Practical Romanticism and the Pursuit of the Whole*. Cambridge, MA: Harvard University Press, 1997.

Brownson, Orestes. "Emerson's Essays." *Boston Quarterly Review* 4 (July 1841): 291–308.

Burkholder, Robert E. "The Contemporary Reception of *English Traits*" in *Emerson Centenary Essays*. Joel Myerson, editor. Carbondale: Southern Illinois University Press, 1982: 156–72.

Cameron, Kenneth Walter, editor. *A Study of Emerson's Major Poems*. Hartford, CT: Transcendental Books, 1973 (articles by Charles Malloy, 1900–1905).

Carpenter, Frederic Ives. *Emerson Handbook*. New York: Hendricks House, 1953.

Cary, Elisabeth Luther. *Emerson: Poet and Thinker*. New York: G. P. Putnam's Sons, 1904.

Channing, William Henry. "Emerson's *Phi Beta Kappa Oration*." *Boston Quarterly Review* 1 (January 1838): 106–20.

Chapman, John Jay. "Emerson, or Sixty Years After." *Atlantic Monthly* 79 (January and February 1897): 27–41; 222–40. Reprinted in *Emerson, and Other Essays*. New York: Charles Scribner's Sons, 1898.

Clarke, James Freeman. "R. W. Emerson and the New School." *Western Messenger* 6 (November 1838): 37–47.

Cooke, George Willis. "Emerson's Literary Methods." Boston *Literary World* 11 (22 May 1880): 181.

———. *Ralph Waldo Emerson: His Life, His Writings, and Philosophy*. Boston: Houghton, Mifflin and Company, 1881. Expanded edition, 1892.

Davis, G. T. "Review of Divinity School Address." Boston *Morning Post* (31 August 1838): 1.

"Emerson" [Special birthday section]. *Literary World* 11 (22 May 1880): 174–85.

"Emerson's Poems." New York *Daily Tribune*. 9 January 1847: 1.

Fuller, Margaret. "Emerson's Essays." New York *Daily Tribune* (7 December 1844): 1.

Gilman, Samuel. "Ralph Waldo Emerson." *Southern Rose* 7 (24 November 1838): 100–106.

Gosse, Edmund. "Has America Produced a Poet?" *Forum* 6 (1888): 176–86.

Harris, Kenneth Marc. *Emerson and Carlyle: Their Long Debate.* Cambridge, MA: Harvard University Press, 1978.

Hawthorne, Julian. "Emerson as an American" in *The Genius and Character of Emerson: Lectures at the Concord School of Philosophy.* Franklin B. Sanborn, editor. Boston: J. R. Osgood, 1885: 68–91.

Hedge, Frederic Henry. "Writings of R. W. Emerson." *Christian Examiner* 38 (January 1845): 87–108.

Heraud, John A. "Emerson's Essays." *Monthly Magazine*, 3rd series, 5 (November 1841): 484–505.

Higginson, Thomas Wentworth. Address at the Concord Centenary Celebration in *The Centenary of the Birth of Ralph Waldo Emerson.* Boston: Riverside Press, 1903: 58–66.

———. "Emerson as the Founder of a Literature." Boston *Literary World* 11 (22 May 1880): 175–76.

Holmes, Oliver Wendell. *Ralph Waldo Emerson.* Boston: Houghton, Mifflin and Company, 1884.

Howells, William Dean. Review of *May-Day and Other Pieces. Atlantic Monthly* 20 (1867): 376–78.

Ives, Charles. *Essays Before a Sonata.* New York: Knickerbocker Press, 1920.

Kernahan, Coulson. "A Half-Made Poet." *London Quarterly Review* 73 (1889): 27–35.

Konvitz, Milton R. and Whicher, Stephen E. *Emerson: A Collection of Critical Essays.* Englewood Cliffs, NJ: Prentice Hall, 1962.

Lathrop, George Parsons. "*Letters and Social Aims.*" *Atlantic Monthly* 38 (August 1876): 240–41.

Malloy, Charles. "The Poems of Emerson." *The Arena* 31–33 (February 1904–March 1905).

———. "The Poems of Emerson." *The Coming Age* 1–4 (January 1899–August 1900).

Mott, Wesley, editor. *Biographical Dictionary of Transcendentalism.* Westport, CT: Greenwood, 1996.

———. *Encyclopedia of Transcendentalism.* Westport, CT: Greenwood, 1996.

Mott, Wesley T., and Burkholder, Robert E., editors. *Emersonian Circles: Essays in Honor of Joel Myerson.* Rochester: University of Rochester Press, 1997.

Myerson, Joel, editor. *Emerson and Thoreau: The Contemporary Reviews,* New York: Cambridge University Press, 1992.

————, editor. *The Transcendentalists: A Review of Research and Criticism.* New York: Modern Language Association, 1984.

Neufeldt, Leonard. *The House of Emerson.* Lincoln: University of Nebraska Press, 1982.

Norton, Andrews. "The New School in Literature and Religion." Boston *Daily Advertiser* (27 August 1838): 2.

Packer, Barbara. "The Transcendentalists" in *The Cambridge History of American Literature, 1820–1865*, vol. 2. Sacvan Bercovitch, editor. New York: Cambridge University Press, 1995: 329–604.

Parker, Theodore. "The Writings of Ralph Waldo Emerson." *Massachusetts Quarterly Review* 3 (March 1850): 200–255.

Parsons, Theophilus. "The New School and Its Opponents." Boston *Daily Advertiser* (30 August 1838): 2.

Peabody, Elizabeth Palmer. "Nature — A Prose Poem." *United States Magazine and Democratic Review* 1 (February 1838): 319–21.

Peck, Harvey Whitfield. "Emerson's 'Brahma'; or, the Poet-Philosopher in the Presence of the Deity." *Arena* 33 (April 1905): 375–76.

Pleasant Hours with American Authors. Philadelphia: American Book and Bible House, 1898.

Poirier, Richard. *The Renewal of Literature: Emersonian Reflections.* New York: Random House, 1987.

Porter, David. *Emerson and Literary Change.* Cambridge, MA: Harvard University Press, 1978.

Review of *The Conduct of Life. Athenaeum* 1929 (15 December 1860): 824–26.

Review of *The Conduct of Life. Knickerbocker* 57 (February 1861): 217–18.

Review of *Essays. Athenaeum* 730 (23 October 1841): 803–04.

Review of *Essays, Lectures, and Orations. Critic* n.s. 6 (18 December 1847): 386–87.

Review of *Letters and Social Aims. Athenaeum* 2516 (15 January 1876): 81.

Review of *Poems. Athenaeum* 1006 (6 February 1847): 144–46.

Review of *Poems. Critic* n.s. 5 (2 January 1847): 9–11.

Review of *Poems. Literary World* 1 (3 April 1847): 197–99.

Richardson, Charles. "Emerson as Poet" in *American Literature, 1607–1885.* Vol. 2. New York: Putnams, 1889: 137–71.

Sanborn, Franklin B. "Emerson among the Poets" in *The Genius and Character of Emerson: Lectures at the Concord School of Philosophy.* Franklin B. Sanborn, editor. Boston: J. R. Osgood, 1885: 173–214.

————, editor. *The Genius and Character of Emerson: Lectures at the Concord School of Philosophy*. Boston: J. R. Osgood.

Slater, Joseph, editor. *The Correspondence of Emerson and Carlyle*. New York: Columbia University Press, 1964.

Stearns, Frank. "Emerson as Poet." *Unitarian Review* 36 (1891): 259–70.

Stedman, Edmund Clarence. *Poets of America*. Boston: Houghton, Mifflin and Company, 1885.

Wasson, David A. Review of *May-Day and Other Pieces*. *Radical* 2 (August 1867): 760–62.

Whipple, E. P., et al. "Tribute." *Literary World* 11 (22 May 1880): 182–83.

Whitman, Walt. "Emerson's Books (The Shadows of Them)." *Literary World* 11 (22 May 1880): 177–78.

Wright, Frank Lloyd and Baker Brownell. *Architecture and Modern Life*. New York: Harper and Brothers, 1937.

4: The Philosophers' Millstone: New Humanism, Modernism and the Marxist Frontier

IN THE LAST DECADE of the nineteenth century, Emerson's image began to resemble one of his own polarities. On the one hand he was the well-known "moral influence" who, in Bliss Carman's phrase, celebrated "the poetry of life." On the other hand, Emerson was the unsystematic thinker whose expression fell far short of "modern" philosophical standards. Eccentrics like Ives and Wright might embrace his innovations, but the growing academic disciplines and the rising cultural critics suggested an alternate path. They advised the serious intellect to move rapidly in the opposite direction.

As the late nineteenth century witnessed the increasing specialization within fields of academic study, each discipline sought a new rigor and a distinct definition for itself. Although philosophical study of the late nineteenth century may still sound decidedly literary to twenty-first-century readers, it was distancing itself from any such alliance. Philosophy, it was argued, specialized in systematic methods and worked through their consistent practice. It relied on a connected pattern of reasoning and failed when such patterns were broken. In short, Emerson neither thought nor wrote like a philosopher, and critics of philosophical persuasion were eager to separate themselves from a figure who was at best an embarrassment to their work. This chapter chronicles Emerson's exclusion from early-twentieth-century philosophical study. With the continued popularity of Emerson in both school and home, the rising intellectual cadres, whether genteel, modernist or humanist, sought to establish their clear difference from Emerson's ideas and the reading communities to which such writings still so widely appealed.

Although he allied himself with the emerging discipline of sociology, John Robertson describes the problems Emerson posed for systematic inquiry in general. In his chapter on Emerson in *Modern Humanists* (1891), he attributes the flaw to Emerson's doctrine of inspiration (which Robertson terms "dogma"). To "lean" on the "secret augury," as Emerson suggests, all too often cracks a surface under which there was no meaning. Inspiration was empty without analytical thinking. The momentary feeling was no better than a fragment unless developed through "connected reasoning." Robertson concedes that Emerson's inspirations were better than most but nonetheless charges the writer with "mental indolence." Emerson refused to do "the drudgery work in thinking," and thus his writing was flawed by irregularity. Such "inveterate indolence" was deadly to philosophy.

When he discussed poetry, however, Robertson begrudgingly offered Emerson a position on the outskirts. He found power in Emerson's provocations: "Certainly no one stimulates as he does." He equates Emerson's writing with a kind of necessary medication. His sentences are "stimulants," and while neither states nor individuals could live on stimulants alone, they "may at times escape death or prostration by them." In the "nervous era" of the century's end, it was not clear whether Emerson was help or hindrance, but Robertson opted for the more charitable assessment of "help." His poetry succeeded where his philosophy failed.

A decade later George Santayana joined Robertson in his evaluation. In his section on Emerson in *Interpretations of Poetry and Religion* (1900), he agreed with Robertson's critique of inspiration, but unlike Robertson he saw an even more dangerous element within it. Unchecked, it lead to "mysticism," which Santayana equated with a static absolute that marred both philosophy and poetry. While later critics would work carefully to reclaim both mysticism and inspiration for critical use, Santayana saw little virtue in either concept. He introduced a different term to describe Emerson's strength. "Imagination," he writes, "is his single theme . . . the art of conception . . . the various forms in which reflection, like a poet, may compose and recompose human experience" (220–23). As long as imagination remained in the realm of artistic composition, Santayana praised its "plasticity" and "spontaneity," but when it moved into the work of philosophy, it was not only out of its element but capable of wide-spread damage. "It loosens our hold on fact and confuses our intelligence, so that we forget that intelligence has itself every prerogative of imagination, and has besides the sanction of practical validity" (225).

Santayana's concern betrays a greater affinity with the Genteel Tradition than he would have cared to admit. While the participants in that tradition worried about Emerson's revolutionary sayings and their effect on a mass audience, Santayana worried about Emerson's effect on the stable order of thought. The emphasis on the imagination could create an insurrection from beneath, suggesting as it did that logical thought was simply one construct among many with no superior claim to truth. Citing Emerson's power of legerdemain, Santayana notes the easy path to delusion: "We are made to believe that since the understanding is something human and conditioned, something which might have been different, as the senses might have been different, and which we may yet, so to speak, get behind — therefore the understanding ought to be abandoned. We long for higher faculties, neglecting those we have" (35). Concern over that imagined neglect governed the cultural critics' commentary on Emerson for the next several years.

This period from the late nineteenth century into the early twentieth century attracted its own group of critics. First among them, H. L. Kleinfield assessed the twenty years between Emerson's death and the centenary celebration in "The Structure of Emerson's Death" (1961). Chronicling "the ascent of Ralph Waldo Emerson to the realm where the gods of culture reigned" (64), he examined the accretion of praise formed around the once revolutionary figure. Charles Mitchell takes that process as the central issue for the early chapters of *Individualism and Its Discontents: Appropriations of Emerson, 1880–1950* (1997). He asks why the idealization occurred and finds the answer in the emerging voices of New Humanism. With their concern for cultural purity, they engaged in a process of gentrification to make Emerson safe for popular consumption.

The concern was long-standing. Although Mitchell's focus does not extend to the earlier part of the nineteenth century, an analogous concern formed part of the early reception. Those who thought of themselves as cultural guardians were always wary of Emerson's meaning. What did self-reliance really advocate? Did its liberty mean license and would its practice ensure a moral community or an anarchic chaos? The focal point was revealing: when critics voiced uneasiness about Emerson, their concern was clear. They were not worried about readers like themselves but about another population. They targeted the common reader. For the individuals deemed vulnerable, Emerson was forbidden fruit. Critics in the early to mid-nineteenth century sought to scare readers away from Emerson by labeling him blasphemer or shame them away by terming him nonsense. Mitchell argues that the turn-of-the-century intellectuals took a different tack. They produced an Emerson whose influence was entirely separable from his words. Praised for the singular excellence of his character, Emerson was accorded a curiously inaccessible place. The question of his originality was turned into an unbending testimony to his uniqueness. Emerson's writings, it was argued, were the product of a unique mind; they belonged to him and him alone. Neither they nor their writer, could be duplicated. The old nineteenth-century paradigm of exemplary character simply would not work in this case because Emerson's uniqueness placed him beyond emulation. Or rather, the individual who followed Emerson did so at peril. The question was *whose?*

Looking at the writings from the turn of the century and from well into the twentieth Mitchell hears a chilling refrain: don't let Emerson get into the "wrong minds" or the consequences will be irreparably damaging. The concern was twofold. The "uneducated" popular reader was clearly the target, as was the "rising intellectual." It was a curious, yet not surprising mix, since both groups were numerous yet disenfranchised. Emerson's words, if read closely, projected a way to power, and those well-established in political or intellectual power were wary of the prospect painted by Emerson.

Thus began a double-edged program to disarm Emerson. As Mitchell illustrates, the Emerson known primarily through his unwavering faith in the moral law was a figure well suited to meet the needs of these turn-of-the-century critics. Voicing dismay over the meaning they feared the general reader might find in Emerson's essays, they sought to replace the inflammatory words with a benign presence to help "educate" this new audience to a "better life." In its educative purposes, the early twentieth century reveals one facet of its concern with Emerson's words. In addition to moving the young white man of privileged background beyond his reading of Emerson, the critics also sought to move a new, potentially disruptive audience away from Emerson's ideas on individual freedom. The second target of the critics was clearly the "uneducated" popular audience, and the unspoken (though in some cases spoken) referent was the black or immigrant reader. The United States' population was rapidly changing, and Emerson's concept of self-reliance was seen as increasingly problematic. Advocating non-conformity, it underscored social unrest. For purposes of assimilation, Mitchell argues, Emerson worked better through his life than with his words.

For the rising intellectual, there was another concern. Emerson, as we have seen, was deemed the stuff of youth. While critics acknowledged his appeal to the young, they invariably ended their comments with the observation that age brought maturity and that with maturity Emerson ceased to be interesting. This implied progression encompassed two types. It charted the supposedly inevitable path of the individual (in this situation always figured as male) but also described the parallel course of American society. The past was increasingly represented as the youth of the country; the present was as emphatically portrayed as its mature adulthood. Keenly aware of their place in the "modern" world, critics including George Santayana, Henry Adams, Paul Elmer More, and William James began stressing the limitations of nineteenth-century writers. The figures of the recent past were seen as outdated, speaking a language for a world that no longer existed. This is the "naive" Emerson of *The Education of Henry Adams*, the man aware of his own limits whom William James celebrated at the centenary; the "sort of Puritan Goethe" of Santayana (*Persons and Places*, 184). From there it was a short step to the thinkers of the teens, twenties and thirties and their out of hand dismissal of Emerson.

The early-twentieth-century contention divided the New Modernists from the New Humanists. Both sought distance from the recent past; each figured that distance differently. As the name implies, the so-called new humanism sought to reclaim the high ideals of pure culture purveyed by the old gentility. Faulting their predecessors for an unconscionable belief in progress, they nonetheless championed their own form of progress. Caught between the bankrupt moral claims of the 1890s and the apparently amoral claims of the succeeding generation, these critics argued that a modern moral standard was not only possible but truly progressive, and not simply a bizarre oxymoron. Maintaining a belief in the power of form, they sought a credible absolute: experimentation was never an end in itself, nor was the utilitarian model recycled through pragmatism. Rejecting the nineteenth century's idealism and the twentieth century's relativism, they championed rigorous aesthetic standards. The educated individual could discern these and aspire to them. Study was essential, characterized by a discipline that firmly governed any motion toward subjectivism.

The New Modernists advocated a simpler solution. There was no use reclaiming the past. When, as Willa Cather said, the world broke in two, there was no plausible hope of uniting the past with the present. They were irrevocably separated, and the New Modernists built their ethic and aesthetic on that separation. The past was more problematic for the New Humanists. They sought voices for the present from within the past, sought to extract a present-day relevance from an earlier time. The voice of a once radical past, Emerson was a complicated phenomenon for them.

New Humanists Paul Elmer More and Irving Babbitt recoiled from the apotheosized Emerson, seeing this position as yet further evidence of the false front of American society. Writing a piece for the centenary, More was clearly uncomfortable with the idea of "tribute." Entitled "The Influence of Emerson," the essay argued the less influence the better. Emerson, the unsystematic thinker, seemingly licensed an intellectual free-for-all in which one idea was as good as another. His essays suggested that anyone could generate insight. His "self-abandonment to ecstasy and the easy acceptance of genius whenever it proclaims itself" resulted, so More argued, in the worst form of banal thought (*Shelburne Essays, First Series*, 82). His target was Christian Science, an attack he made brutally personal. In his words, Mary Baker Eddy was a provincial "ignorant woman" (79). Throughout the essay, More's concern lay with the application of Emerson's ideas, ideas he felt were never firmly developed in the first place. Emerson, "like all teachers of spiritual insight . . . was profoundly impressed by the ubiquitous dualism of life" (74), but he failed to make such dualism philosophically credible. More faulted Emerson for his unwillingness to bridge the gap between a perceived whole and an experienced fragmentation. He writes, "He was content to let them lie side by side unreconciled, and hence his seeming fluctuations to those of shallow understanding. . . . Not only does he make no attempt to connect them logically, but he is satisfied to apply now one and now the other of them to the solution of a thousand minor questions without much order or method" (75, 76). In consequence, Emerson's readers chose what they wanted, producing a fatally flawed "Emersonianism" associated with "facile optimism" (72, 81).

Babbitt shared More's profound distrust of "the influence of Emerson as it works on large masses of men" (More's phrase, 72). Babbitt located Emerson's fatal flaw in his endorsement of the individual. Acknowledging that Emerson himself attempted to guard self-reliance from becoming self-indulgence, he felt those attempts were finally unsuccessful: "We also have to face the fact that Emerson, who has emphasized more happily perhaps than any other recent writer the need of selectiveness in the individual (as, for example, in his poem "Days"), and also the wisdom of the selections embodied in tradition, nevertheless gave undue encouragement to the ordinary man, to the man who is undisciplined and unselective and untraditional" (*Modern French Criticism*, 1912, 354–55). Commenting on Emerson's apparent endorsement of the "ordinary untrained individual," he plays out the consequences: "when the man in the street thus sets up to be the measure of all things, the result is often hard to distinguish from vulgar presumption. The humanitarian fallacy would be comparatively harmless if it did not fit in so perfectly with a commercialism which finds its profit in flattering the taste of the average man, and an impressionism that has lost the restraining sense of tradition and encourages us to steep and saturate our minds in the purely contemporaneous. As it is, these elements have combined in a way that is a menace to all high and severe standards of taste. To use words as disagreeable as the things they describe, literature is in danger of being vulgarized and commercialized and journalized" (353–54). For Babbitt, restraint and discipline were essential to human thought. While Emerson provided that discipline in his Platonist side, he nonetheless failed, by Babbitt's account, both in manner of thinking and style of expression. Falling prey to the "humanitarian fallacy," Emerson underwrote one mistake with another. His thinking not only lacked method but "that more essential consistency which would have enabled him to knit together the two main aspects of his work" (358). Echoing More's criticism, Babbitt faults Emerson for his unreconciled dualism. He failed to create an effective dialectic. For the reader Emerson's words all too readily became the intoxicant without the corrective. Babbitt's imagery looks back to Robertson's earlier comment on Emerson as "stimulant." This quality would in turn become the focal point for Alfred Kreymborg's later defense of "The Intoxicated Emerson."

For Babbitt, however, no good could be said of such intoxication, although he almost exempts Emerson from his own failing. He refuses, however, to exempt the "Emersonians." When translated back into real people, the members of this group are the moderately educated and easily disparaged adult learners. More often than not they are women; in all cases their presence in early-twentieth-century criticism articulates the growing divide between general and professional readers. As Babbitt and More struggled to defend a "severe" and "critical standard," they launched their most vitriolic attacks against individuals of common education. Little wonder that many of the attacks now ring with blatant misogyny. Women were precisely the individuals entering the turn-of-the-century conversations in an increasingly public manner. Paul Elmer More would keep such matters private. He advocated a readership where the individual never stepped outside the polite bounds of her own perception. Damning "Emersonianism" — "this self-deceit of a facile optimism" (83) — he nonetheless recuperated Emerson for the individual who needed a private, literary friend. "I would not imply that the individual reader of Emerson may not go to him for ever renewed inspiration and assurance in the things of the spirit" (72). He concludes his centenary tribute, by placing reverence before reading. He assures his reader that he will make no disparaging remarks against the "sweet spirit of Emerson" (83). His writing is another matter.

From the vantage point of the New Humanists, Emerson was irretrievably associated with the most recalcitrant parts of the American past. Depending upon one's critical standpoint he gave either too much or too little power to the individual. He was either complicitous with American materialist culture or the ineffectual voice of protest against such materialism. As the New Moderns battled against the New Humanists, Emerson was caught in the critical crossfire. T. S. Eliot labeled his essays "an encumbrance," something Santayana said more politely in 1900 when he jettisoned Emerson from the field of philosophy. Regardless of their differences, the cultural critics in the first forty years of the twentieth century found Emerson mostly useful by way of rejection. This story dominated Emerson studies: the voices of writers such as Eliot and H. L. Mencken were powerful. Their critical frameworks shaped the century's understanding of literature. In the history of literary and cultural criticism, their influence was enormous; yet their engagement with Emerson's writings was infrequent at best. As is increasingly apparent, these critics did not spend much time reading Emerson's words.

Early in the century, Emerson was still worth celebrating for his remarkable character even though he was rapidly becoming a dead question in terms of writing or thought. The benign Sage of Concord became almost as grandfatherly as Longfellow and served the emerging moderns well in their own self-definition. Their assertions proceeded most successfully by negation. From our late-twentieth-century vantage point, we might well be eager to invoke Harold Bloom at this point and show how his writing about the "anxiety of influence" describes both New Humanist and Modernist response to Emerson. He was the great forefather they needed to silence. Reading a sentence at a time from essays by Barrett Wendell, Irving Babbitt, and T. S. Eliot (not to mention Robert Penn Warren and Yvor Winters), war is decidedly declared. This diatribe against Emerson is the most familiar piece of Emerson's reception history, perhaps better known than Emerson's essays themselves. With the damnation by Eliot, so the story runs, Emerson fared increasingly poorly at the hands of the intellectuals. The New Critics found his writing intractable, flawed in terms of genre and subject. The poets, who were in the Southern Agrarian circle and moved between poetry and criticism, clearly wanted no part of an Emersonian prototype. Winters was the most infamous in his claims, single-handedly convicting Emerson of Hart Crane's suicide, but Allen Tate and Robert Penn Warren also noted the faults they saw in Emerson's work.

Such quotations make for a good story, and the story's reputed power has certainly been seen in the diminished academic study of Emerson in the thirties, forties, and — despite watershed books in the fifties and sixties — even until the seventies. To this day, critics such as Michael Lopez and Charles Mitchell show how powerful that hold apparently was. The frequent point of departure for today's Emerson criticism and indeed sometimes its topic are the dismissals of the past. Whether Lopez's discussion of how we get out of that old pattern only by "de-transcendentalizing" Emerson or Mitchell's assertion that the quarrels of the past were generally innocent of close readings of Emerson, the late twentieth century found that the first forty years of the century shaped the next sixty.

Less well known are the voices that continued to praise Emerson's revolutionary words. While an anonymous reviewer for the *Ethical Record* complained that the centenary comments were so bland as to be virtually thought-deadening, not all of the centenary remarks were dutiful tributes. While Emerson was steadily becoming the albatross around philosophy's neck, one voice as steadily argued that a place be kept for him in the field. John Dewey, who himself would come in for much philosophical discrediting, maintained that Emerson's rejection from the discipline was more often than not a necessary strategy on the part of the writer. It had little to do with Emerson's work. This work contained a "finely-wrought" logic that was part and parcel of his aphoristic method. In his 1903 essay "Emerson — The Philosopher of Democracy," Dewey comments, "I am not acquainted with any writer . . . whose movement of thought is more compact and unified, nor one who combines more adequately diversity of intellectual attack with concentration of form and effect" (405–06). Delivered first as an address for the Emerson Memorial Meeting at the University of Chicago, Dewey's piece is argumentative in its emphasis. The separation of Emerson from philosophy stood on the false ground of a suspect division between poetical and philosophical work.

In Emerson, Dewey saw an individual interested in the work of creation: he was the "maker," not the "reflector" (406). He used these designations to ally Emerson with the poet. He would not, however, close the doors of philosophy to him. Emerson's subject remained quintessentially philosophical. His work was nothing less than philosophy rendered in poetry: "a hymn to intelligence, a paean to the all-creating, all-disturbing power of thought" (409). Dewey found even this formulation unsatisfactory. The poet-philosopher was all too readily dissolved back into the poet. He took one further step — a step that mid-twentieth-century critics refused and late-twentieth-century critics endorse. Dewey writes, "the coming century may well make evident what is just now dawning, that Emerson is not only a philosopher, but that he is the Philosopher of Democracy" (412). For many years of the century, Dewey's comments were either dead-end or embarrassment. If Emerson showed anything about democracy, it was its patent limitations, whether those limitations were seen in Emerson's distrust of the masses or his supposed sponsorship of the "imperial self." Every decade of the twentieth century produced its own denunciation of Emerson's philosophy of democracy. The final decade of the twentieth century, however, saw this issue differently. John Dewey's comments sound remarkably current when played through the democratic individuality of George Kateb's discussion of *Emerson and Self-Reliance* (1995).

Emersonian individualism was clearly up for definition during the centenary celebrations. For many, the Emerson memorials were best delivered as social criticism for the current day. Even the hometown effect of the Concord celebrations did not cause a retreat to polite discourse. Moorfield Storey called his hearers to account, using the celebration of Emerson's birth to remind them of the United States' failure to express a "living faith" in the ideas of the man they were supposedly honoring. His questions were unmistakably specific: "Are the sons of your fathers indifferent to the struggles of other men for freedom? Are they content to stand silently by while their fellow citizens in this country are denied their equal rights? Are they willing to help deprive another people of that liberty which is the birthright of all human beings?" (*Centenary of Ralph Waldo Emerson*, 109). Emerson's son Edward echoed the concern with his own criticism of an earlier omission. Calling attention to the festivities of the morning, he reminded his hearers that some of his father's words had been left out, ostensibly due to the constraints of time. In singing the Independence Day Ode written by Emerson in 1857, the high school students omitted two verses, the very verses that had been unsettling in the late 1850s and, Edward Emerson suggested, still proved disturbing. The verses directly criticized the United States. Too often it was a country that spoke high principle and enacted unsavory deeds. What had not been heard that morning were the following lines:

> United States! The ages plead, —
> Present and past in under-song, —
> Go put your creed into your deed,
> Nor speak with double tongue.

> For sea and land don't understand,
> Nor skies without a frown
> See rights for which the one hand fights
> By the other cloven down.

The son made certain that the father's words were heard at least once that day, reciting them for his audience and prefacing them with the reminder of current affairs. "They were lasting truths that he announced — as true from 1898 to 1903 and onward as in the dark days of the Civil War" (122).

Storey and Emerson were not the only ones to bring discord to Concord. Though veiled in politer terms, Caroline Hazard, then president of Wellesley College, honored Emerson for "the work which [he] did for women" (100). Her work faced no small task, because Emerson's own ambivalence about a woman's place outside the domestic sphere made his comments about women often problematic at best. Hazard chose to focus on the implications of Emerson's thought. Self-reliance, she made clear, was not necessarily a gendered concept. She comments, "The dignity which he gave to the individual with his call to awake and arise — this splendid call to personality — sounded not only for men but for women" (100–101). While her emphasis on personality was hardly in keeping with Emerson — that was a word that he would no more ascribe to man than to God — Hazard saw in it an eminent fit and useful application to women's lives. Were "personality" licensed, and yet still couched within the form of "service," then the longstanding ethic and aesthetic of womanly self-denial could finally be overturned. She reads the lesson out loud for women of the previous generation as well as for her own: "There were many women who were content with their daily round of duty, who found in it certainly all the room they could ask for self-denial; but the call to awaken to their own personality, to a conception of the worth of their own souls and the right that they had to live their own lives, — this call came with an especial force, as it seems to me, to the women of his day. We hope we have learned the lesson" (101).

Hazard speaks for one of the audiences often rejected in and by Emerson criticism. No less serious than the critic, these individuals championed Emerson's writing for its life-altering power. (So too, of course, did Nietzsche and Porte and Poirier and Cavell.) Represented by the women and men in the numerous Emerson Clubs, their approach should not be confused with the vindictive representations rendered by More or later by Mencken ("debased Transcendentalism rolled into pills for fat women with vague pains and inattentive husbands," *Prejudices, First Series*, 194). In an age of limited access to higher education, the reading clubs offered a program of systematic and often cumulative study. Beyond these programs, the emerging field of curricular reform advocated a greater use and less traditional inclusion of Emerson in the public schools. Numerous books for school study were developed, foremost among them was Eva Tappan's *Emerson: Select Essays and Poems* (1898) and Bliss Perry's *The Heart of Emerson's Essays* (1914). A professional and public voice for these readers emerged in the 1920s with writers as various as Stuart Sherman, Bliss Perry, Alfred Kreymborg and Samuel Crothers. While their studies were clearly written in response to the attacks on Emerson — New Humanist and New Modernist alike — they were at the same time the heirs to two studies of Emerson that deliberately eschewed contention.

The best known of these lesser known critics is O. W. Firkins. His *Ralph Waldo Emerson*, published in 1915, was the first book-length work to make use of the recently published *Journals*. It builds from the life and works model of the nineteenth century, but in this case, the works dominate the life. Firkins' book is divided into two sections. The first third is biographical; the rest of the book is devoted to a detailed discussion of the works. Beginning with a chapter entitled "The Harvest," Firkins provides interpretive summaries of the prose works, complete with numerous quotations and frequent commentary on the essays themselves. He then examines the prose and poetry in turn, focusing on the separable elements of style. From poetry he turns to philosophy, quietly making his assertion that Emerson could still be seriously considered under that rubric. He ends with a chapter entitled "Foreshadowings," in which he addresses the common objections to Emerson's thought and suggests that a careful reading of Emerson would be a thought-provoking means for resolving the seemingly irreconcilable differences of the present day.

While Firkins directly refers to the events leading up to World War I and locates the divisiveness in the unresolved tension between the demands of force and the "undisplaced claims of morality" (366), he also identifies a problem closer to home in the practice of criticism itself. Critics fail to recognize the source of their resistance to Emerson's ideas, terming Emerson an "aberration," when in fact he "represents an extraordinary intellectual and moral development" — so extraordinary that his thought necessarily demands a reevaluation of the old values (360). In place of such reevaluation, however, Firkins sees only repetition of secondhand truisms: "The world adopts Emerson's sagacities, chants his verse, savors his pungencies, and reveres his character: meanwhile it ignores his philosophy: he is at the same time honored and forsaken" (373).

He faults the prevalent style of criticism. Examining the debate over Emerson's poetry, Firkins finds that the controversy yields little about the poems themselves, although it speaks volumes about the "psychology of readers." Truculence provides a certain "contentious piquancy" and entertains its readers with "pungent implications" about the intellects of the critics who value or disparage a certain aspect of Emerson's writing. Firkins counsels against contention, and suggests that, at any rate, the relentlessly worked topic of Emerson's poetry offers little for the immediate future.

His discussion attempts to strike a balance among the various considerations of Emerson's writing. While he claims that Emerson's ideas are the most important element for the contemporary reader, he in no way diminishes the importance of literary considerations. His discussion of the stylistic elements in Emerson's essays and poems is exhaustive, divided among various literary devices with numerous examples. He is one of the first to argue for the structural coherence of Emerson's essays, disputing the long-held assumption that Emerson assembled his essays as a simple collection of sentences. While he defines the sentence as the basic unit of Emerson's compositions, he also draws attention to the form of the paragraph and the relation of those paragraphs within a given essay. He highlights the rhythms in the prose and suggests that the vaulting rhythm between extremes was one of Emerson's many methods for suggesting the whole through its parts.

In contrast to earlier commentary that made the poetry and the prose all of one piece, he distinguishes the genres, calling them complementary yet distinct. He sees the poetry as "correlative and corrective to the prose." Where the essays follow a whirlpool-like method of abstraction illustrated by a rapid succession of fragmentary but concrete images, the poems serve as parables, taking the single image and enlarging it into its own expanded moment. He cites "Days" as the best example of this process, but admits that Emerson's poetry is rarely so sharply focused. While Firkins himself is not entirely able to value the poetry he describes, he nonetheless provides a canny description of Emerson's poetic practice: the poems work as a "succession — not properly a series . . . of self-sufficing moments" (281).

That sentence identifies both the essay and the idea Firkins deemed central to his interpretation of Emerson. In his summary of Emerson's works, he terms "Experience" "one of the boldest essays in literature." Later generations of Emerson critics fully agreed with that assessment. Firkins writes, "It is a provoking, unsettling, aggressive, half-mephistophelean essay; it acts as pry or wedge; it loosens, dislodges, and upheaves. It shows Emerson's faculty for turning his own flank and assailing himself, as it were, in the rear" (193). Both here and in reference to the poetry, Firkins praises Emerson's ability to show his own limitations. Reminiscent of William James's comments about Emerson's wise obedience to his own constraints, Firkins takes this a step further and sees such acknowledgement as part of Emerson's repertoire of stylistic elements. He also links it with the idea he places at the center of Emerson's work.

He opens the section on Emerson's philosophy by telling the so-called "secret of Emerson." He says it may be "conveyed in one word" though he himself has difficulty keeping it to that. In his reading of Emerson, the central point is "the superlative, even the superhuman, value which Emerson found in the unit of experience, the direct, momentary, individual act of consciousness" (297). Firkins combines experience and consciousness into a single act. What matters is the power of the moment. He terms it an "isolative philosophy" in which individual moments take precedence. "The supreme good is the integrity of the moment" (311), he writes, and reminds his readers that such a philosophy has little use for conventional logic. As in his discussion of Emerson's compositional practices, he refutes the charge that Emerson's inability created his lapses. Emphasizing Emerson's own mastery of logic through the Harvard curriculum as well as in certain pieces of his essays, Firkins argues that the absence of logic was a deliberate refusal. Logic did not fit with the philosophy of the moment. That required a very different approach: experience demanded endless experiment.

For Firkins, the future of Emerson studies lay in the philosophical aspect. To arrive at philosophy, however, he found it essential to establish Emerson's works on firm literary ground. First and foremost, he argued, the essays and the poems required close and careful reading. Citing the progress that fifty years effected, he warned his audience that their job was not finished. What was obscure to the first readers gradually cleared over time. "Fifty years of approach have lightened many difficulties" (234). The same idea could be applied to the individual reader. The more one read and analyzed Emerson's writing, the clearer one's understanding became. Without such study, Firkins warned, Emerson's works would once again be as opaque as they were to their original reviewers. In a comment whose cautionary note can now be read as prescient prediction, Firkins wrote, "and one reflects curiously that fifty years of recession, should they occur, might involve our grandchildren in the same perplexities which befogged our grandsires" (234). Depending upon how you read Emerson criticism, Firkins was off by a mere ten years — either way. For those who see the breakthrough in Emerson studies occurring with Whicher in the 1950s, there were a mere forty years of fog; others might say the fog lifted in the 1970s as the effect of the *Journals and Miscellaneous Notebooks* finally freed critics from the repetition of the past.

Firkins's book received relatively little attention at the time of its publication, in large part due to the war, in small part to the continued interest in what Firkins called "contentious piquancy." H. D. Gray, however, mentions Firkins in his *Emerson: A Statement of New England Transcendentalism as Expressed in the Philosophy of Its Chief Exponent* (1917). Although the bulk of Gray's book was written before Firkins's, he does add Firkins's voice to his own argument. Firkins's emphasis on Emerson's philosophy was clearly a welcome sign for Gray. Approaching the philosophy as many had the poetry, Gray acknowledges its "amateur" appearance: "lack of system, of philosophical consistency, indeed of that

logical soundness which is essential to an original thinker worthy of any
serious consideration" (26). Well aware of the Robertson-Santayana
criticism of Emerson's unsystematic thought, Gray sought to establish
his claim without skirting its real obstacles. By comparing Emerson
with accepted philosophers, he countered the critics who denied Emerson his discipline. He realized the limitations of such an approach, for
comparison easily became the pale cover of imitation. He linked Emerson to the German philosopher Schelling only to back away from the
comparison and remind his reader that Emerson was an "original
thinker, and arrived at his conclusions by very much the same methods
as all other philosophers have done" (31). Emerson, he claimed, thought
like a philosopher. Frederic Henry Hedge had asserted the same in
1845; Stanley Cavell turned that assertion into long-term discussion in
the late twentieth century.

Gray's central concern is Emerson's contribution to philosophy. He
never wavers in asserting its reality. Regardless of the apparent stylistic
differences from other philosophers, Emerson posed a convincing answer
to one of the most troubled questions in Idealism which Gray phrases as
follows: "how a real individual may exist in a world of universal spirit"
(41). Examining Emerson's individualist based idealism, he locates Emerson's original contribution in evolution. He clearly distinguishes this from
a Darwinian meaning, setting his argument apart from those who attempted to conflate the two. For Emerson, he argues, evolution supplied
a dynamic of change to an otherwise static world of the ideal. The ideal
world could incorporate the real individual through an emphasis on
change, or using Emerson's vocabulary, "metamorphosis" (45).

Like Firkins, Gray's emphasis strikes a note that late-twentieth-
century critics would turn into the chordal structure of Emerson studies. Firkins called it the "secret of Emerson" uncovered in the importance of the moment. Gray restricted this moment to Emerson's
comments on ecstasy and used them to study Emerson's epistemology.
Explicating the troubling statement from "Experience" — "the individual is always mistaken" — Gray finds its meaning in the relationships
Emerson posits among nature, the individual and divine force (or soul).
We emerge from nature, he says, but until distinguished by the "development of the intellectual faculties," we are not individuals. With that
development, however, we not only gain individuality but lose our un-
failing connection with nature. Thus is "the individual always mistaken." Gray then takes one further step: "therefore our prime duty is
to 'surrender' our will, that is to remove the inhibitory effect of the understanding upon the divinity within us; in other words, to go into a
perpetual state of 'ecstasy'" (60). Gray notes the philosophical difficulty

involved in such a demand: it creates a "complete dualism in the mind of man." To resolve such dualism, Gray turns to Emerson's mysticism. While this sounds like an open admission of defeat, Gray argues its power on philosophical grounds. Emerson's development of the concept came close to turning mysticism into philosophy.

Gray's final concern was Emerson's contribution to ethics. The sticking point was Emerson's much discussed optimism. He sided with those who connected optimism to Emerson's concept of evolution, and he pointed out the number of times Emerson reminded his readers that the particular individual was readily expendable. Gray finally could not get over the hurdle himself and maintained, with Santayana, that Emerson's optimism had "no philosophical basis" but was due to "religious instinct" (78). The best he could say was that this optimism was a fully developed conviction on Emerson's part, in no way denying the existence and power of evil, yet invariably upholding the individual and championing an unshakable moral order within the universe.

In the World War I world, such words played an elusive tune for their readers. An article that appeared in the *Nation* in 1919 suggests just how unsatisfactory Emerson's apparent philosophy was to certain members of its audience. Written by a recent immigrant from Russia, the article attacked Emerson's "doctrine of Compensation." Maria Moravsky found Emerson out-dated at best, an unwittingly cruel coward at worst. His assertion that "justice is not postponed" fit the system he needed, but it was a system that existed only in his own mind. Paralleling the philosopher's with the embroiderer's work, she maintained that the intellect stood to learn much from the home: "A philosopher draws a design of his world exactly as a sweet maiden in the old-fashioned home would draw a design of embroidery. The maiden has thousands of multicolored beads; she selects them carefully and puts on her needle one after the other. . . . So a philosopher works with facts. He carefully selects only those which fit his design, his outline of the universe. And then he makes a harmoniously colored theory of life. But the sweet maiden grows old, and when she is a grandmother, her little grandchild finds the dusty embroidery and breaks all the weakened threads with her irreverent fingers, and the flowers and letters of the old design again become just a mass of multicolored beads — material for new designs" (1005). Emerson failed, as did others, by holding to a design well past its temporary usefulness. Witness to the Russian Revolution, Moravsky saw little to salvage from Emerson. His writing, she admitted, was beautiful. It was "sweet music" yet carried within it "strange dissonances" (1004). Her present age required a different "system of life," one that would take into account the actual pain and manifold limitations of individual human experience: "the human race does not consist of Emersons. Most of us are weak. We are never fully responsible for our actions. We need pity and forgiveness. We cannot pay two cents for two cents all our life, and even if we could, it would be a poor life" (1005).

By the end of the century's second decade, consensus about Emerson was crumbling. In the late teens, early twenties, H. L. Mencken commented extensively on Emerson in his several series of essays, tellingly entitled *Prejudices*. In Emerson he found a useful example of his own theory of American failure. Noting that the Emerson-like prophecies of a coming American literature never materialized, he placed the blame on American culture 'in general and the New Humanists in particular. There was no intellectual depth to American thought, no vigor in American writing because an ethical bent warped expression. The "decaying caste of literary Brahmins" (*Prejudices*, Second Series, 21) remained in power, and in consequence, no writer could create an authentic expression of American life. In Mencken's terms that life offered the unfettered writer lush opportunity: "the whole, gross, glittering, excessively dynamic, infinitely grotesque, incredibly stupendous drama of American life" (23). Mencken freely denounced American society for its superficiality. In his reading, Emerson stood as its signal victim. In his long reflection on national literature (*Prejudices*, Second Series), he called Emerson "the victim of gross misrepresentation" (58) and blamed the "enthusiasts" who "read into him all sorts of flatulent bombast" (58).

A year earlier in his short piece "The Unheeded Lawgiver" (*Prejudices*, First Series), he underwrote the separation that would last several generations. Mencken presented Emerson's thought as the mutually exclusive opposite of American pragmatism. "On the side of ideas," Emerson was quintessentially a writer interested in "first causes . . . interior and immutable realities" (193). The United States' reality, however, followed a far different approach. Mencken comments, "But the philosophy that actually prevails among his countrymen — a philosophy put into caressing terms by William James — teaches an almost exactly contrary doctrine: its central idea is that whatever satisfies the immediate need is substantially true, that appearance is the only form of fact worthy the consideration of a man with money in the bank" (193).

The 1920s saw a much greater activity in specific discussion of Emerson than had any period since 1903. The short and long studies as well as the various editions were clearly the outgrowth of a combined group of influences. The publication of Emerson's *Journals* (1909–14) broadened the audience for Emerson as well as offering new material for a scholarly audience. Edited by Edward Waldo Emerson and Waldo Emerson Forbes, the volumes served as a catalyst for the wholesale rereading Firkins challenged his audience to undertake. The challenge would not end in the 1920s. A similar phenomenon would occur sixty years later with the modern editions of Emerson's work. There was also a group of new poets who claimed their own relation to Emerson and critics who saw in that relationship another aspect of their own argument.

This argument would once again turn away from philosophy and back to poetry. In the 1921 introduction to his edited volume of *Essays and Poems of Emerson*, Stuart Sherman concluded his remarks by discussing Emerson's poetry. He dismissed the "popular errors" that clouded a clear understanding of Emerson's aesthetic development. Arguing against Gray, he maintained that Emerson was not primarily an ethicist, but a God-intoxicated individual for whom "ecstasy" meant artistic expression, not epistemology. He also countered the charge of "Puritanism" that had been leveled against Emerson since the first attacks on the Genteel Tradition. Emerson, he maintained, was no Puritan "decadent" but a "renascence and fresh flowering" (reprinted in *Americans*, 1922, as "The Emersonian Liberation," 107). As he defined this "renascence," Sherman showed the source from which he developed his ideas. A student of Babbitt's, he retained the category "humanist," applying it to Emerson; yet his Emerson was not Babbitt's. Embracing Emerson's liberating force, Sherman betrayed no fear of the democratic leveling Babbitt condemned. Sherman's Emerson freed artists, American and otherwise, to wrestle independently with the problems of their art. He reminded the reader, "In 1831, long before Flaubert or Pater had announced it, [Emerson] committed to his Journal the doctrine of the 'unique word'" (114). He anticipated the other aestheticians of the age.

Sherman begins his discussion with Emerson's influence; he ends with the poetry itself. Arguing its excellence, he challenged his readers to reevaluate their assessment. He attributed Emerson's "underrated" status as a poet to his unwillingness to write for an audience. He did not "practice dilution," and in consequence the common reader found his attention taxed beyond its limit. Extending his commentary to the essays, Sherman noted a similar effect. Emerson's practice of economy — whether in the sentence or the line — proved difficult to the "ordinary mind." He does, however, hold out those same lines to the aspiring poet. Quoting the first lines of "Hamatreya," he suggests that the Chicago School of poets could not find a better model (114–18).

Sherman called Emerson "an unspent force in our own times" and encouraged his reader to tap into that force through a particular type of reading. Not only would multiple readings be necessary, but the approach could not be limited to a single dimension. Tweaking the noses of his fellow professors, particularly those for whom literary study featured the history of ideas, he announced, "To know him is not mere knowledge. It is an experience; for he is a dynamic personality, addressing the will, the emotions, the imagination, no less than the intellect. His value escapes the merely intellectual appraiser" (64).

Sherman assumed an audience of both professors and students. While his target was clearly the younger readers, he did not address them directly. Well aware of his other, resisting readers, he turned the criticism against Emerson in Emerson's favor. Citing Arnold, he reminded his readers that the criticism also included one stunning superlative: Emerson's essays were the "most important work" of nineteenth-century prose. Even the phrase, "friend and aider of those who would live in the spirit" becomes something more than a moral salve to bind up the wounds left by Arnold's judgment. In Sherman's reading, Emerson was a distinctly necessary "aid" who freed the younger generation from the older. One can certainly read such assertions biographically as Sherman declares independence from Babbitt, but Sherman's focus remains the importance of Emerson to a young person's "intellectual emancipation." He insists that such freedom is no mere rebellion, no post-war frivolity. Emerson is "the true liberator" who "strikes off the old shackles but immediately . . . suggests new service, a fuller use of our powers" (78).

Speaking to the students who would be using his collection of Emerson's writing, Sherman also spoke to the "new poets" for whom Emerson's poetry and poetic theory held the key to their emancipation. Sherman's selection of poems is generous for the size of his edition: thirty-five poems with a range from "Days" to "The Snow-Storm" to the "Boston Hymn" to "Voluntaries." The poems conclude the volume, following a section of essays entitled "Men of Action." The call was clear, and at least some of the new poets responded accordingly.

In 1929, Alfred Kreymborg published *Our Singing Strength: An Outline of American Poetry, 1620–1930*. A poet himself, Kreymborg eschewed the company of "critics" or "historians" (1). Questioning the possibility of "objective criticism" (2), his introductory remarks point the way to a late-twentieth-century perspective. Such prescience was his hoped-for end. He reminded his audience that the past wielded a dangerous power; it privileged one form of literary kinship over another. The "student" of poetry was "liable to see most intimately the aims and achievements of the era he lives in, to overpraise the men and women for whom he feels the closest kinship, and almost to miss altogether the at least equal values of the past we derive from" (3). Encouraging his readers to pursue all forms of kinship, Kreymborg endorses their individual work — to re-envision their perspective on the past and their imagined expression for the future. He also offers an identity for both reader and writer. They are students, as the passage says, but they are also, and above all, amateurs, who refuse the temptation to speak as an authority. From Kreymborg's view, once *authority* speaks, a fatal confusion enters. The subjective perception is set forth as the objective truth, and in consequence past writers will always be heard for their limitations.

Following his announcedly different path, Kreymborg nonetheless addresses the immediate past and its various Emersons (the cold dispassionate Emerson and the cheerfully optimistic model). He finds a different image in Emerson's poetry and journals. In the age of Prohibition, his is "the intoxicated Emerson." That phrase gives his Emerson chapter its title. It also articulates the unconventional power of Emerson's poetry. Kreymborg returns to the claim launched as early as 1841 by John Heraud. Emerson refused to conciliate his reader. Representing Emerson's poems as a dynamic equilibrium between poetry and philosophy, Kreymborg describes moments when the two merge and moments where the two part. "The dialectic," he says, "is dazzling" (69). It is also inflammatory and intoxicating: "fire abounds all through Emerson, fire kindled through a fearless contact with Nature" (73); "There is no poet among us whose drunken poems equal Emerson's" (78). He allies both images with Emerson's form-breaking style and claims that such breakage became the one firm foundation for American poetry.

Kreymborg's intoxicated Emerson fits strangely with Bliss Perry's "serene visionary." In the introduction to his edition of Emerson's essays (1926), Perry presents a figure far different from either Sherman's or Kreymborg's. Like Sherman, he sought a wider audience for Emerson, assuming that many varieties of student would be interested in his volume. He maps out an itinerary for their study depending upon their experience. He guides the new and bewildered reader to and through the voluminous amount of published Emerson (a massive twenty-two volumes by their standards; a mere twenty-two volumes by the standard of the late twentieth century's insurmountable fifty). He suggests that the reader new to Emerson begin with the biographies: "Holmes or Cabot or Garnett or Woodberry." (Firkins is not mentioned.) If biography does not readily appeal to the reader, he advises Samuel Crothers' *Emerson: How to Know Him*. For the student with some prior knowledge of Emerson, he advises the Journals, and for all readers, he suggests a slow chronological reading of the twelve volumes of essays.

Perry assumes readers will find a writer of decidedly private concern who speaks to individuals of a particular class: "endowed with intelligence, will-power, and a sense of right and wrong" (6). Echoing the concerns of the Genteel Tradition, Perry emphasizes the identity necessary for the "good" reader of Emerson. He quotes Matthew Arnold with approval, turning the comment into a statement about substance over surface: "He is looking at the object of writing rather than at the technique" (8). Perry concludes by citing Emerson's definition of his audience: "Men and women of some religious culture and aspiration, young or else mystical" (8). From this group he excludes the writers and the critics.

Perry's publishing efforts in the first thirty years of the twentieth century included four different editions of Emerson as well as the Princeton Vanuxem Lectures published in 1931 as *Emerson Today*. Advocating an expanded audience for Emerson, Perry produced two similar yet not identical collections of Emerson's prose. Published in 1926, *Selections from the Prose Works of Ralph Waldo Emerson* was part of Houghton Mifflin's Riverside college series. *The Heart of Emerson's Essays* appeared in two editions separated by twenty years. First published in 1914, it was reissued in an expanded version in 1933, following the popularity of the journal selections Perry edited in 1926 (*The Heart of Emerson's Journals*). In the school edition, Perry included a selection from Emerson's letters: fifteen letters to Carlyle, three to John Sterling, five to Samuel Gray Ward, and the famous "I do not know what arguments mean" letter to Henry Ware, Jr. The letters are omitted from the popular edition and in their place are two additional essays: "Country Life" and "Concord Walks," first published in *Natural History of Intellect* (1893). The 1926 and 1933 editions contain the same footnotes and each includes the same bibliography. The placement of the bibliography differs between volumes: in the student edition it appears immediately after the introduction; in the popular edition it is placed at the back of the book. In the editions I consulted, the student volume, housed at Carleton College, had many of its pages uncut. The introduction had never been read and neither had the notes. The popular edition was well worn, rebound and generously underlined — even in the notes and bibliography. It too had resided in a school library, a teacher's college in upstate New York.

Perry's project of making Emerson accessible to a wider audience gained momentum with his selection from the Journals. His purpose, however, was never to alienate Emerson from the professors. To further the study of Emerson he championed the publication of the unpublished works, in particular the letters, and advocated the more careful study of the Journals. The fiction he hoped to preserve was that the various audiences for Emerson were finally not that different.

That fiction would not last long. The 1920s and 1930s saw the increasing separation between different groups of readers. A general audience remained viable, as is patently clear by the number of editions for the general reader. The difference between college student, high school student and general reader at this point was a distinction of degree, not of kind. It was still assumed that a textbook would appeal to the adult who sought to further his or her education and that a text for college need not be substantially different from a text for high school. The growing gap appeared in the difference between publications for the rising "scholarly" journals and discussions aimed at the general reader.

No better demonstration of the emerging difference can be found than in the contrast between Crothers' *Emerson: How to Know Him* and Norman Foerster's "Emerson On the Organic Principle in Art" (1926). Foerster emphasizes analysis; he constructs an argument as the best means for examining Emerson's theory of art. While he includes references to the present, he mutes them. They never become the announced premise from which he thinks. For Crothers, however, it is precisely the present and immediate past that form the context of his discussion. He begins his book by criticizing the critics. In an introductory chapter entitled "The Approach to Emerson," he tells his reader to set aside the customary critical practice of "building systems" (2). Instead, he maintains, as did Sherman, that reading Emerson requires experiential knowledge. He suggests a process of "comparing notes" (2). He cautions the reader against biography. From his vantage point, Emerson's writing was largely independent of the life. He further classes Emerson with the "geniuses" who are "essentially timeless. They owe very little to their immediate environment. They might have lived anywhere or at any time, and the substance and manner of their thinking would have been very much the same" (3).

In contrast, Foerster set his discussion of Emerson distinctly in Emerson's immediate environment. The article begins and ends with a comparison to Poe. As Foerster considers Emerson's poetics, he concentrates heavily on influence, citing the aesthetic theory of Benedetto Croce and its popularity with Coleridge and the Romantics and then narrowing the focus to the Platonic source for Emerson's doctrine of inspiration. Foerster's approach clearly signals the scholarly future. With his attention to source study and his point-by-point argument, he adopts what would become standard practice for the critical essay during the next fifty years.

Reflecting the growing critical interest in "organicism," Foerster turned to Emerson's aesthetic theory as an eminent example. Ten years earlier, Firkins discarded the concept; it was imprecise and therefore not useful. Beginning in the twenties, however, a number of critics interested in Romanticism sought to give this concept critical mass. At the same time, those who would become known as the "New Critics" were shaping their views on the inviolable integrity of the artistic work. Organic became their word. Foerster was among them and found in Emerson an excellent possibility for illustrating the complex dimensions of the "organic principle." In Foerster's discussion, it was clear that organicism was no simple principle of growth.

Foerster was interested in Emerson's ideas about poetry rather than in the poems themselves. He unapologetically identified himself with those who found the poems a failed practice of an interesting theory. He comments, "his essays and poems are badly organized, the parts having no definite relation to each other" (195). Foerster is quick to add that inability to "observe the law of organic form" did not mean failure to "interpret" that law with insight. His article takes that interpretation as its province, creating two categories within which to understand Emerson's "philosophy of art." He writes, "Thus the poem, we may say — though Emerson does not use the terms — has organic beauty in a twofold sense, qualitatively and quantitatively" (196). He locates the "qualitative" in the kind of intuition the poet received; the "quantitative" in the "success" with which the poem expressed that intuition.

Foerster assures his reader that such a distinction "clarifies" and does not "distort" Emerson's writing, and in that assertion, he speaks for the growing literary critical interest in creating explanatory structures for the analysis of texts. Moving away from the appreciative and largely descriptive narrative, this new group of critics sought to place their work on a more "scientific" ground. They did not simply respond to poems but analyzed them. At the same time, they distinguished their work from the time-honored explication de texte. In contrast, to the specific parsing of lines, often with a decidedly philological bent, they defined their work through the application of large principles. They created (hypo)theses which they in turn examined through the works of a particular author or group of authors.

Foerster's focus served Emerson critics well. A clear line of interest in "organicism" can be traced from Foerster to Matthiessen's discussion of Emerson in *The American Renaissance* (1941) to Vivian Hopkins' study of Emerson's aesthetics in *Spires of Form* (1951), Sherman Paul's focus on correspondence in *Emerson's Angle of Vision* (1952) and Richard Adams' discussion of the dynamic element of organicism in "Emerson and the Organic Metaphor" (1954) and "The Basic Contradiction in Emerson" (1969).

This fifty-year project of creating unity for and from Emerson depended upon a singular, often precarious, solution. The bristling tension between extremes — the defining force of Emerson's dualism — required a thorough revision into a stable middle ground. Emerson was presented as the reconciler, the individual who held contradictory ideas within a single continuous thought. Dualism yielded unity. Development was the key. Under its rubric, opposition did not mean a sharp division into mutually exclusive extremes. Gray cast it as *evolution*; Foerster located it in the *organic principle*; Matthiessen, almost despairing of Emerson's ability to escape the "confusing alternation" between the two halves of his consciousness, borrowed Sherman's concept of *parable* to illustrate how Emerson created an artistic whole. Hopkins blended the concept of *evolution* and *organicism* to illustrate the dynamic moment of *wholeness* created through the progressive development of the parts. Life and work were in turn seen to mirror each other. Whicher created a two-part structure for Emerson's life in which the opposite halves were presented as complementary. By studying a mind in its process of thought, the particular contradictions became a part of the process.

Whicher marks both the epitome of the organic theory and its end. While his emphasis on Emerson's process clearly tied into the concept of development, his two-part division returned criticism to the prospect of two halves that finally were irreconcilable. The continuity between Emerson's idealism and his skepticism existed only in the life. In the writing, the positions remained what they always had been: an expression of dualism. Whicher's emphasis on the process of thought similarly pointed the way to a future in which process would dominate critical discussion. While the structures of critical inquiry came increasingly into question, so too did the structure termed unity. An emphasis on process did not necessarily envision reconciliation as its end.

That interest in reconciliation could not be sustained as the century waned. By the 1970s, the concept of *unity* became increasingly untenable. What had been built up in those fifty years was slowly (or in some cases swiftly) being taken apart. The very elements of a critical approach were under question. Foerster's assumption that the objective study of a writer could necessarily be mastered through a particular kind of argument no longer held sole authority. Premises again shifted and works dismissed earlier looked interesting once again.

The very title of Crothers' 1921 book made it highly suspect for the growing "scholarly" debates of the 1920s and ever more marginal in the subsequent decades. As the New Critics would so emphatically show, the goal of literary criticism was not acquaintance with an author but a very different type of knowledge. The focus was the work and its form; the role of criticism was to develop methods that would best evaluate this formal expression of ideas. Crothers' approach might be fine for the amateur, but the professional reader of literature required something more rigorous. For twenty-first-century criticism, however, Crothers' "unscholarly" approach is interesting for its many anticipations of the late-twentieth-century Emersons. Refusing to "harmonize the views of Emerson," Crothers maintains the distinctness of "each separate view" (14) and leaves opposing views unreconciled. From his perspective, unresolved opposition in no way compromises Emerson's writing or the philosophy on which it is based. Ongoing opposition was a method in itself. Unsystematic it might be, but deliberate it certainly was.

While Crothers quotes too often and interprets too little for current taste, his interpretive sections look markedly contemporary. He locates Emerson's philosophy in antagonism and comments, "It [the mind] must assert its sovereignty, and in its resistance it makes the discovery of its power." The philosopher of power studied by Emerson critics in the 1990s was part and parcel of this "general discussion" in the 1920s.

Crothers' comments on Emerson's poetry are similarly prescient of recent debate. He writes, "He was the poet of the 'rushing metamorphosis'" (85). Like his peers, he found Emerson's poems less successful than the ideas behind them, but unlike them, he gave a lively description of these so-called faults. He described the experience of reading Emerson as a kind of electric shock; the reader frequently encounters a "metrical jolt" (76). He laments Emerson's inability to embrace free verse, and yet, when he articulates the "distinctive quality" (80) of Emerson's poetry he creates a different effect. Citing the limitations of human perception, he reminds the reader that what we perceive is already past, that what we recognize as current is "not strictly contemporaneous" (83). He comments, "The great illusion is that of arrested motion. Things seem to us to stand still, which in reality are whirling about with inconceivable velocity" (83). He cites the sciences as undoing that illusion of the "standstill" and then celebrates Emerson's endorsement of nineteenth-century science. "Emerson was profoundly stirred by thought of the explosive power of nature. Indeed his world was always exploding. He attempts to express the sense of these sudden happenings in his poetry. He is preeminently the poet of swift motion" (84). Crothers quotes generously from "Woodnotes," "Initial, Daemonic, and Celestial Love," and "Threnody." His final observation suggests why his words offered little to the literary establishment of his day, why they speak as a living voice to ours. He comments, "permanence is not of form but of force" (92).

For the New Critics of the 1930s, such a statement held little meaning. The only form of force was form itself. To somehow separate force into its own category made as little sense as valuing the poet's intent over the poem. Crothers did not speak with the voice that became dominant. It belonged to the New Critics, and their peculiar inflection of Emerson forms the substance of the next chapter. According to their appraisal Arnold succeeded on two counts, failed in one. As he said, Emerson was neither poet nor philosopher, but as he failed to say, his "friend and aider of those who would live in the spirit" was a fairweather companion, lasting only as long as an untenable optimism.

Works Cited

Anon. "The Emasculation of Emerson." *Ethical Record* 4 (1903): 189–91.

Adams, Richard P. "Emerson and the Organic Metaphor." *PMLA* 69 (March 1954): 117–30.

———. "The Basic Contradiction in Emerson." *ESQ: A Journal of the American Renaissance* 55 (1969): 106–10.

Babbitt, Irving. *Masters of Modern French Criticism*. Boston: Houghton Mifflin, 1912.

The Centenary of the Birth of Ralph Waldo Emerson. Boston: Riverside Press, 1903.

Crothers, Samuel McChord. *Emerson: How To Know Him*. Indianapolis: Bobbs-Merrill Company, 1921.

Dewey, John. "Emerson — The Philosopher of Democracy." *International Journal of Ethics* XIII: 4 (July 1903): 405–13.

Eliot, T. S. "American Literature" (review of the *Cambridge History of American Literature* vol. 2). *Athenaeum* 4643 (25 April 1919): 236–37.

Emerson, Edward Waldo. Speech at the Concord Centenary Celebration in *The Centenary of the Birth of Ralph Waldo Emerson*. Boston: Riverside Press, 1903: 119–27.

Firkins, O. W. *Ralph Waldo Emerson*. Boston: Houghton, Mifflin and Company, 1915.

Foerster, Norman. "Emerson on the Organic Principle of Art." PMLA 41 (1926): 193–208.

Gray, Henry David. *Emerson: A Statement of New England Transcendentalism as Expressed in the Philosophy of Its Chief Exponent.* Stanford: Stanford University Press, 1917.

Hazard, Caroline. Speech at the Concord Centenary Celebration in *The Centenary of the Birth of Ralph Waldo Emerson.* Boston: Riverside Press, 1903: 99–103.

Hopkins, Vivian C. *Spires of Form: A Study of Emerson's Aesthetic Theory.* Cambridge, MA: Harvard University Press, 1951.

Kateb, George. *Emerson and Self-Reliance.* Modernity and Public Thought, vol. 8. Thousand Oaks, CA: Sage Publishing, 1995.

Kleinfield, H. L. "The Structure of Emerson's Death." *Bulletin of the New York Public Library* 65 (January 1961): 47–64.

Kreymborg, Alfred. *Our Singing Strength: An Outline of American Poetry, 1620–1930.* New York: Coward-McCann, 1929.

Lopez, Michael. "De-Transcendentalizing Emerson." *ESQ: A Journal of the American Renaissance* 34: 1–2 (1988): 77–139.

Matthiessen, F. O. *American Renaissance: Art and Expression in the Age of Emerson and Whitman.* New York: Oxford University Press, 1941.

Mencken, H. L. "An Unheeded Law-Giver" in *Prejudices,* First Series. New York: Alfred A. Knopf, 1919: 191–94.

———. "The National Letters" in *Prejudices,* Second Series. New York: Alfred A. Knopf, 1920: 9–101.

Mitchell, Charles. *Individualism and Its Discontents: Appropriations of Emerson, 1880–1950.* Amherst: University of Massachusetts Press, 1997.

Moravsky, Maria. "The Idol of Compensation." *The Nation* 108: 2817 (28 June 1919): 1004–05.

More, Paul Elmer. "The Influence of Emerson" in *Shelburne Essays,* First Series. Boston: Houghton, Mifflin and Company, 1904: 71–84.

Paul, Sherman. *Emerson's Angle of Vision: Man and Nature in the American Experience.* Cambridge, MA: Harvard University Press, 1952.

Perry, Bliss. *Emerson Today.* Princeton: Princeton University Press, 1931.

———. *The Heart of Emerson's Essays.* Boston: Houghton Mifflin, 1914.

———. *The Heart of Emerson's Journals.* Boston: Houghton Mifflin, 1926.

———. *Selections from the Prose Works of Ralph Waldo Emerson.* Boston: Houghton, Mifflin, 1926.

Robertson, John M. *Modern Humanists: Sociological Studies of Carlyle, Mill, Emerson, Arnold, Ruskin, and Spencer with an Epilogue on Social Reconstruction.* London: Swan Sonnenschein, 1891.

Santayana, George. "Emerson" in *Interpretations of Poetry and Religion.* New York: Charles Scribner's Sons, 1900.

————. *Persons and Places.* New York: Charles Scribner's Sons, 1944.

Sherman, Stuart P. "The Emersonian Liberation" in *Americans.* New York: Charles Scribner's Sons, 1922.

————, editor. *Essays and Poems of Emerson.* 1921.

Storey, Moorfield. Speech at the Concord Centenary Celebration in *The Centenary of the Birth of Ralph Waldo Emerson.* Boston: Riverside Press, 1903: 104–10.

Tappan, Eva March, editor. *Select Essays and Poems of Ralph Waldo Emerson.* Boston: Allyn and Bacon, 1898.

Wendell, Barrett. "Ralph Waldo Emerson" in *A Literary History of America.* New York: Scribners, 1900: 311–27.

5: Emerson and the Dilemma for New Criticism

CONTENTION MARKS EMERSON commentary from its beginning, but if any period takes precedence, it is the thirty years between 1930 and 1960. There is far more than one generation's-worth of struggle in these three decades, and if the tone of the criticism sounds a note of greater urgency, it may well be that never before had Emerson's place been so keenly threatened. The old debate between poet and philosopher acquired a super-charged tone. The stakes were different. No longer were the debates about academic disciplines. Emerson was deemed more culpable than a mere "encumbrance." He was charged with giving an ugly consent to American materialism. He was faulted for an optimism that had no place in light of death camps and atomic bombs. Self-reliance was equated with a predatory individualism in which the bottom line was all too powerfully present. He provided the voice of capitalist exploitation; he turned a blind eye to the very real presence of evil in the world. And even art could not save him, for when critics turned to his aesthetic, many found a fatal flaw in the theory. By subordinating form, Emerson inescapably marred his content.

The attacks broke into three overlapping yet distinct categories: the socio-economic, the artistic, and the moral. The last category might well have come as a surprise to the critics of the era, for in part, they were separating themselves from the so-called moralism of an earlier time. In retrospect, however, the attacks on the economic implications of self-reliance and philosophic implications of Emerson's optimism were deeply rooted in questions of right and wrong. For the Marxist critics of the 1930s, Emerson's self-reliance was the inevitable companion of exploitation. For those who despaired over Emerson's apparently sanguine view of the universe, his vision of "the good" was not only inhuman but dangerous. Even the criticism on artistic grounds participated in this moral argument against Emerson. In Emerson's failure to respect form, he betrayed the power of art. His seemingly cavalier attitude toward the shape of meaning offered little hope to those who sought to shape a shattered meaning back into existence.

This chapter begins and ends with the sharp differences dividing the 1930s from the 1950s. These divisions cut in multiple directions. To borrow the image that shaped the times, Emerson's stock crashed in certain intellectual markets, a plunge that could in retrospect be expected from the inflated praise and extravagant blame he had received in the post World War I years. At the center of Emerson's devaluation was a powerful combination of societal circumstance and interpretive method. With the rise of New Criticism, Emerson's value could only fall. Its fundamental premises were a particularly poor fit for Emerson's writing, and thus, the burden of this chapter is the thirty-year struggle to make Emerson and New Criticism compatible. During those warring years, however, another side of the criticism was continuing, albeit slowly. The final section of this chapter returns to the 1930s: its work in editing was the way of the future. The late 1930s began what only the twenty-first century could finish: the behemoth task of publishing the unpublished Emerson (journals, letters, lectures, sermons) and bringing what had been published into modern editions.

While the 1920s attempted to recommend Emerson as the tonic for a post-war era, the late 1930s made clear that the so-called tonic was nothing but a narcotic. Arnold's claim, so often recycled, was savaged as a highly culpable indulgence. To live in the spirit was no longer a viable option for a responsible individual whose society was struggling out of one war and toward another. Earlier periods could afford to dismiss Emerson as naive or elevate him to a non-threatening and passive idol. Such strategies seemed poorly devised for the middle decades of the twentieth century. The massive damage done by the Depression in the United States; the rise of Fascism in Hitler's Germany and Mussolini's Italy; a second World War; the beginning of the atomic age; for the United States, another foreign war in addition to the war at home known now as the McCarthy Era — all of these shook definitions of "America" in ways the earlier years could not have known.

No better example of the difference between the Emerson of 1930 and the Emerson of the 1950s can be seen than in the contrasting tones of Frederic Ives Carpenter's 1930 *Emerson and Asia* and his 1953 *Emerson Handbook*. In 1930, the criticism of Emerson appeared to be settling into a solid ground of ongoing scholarly debate. With the work of Firkins, Foerster, Sherman and Perry, Emerson's place within the academy seemed a matter of course. Sherman's and Perry's anthologies set a standard for the college textbook. Foerster's work on Emerson's "organic form" paved the way for future studies of Emerson's aesthetic. Perry's highly successful *The Heart of Emerson's Journals* skillfully bridged the difference between scholarly and popular work, presenting a highly readable Emerson who was at the same time deemed essential to the academic reader. Surveying the field in 1931, Perry compared Emerson's critical fate with other nineteenth-century figures and declared the patient healthy. Emerson weathered the late-nineteenth and early-twentieth-century reevaluations better than many of his contemporaries.

Given this climate, Carpenter situated his 1930 study of influence without apology. He presented his work as an uncontroversial piece in the ongoing scholarly study of sources. By no means unique to Emerson, this source study was well-established when Carpenter undertook his work. The justification of his project was solely internal. The role of the "Orient" in Emerson's thought had not been fully studied. To understand Emerson, whether as poet or philosopher, meant understanding what he took from his reading.

Carpenter's particular focus responded to an absence in the earlier criticism. He provided the corrective to the still predominant emphasis on the British romantics and the German idealists. He also argued for a firmer acknowledgment of Emerson's influence on the development of comparative religious and comparative literary study. He reserved his final thoughts for the future, a future in which Emerson's favorable force loomed large. He compared Emerson to Petrarch, suggesting that each stood in similar relation to a similar "Renaissance." For Carpenter, the "American Renaissance of Orientalism" was just coming into its own, as witnessed in the Chinese translations of Amy Lowell, the poetry of Carl Sandburg and Stephen Vincent Benet and the plays of Eugene O'Neill. Emerson's work was its long foreground (251–55).

Two decades later, Carpenter faced a different world. Emerson was now a writer whose general acceptance could no longer be assumed. He begins his *Emerson Handbook* by quoting Oswald Spengler's *Decline of the West* and remarks that the form of a handbook itself suggests decay. He clearly hopes to prove that conclusion wrong and pointedly identifies his work as a systematic, almost scientific, study. He sets out to "itemize [Emerson's] life, catalogue his books and analyze his techniques" (x). As has been seen in Chapter Two, he painstakingly distances Emerson from Nietzsche and argues for Emerson's relevance at a time when the American government was policing its citizens' thoughts. He devotes twice as many pages to Emerson's "ideas" as to his "prose and poetry." Although he acknowledges that "the problem of form in Emerson's writing is even more difficult than the problem of idea" (74), he focuses the greatest attention on making those ideas credible to the modern reader. The key, he argues, rests in Emerson's "dualism" and its varied attempts to reconcile apparently irreconcilable differences. He writes, "the 'two laws' of Emerson's philosophy always remained 'unreconciled.' The strong Yankee realism and the ethereal transcendental idealism cohabited in his mind, but never formally joined. And this informality has always troubled critics and philosophers" (109).

Carpenter's words articulate the trouble within the criticism of these decades. Those who found something of worth in Emerson's work tended to emphasize the reconciling forces within Emerson's dualism. Those who found Emerson's work irremediably flawed argued that the dualism was simply one symptom of a failed system. The most vehement criticism occurred within the 1930s and centered around the economic and aesthetic implications of Emerson's writing. While the particular point of the criticism was hardly new, its packaging was decidedly different. The comments appeared in large studies of American history and literature; they presented themselves as the inarguable interpretation of the past.

This was undoubtedly criticism with a social agenda, and its intent was clearly seen in the Marxist intellectuals of the 1930s. Self-reliance had long been suspect, but the moral issue of the nineteenth century (few individuals are, by nature, good enough to be self-reliant) took a different turn in the twentieth. Self-reliance was identified with the worst abuses of capitalism. Emerson came under attack for his implicit support of a laissez-faire system in which individuals were justified in taking advantage of any and every situation to forward their economic standing. The individual who supposedly sought to free his fellow Americans from the trap of materialism effectively wrote them right back into the system. V. F. Calverton commented, "the philosophic idealism embodied in the doctrine of self-reliance was but a subtle camouflage, however unconscious, for the petty bourgeois materialism which was concealed beneath its inspiration" (254).

Calverton's remarks appeared in his 1932 book *The Liberation of American Literature*. He situated Emersonian self-reliance in a singular environment. Countering the image of Emerson's "pure" idealism, Calverton's Emerson keenly followed the practical implications of his thought. "Emerson understood the practical philosophy of the petty bourgeoisie much better than most of his critics have realized. . . . It was this petty bourgeois philosophy of individual possession which he believed in and encouraged; it was this petty bourgeois conception of life which made him suspicious of social movements" (248). Dismissing the European or "Eastern" influence, Calverton claimed Emerson as a wholly American product whose guiding force was the frontier. He writes, "Emerson extended the petty bourgeois philosophy of the frontier to its farthest anarchical extreme, extolling at times attitudes that were as definitely antisocial in their implications as the activities of the frontiersmen who early defied every semblance of state, authority, and tradition" (249). Later critics would extend that link. Its culmination might best be seen in Quentin Anderson's 1971 book *The Imperial Self*, and remains current in the various descendants of Marxist criticism. The late twentieth century would indeed revisit many of the questions raised in the 1930s.

Calverton was not alone in his frontier emphasis. As he himself acknowledged, others preceded him into that territory. Ernest Marchand's lengthy article "Emerson and the Frontier" (1931) appeared the previous year. A year later, Granville Hicks tied Emerson to the frontier but moved readily through its importance, treating it as a given. The first provoking study had been published a few years earlier in 1926. Lucy Hazard's *The Frontier in American Literature* brought together the emergent thought on the frontier's role and laid the groundwork for future studies. Situating her study as a defense of American literature, she identified a two-pronged attack: the European critics who continued to see mediocrity in American literature and the genteel critics who celebrated the unsullied purity of "literature." Arguing that the more interesting emphasis was on "American," not "literature," she divided her study among three types of pioneering: regional, industrial and spiritual. In each case, the issue was control, and in the first two, one question raised yet another. How much did these attempts to control an environment reveal an unwitting control by it? In the case of the Transcendentalist writers, she argued that self-determination was its own fiction. Reminding her readers of a contemporaneity conveniently forgotten, she firmly linked the western explorers (Kit Carson and John Fremont) with the world inhabited by Emerson and Thoreau. Transcendental idealism and the open land were partners engaged in the same venture.

In contrast to the Emerson "who smiles benevolently from the pictures of 'Our Poets' and moralizes epigrammatically in the 'Selections from American Literature,'" she offers a different image (159). Her Emerson underwrites both material gain and subversive action. Matthew Arnold's "friend and aider," Paul Elmer More's "sweet spirit" collapse when a reader looks at the Emerson of "The Young American," "The Progress of Culture," "Resources," "The Fortune of the Republic," "Social Aims." "It is time," Hazard writes, "to decanonize Emerson; to recognize that however truly he may have been 'the friend and helper [sic] of those who would live in the spirit,' he is just as truly the friend and helper of those who want to annex a territory, or corner a market, or spread heretical propaganda. It is time to strip from the Emersonian hero the decorous toga and conventional mask . . . 'the heir of Plato's brain' was no mystic recluse, but a man of action well fitted to play a leading part in the drama of pioneering" (152–53).

Hazard remains firmly committed to the individualist model: the artist was the spiritual pioneer who would redeem the concept of the frontier. For later critics, especially those who readily identified themselves as Marxist, her return to the individual prompted their most pointed response. Agreeing with her assessment of the frontier, noting Transcendentalist complicity with capitalist gain, critics like Calverton and Hicks stopped short at the individual. Hicks comments, "Emerson's great faith in humanity was based upon a historical reality, the emergence, especially on the frontier, of the common man. But that movement was merely a preliminary skirmish, leading to a realignment of forces, to a new division of classes" (29). Calverton's assessment was less polite: "the faith in the common man which Emerson and Whitman entertained was faith in him as an individual and not as a mass. It was faith in him as an individualist and not as a collectivist. In that sense, their faith was founded upon a false premise; fitting and persuasive enough in their generation it led only to disaster in the next" (479–80).

In answer to these "false premises," several critics argued a different reading of Emerson's economics. In his 1940 "Emerson and Economics," Alexander C. Kern reminded his readers of a still recent, respected assessment of Emerson's position. Vernon L. Parrington's monumental history of American thought (*Main Currents in American Thought: An Interpretation of American Literature: The Romantic Revolution in America*, 1927–30: 386–99) identified Emerson as a "shrewd," "severe," and "almost savage" critic of American materialism. An unabashed apologist for Emerson, Parrington affirmed the credibility of Emerson's thought and argued that Emerson's best contribution was as a social critic. No "jaunty optimist," he rejected economic determinism, putting in its place a "transcendental theory of politics" that bordered on philosophical anarchism (391, 393). The latter was little help to Kern, but Parrington's consistent narrative of argument and quotation firmly supported his own point about Emerson's critique of materialism.

At the same time that V. F. Calverton identified him as the sponsor of the petty bourgeois and Lucy Hazard equated Emerson's individualism with the necessary justification for unchecked expansionism (individual and societal), Kern argued the opposite position. He returned to the "fixed principles" in Emerson's thinking: "correspondence, melioration, individualism, and, to a lesser extent, compensation" (678–79). Acknowledging the difficulty of his task, he cited "correspondence" as the key to unraveling the apparent identity between self-reliance and "a grasping, predatory, and exploiting bourgeois individualism" (681). Drawing from passages in both the essays and the journals, Kern built his argument on the weight of the written evidence. Not only does the bulk of Emerson's writing treat material wealth with suspicion, but the role wealth played within Emerson's vision of self-reliance made clear that the goods alone never delivered — and more often than not hindered — the individual. In the end, he suggested that Emerson's words about economic issues always operated more as metaphor than program. Readers endorsed an isolated part of Emerson to justify their materialism, but Emerson should not be held responsible for their misappropriation of verbal funds.

Seeking to free Emerson from his critics' positions, Kern joined the long debate over Emerson's responsibility for his readers' interpretations. The nineteenth century often questioned the feasibility of Emersonian self-reliance. In the words of one reviewer, "try it by the test of experience. . . . Let each man take to himself this new gospel — "Rely on thyself". . . . What will the countless thousands who now *choose* to violate their conscience, do with such a maxim as this" (1849, *Contemporary Reviews* 197). The twentieth century heightened the demand, making the implications more difficult to escape. Given the various determinisms at work — psychological, economic, cultural — Emerson could not avoid complicity. Part and parcel of the times, his thoughts had been shaped by his circumstances. In Calverton's words, Emerson may well have been "unconscious" of endorsing behavior that sounded far different from his ideas, but the connecting link of the economic system inevitably supported the culture's dominant ideology.

Daniel Aaron explored that support — unconscious and otherwise — in his post-war study of American thought, *Men of Good Hope* (1951). He identified Emerson as "the real prophet of the progressive tradition" (7), equating Emerson's meliorist position with the later reformers. As he described the progressives, the connection was clear: "Society, they felt, needed to be reformed, to be brought into closer correspondence with American democratic precepts; it did not need to be uprooted" (19).

Aaron's version of Emerson rings the familiar note of reconciliation: Emerson brings together disparate elements of experience and idea. Drawing upon Henry Nash Smith's 1939 discussion of Emerson's "problem of vocation," Aaron locates this reconciliation in biography. He comments, "After a period of worry and doubts, the Emerson who agonized over the choice of his vocation was able to reconcile the divergent appeals of practical action and reflection in the vocation of the scholar, which became for him a symbol of dynamic passivity" (12).

Aaron's concluding phrase may well give the reader pause, and Aaron himself used it to show the strange and strained connection between Emerson and "business principles." With Kern, Aaron termed this connection a working metaphor in which the equivalence was not exact. Business principles offered usable material and a particularly unexpected way of characterizing the scholar's demanding work. Aaron, however, was less willing than Kern to separate the critic of materialism from the participant who "enjoyed almost sensuously the plump and solid tangibles" (11).

Aaron's Emerson is decidedly double-sided: "transcendental democracy" coincides with "aggressive individualism" (96). While he spared Emerson the responsibility, he nonetheless acknowledged that such interpretations were entirely plausible. Emerson invariably offered many possibilities in his writings, and the individual might well stop to develop one over another. From Aaron's standpoint, the final possibility, the "logical conclusion" of Emerson's individualism was "anarchism," though few readers followed him to that frontier (14–18).

For Aaron, as for Perry Miller two years later, Emerson's treatment of Napoleon was central to understanding the United States political economy. Aaron comments, "The portrait of Napoleon in *Representative Men* is perhaps the best illustration of Emerson's ambivalent attitude toward aggressiveness and self-seeking" (9). Emerson praised Napoleon's "practicality, prudence and directness," and thus "underscored precisely those attributes that made up the American success code." At the same time, the praise was tempered by Emerson's merciless comments about "the blowhard, the strutting egotist, the low vulgarian." Aaron ended his discussion with ambivalence, quoting a final word of praise from Emerson. He does not address the devastating indictment of American society delivered in that praise, a point Perry Miller makes central in his essay "Emersonian Genius and the American Democracy" (1953). Where Aaron distanced Emerson's transcendental democracy from its capitalist counterpart, Miller separated Emerson from the aristocracy of the Genteel Tradition and allied him with a firm, and given his background surprising, commitment to democracy. Napoleon figured into his argument for precisely the point Aaron left unaddressed. There would always be Napoleons to lead ineffectual revolts as long as the United States remained a civilization of "property, of fences, of exclusiveness" (Miller quoting Emerson, 42).

For Miller, Emerson's Napoleon represented his complex understanding of the relationship between genius and democracy. Turning to the Harvard of Emerson's college days, he shows how the expected path for Emerson would have been straight from Harvard ennui to

Whiggish aloofness. "Nothing would be easier," Miller comments, "than to collect from the Journals enough passages about the Democratic party to form a manual of Boston snobbery" (29). Such a collection, however, would touch only one surface of Emerson's thought. He was never quite the Brahmin. As much as Emerson criticized Andrew Jackson, he was a Jacksonian force in literature, extending his faith in the individual beyond the educated few to include the many. In short, Miller argues, Emerson democratized genius without debasing it. The "genius" was defined by his use; he was representative rather than unique. To prove his point, Miller draws heavily upon Emerson's journals and early lectures. He cites the proximity of topics in the journal entries: "over and over again any mention of genius is sure to be followed, within an entry or two, by a passage on democracy, the Democratic party, Napoleon" (35). Miller ends his piece with a pointed comment for his present readers. Emerson, he writes, was "a serious man who could finally run down the devil of politics . . . who understood as well as any . . . that magnificent but agonizing experience of what it is to be, or to try to be, an American" (44).

The double notes of "American" and "democracy" were frequent elements in the criticism, not simply for those who took a socio-political view of Emerson's writing in the Depression 1930s or the McCarthy 1950s but also for those who worked with the style of Emerson's poetry and prose. In her study of Emerson's aesthetic theory, Vivian Hopkins allied that aesthetic with democracy. Anticipating Miller's study, she distanced Emerson's "artist" from the "lonely genius" who "shrinks from the touch of ordinary persons" (16). In Emerson's aesthetic system, the artist's works are designed "for the nourishment which they can give to all men's spirits" (104). Ten years earlier in a study that remains a monumental force, F. O. Matthiessen equated Emerson's central idea with a democracy manifest in both thought and expression. Near the opening of *The American Renaissance* he comments, "[Emerson's] belief in the infinitude of the private man was also a democratic doctrine. He shared in that revolution too, and held it responsible for the great extension of the scope of literature" (13).

The focus on democracy in these decades speaks readily for the ongoing concerns within American society. At the same time, a democratic aesthetic won little favor for Emerson in the emerging world of New Criticism and the dominant creative voice of the Southern Agrarian poets. Although not truly part of either, Yvor Winters has often served as the spokesman for the critical assessment of Emerson in these years. His polemical style certainly gave later critics much to react against. Whether blaming Emerson's ideas for Hart Crane's suicide or claiming self-reliance as a license for murder, arson and incest, Winters never chose to measure his words. Beneath the extremism, however, played a common note: Emerson's fascination with change in and of itself wrought havoc with art. In an essay that reevaluated Jones Very's poetry, Winters faulted Emerson for an unchecked reliance upon emotion-induced impulse: "his central doctrine is that of submission to emotion . . . it eliminates at a stroke both choice and the values that serve as a basis for choice, it substitutes for a doctrine of values a doctrine of equivalence . . . so that Emerson's acceptable acts of expression are accidental poems or epigrams" ("Jones Very and R. W. Emerson: Aspects of New England Mysticism," 267). For Winters, the problem was constitutional, an insurmountable difficulty situated in the definition of art itself. From his vantage, art was never "accidental." Its base was form, a structure shaped by the perception of absolute values. Emerson's apparent relativism was simply unacceptable, and Winters made no apologies for his firm conviction: "Emerson at the core is a fraud and a sentimentalist, and his fraudulence impinges at least lightly upon everything he wrote: when it disappears from the subject, it lingers in the tone; even when he brings his very real talent to bear upon a thoroughly sound subject, he does so with a manner at once condescending and casual, a manner of which the justification, such as it is, may be found in his essays, but of which the consequence is a subtle degradation of the poetic art" (279).

In his anatomy of Hart Crane's failure, Winters traces the not-so-subtle effect of this so-called degradation. For Winters, there was no greater implausibility than Emerson's assertion that the divine and the human were inseparable. This conflation or as Winters saw it, confusion invariably compromised human achievement, turning the individual into a creature of the moment, no better than an automaton. In his essay "The Significance of *The Bridge,* by Hart Crane or What Are We to Think of Professor X," Winters faulted Emerson's "view of art" (that "true art is never fixed, but always flowing"). It rested on the flawed "assumption that man should express what he is at any given moment; not that he should try by all the means at his disposal to arrive at a true understanding of a given subject or to improve his powers of understanding in general" (583). For Winters, Emerson's shape-shifting aesthetic invariably sacrificed "true understanding" to self-indulgence and self-ruin. The consequences appeared in the quality of expression. From this discussion of Emerson's immediacy, he turns to "automatic writing," a subject he treats with wary interest.

Whether poets or critics, writers of the 1930s and 1940s consistently faulted Emerson for his inadequate aesthetic, and as was often the case in this period, poet and critic were one. The aesthetic they shaped in their poetry was in turn the standard they defined for assessing literary works. Emerson was tough material to make palatable to the New Critics. In fact, one could create a Henry James litany of negations to describe the mismatch between Emerson and the New Critical aesthetic. Where New Criticism valued the perfection of form, Emerson remained relentlessly experimental, not simply across works but within the poem or essay itself. New Criticism equated rhetorical irony with the height of linguistic power. Emerson used irony for purposes of societal condemnation but generally engaged in a much different rhetorical practice. His work was dominated by analogy, a technique that found little use in the poems praised by the New Critics. Analogy was an invariably messy method. Always capable of addition, it resisted containment. Emerson's writing appeared like a poor relation in elegant company. The gorgeously crafted structures of the poetry of the 1930s seemingly put to shame Emerson's exuberant experiments. He was an amateur among highly accomplished professionals. His topics said as much. His ideas were of questionable import. Critics took their refrain from one of the poets their work celebrated. In William Butler Yeats' words, Emerson "lack[ed] the Vision of Evil" ("The Trembling of the Veil," 1922).

To create common ground where there was virtually none available, several critics turned to full-scale consideration of Emerson's poetic theory. Fighting against the odds, these critics acknowledged the difficulty but also recognized that by focusing on questions of style, they could circumvent the common complaint about outdated or flawed ideas. The period witnessed a slow but steady emphasis on Emerson's writing itself. In terms of stylistic analysis, the poetry received more attention than did the essays. Gay Wilson Allen's chapter on Emerson appeared in his *American Prosody* in 1935. Arguing against the general impression that Emerson's poems were best described by their formal "irregularities," he illustrated Emerson's skillful use of his own prosodic theory. Admitting that Whitman was still the better practitioner, he nonetheless argued the importance of a systematic study of Emerson's style. Focusing on metrics, he allied the structure of the line with a rhythmic demonstration of meaning.

A similar issue occurred with Emerson's use of rhyme. Clarence Stratton argued that Emerson's rhymes were irredeemably poor ("Emerson's Rhymes," 1944). In the April issue, Thomas Mabbott and Isabel Kadison came to the defense of Emerson's rhymes ("Emerson Rhymes" and "Emerson followed Webster," 1945). This "local" argument went before a larger audience in 1948 with Kathryn McEuen's

Rhymes" in *American Literature* (vol. 20, March 1948: 31–42). Individual poems received some attention, most notably "Days" after Matthiessen's compelling discussion in *The American Renaissance*. But in all cases the stylistic study proceeded slowly. Sustained work on the prose would wait, eventually becoming a long-term project begun in the 1960s. From the 1930s well into the 1950s the essays were considered primarily for content, not form. They remained a place to mine Emerson's ideas.

A few critics did turn to the essays themselves. Focussing on the First Series essay "Art," Walter Blair and Clarence Faust defined Emerson's literary method as a version of Plato's twice-bisected line ("Emerson's Literary Method," 1944). Emerson, they argued, used that image as a model for constructing his own prose. He built his essays in three sections, each representing one part of the division between, yet relation within, the visible, intelligible world. Each section was governed by a movement from multiplicity to unity. The final effect was a moment of unity in which the "Artist," the "Beholder" and the art work itself were united in the larger concept of "Art."

Nothing can sound more different in tone than Faust and Blair's detailed explication of Emerson's literary method and F. O. Matthiessen's careful contextualizing of Emerson's "quest for form" or Vivian Hopkins' narrative discussion of Emerson's aesthetic theory, but the different approaches belie a shared concern. Each offered a systematic organization of Emerson's literary method. Against charges of Emerson's failed form, critics like Blair and Faust, Matthiessen, Hopkins, and Sherman Paul presented a unified theory behind Emerson's poetics.

For more than just its opening section on Emerson, F. O. Matthiessen's influential *American Renaissance* (1941) remains the best known example of this mid-century work. He begins by acknowledging the hard times on which Emerson had fallen: wherever his work is mentioned, it meets with "the usual academic dismissal" (4). He uses this phrase not simply in reference to his own time, but specifically to John Dewey's apparently failed argument that Emerson was both artist and philosopher. To avoid such failure Matthiessen carefully defined the limits of his argument. He vehemently dropped the Arnoldian approach. There would be no help from phrases such as "friend and aider." "Sixty years later," Matthiessen comments, "such a judgment helps us not at all. We have witnessed altogether too many vague efforts to 'live in the spirit,' following in the ruck of Transcendentalism and disappearing in the sands of the latest theosophy" (5). Sharing the distrust of idealism common to his period, he likewise refused to argue for Emerson's philosophy. He judged Emerson "as a writer," all the while acknowledging the assumed "failure" of Emerson's individual essays and poems.

Taking the attention away from the products of Emerson's theory, he focused on the theory itself, and most specifically on its development. With this approach, he effectively defined the method for reading Emerson that would remain standard for the rest of the century. To trace the development of Emerson's style, he relied heavily on the journals, drawing upon the cognate passages within the essays to show how a particular idea took shape over time. By the same token, Matthiessen's approach was firmly embedded in the history of ideas. Although he would not seek to reclaim Emerson's ideas themselves, he firmly situated Emerson's aesthetics within the dominant elements of Emerson's thought.

Dualism was the primary element. He defined Emerson's version as an ongoing opposition between the "now" and the "eternal" and turned the abstraction into a particular element in Emerson's life. Emerson wanted to embrace "absolute life" without abandoning the material present. Matthiessen calls attention to the subject-defining moment in Emerson's journals. In 1840 Emerson had written, "In all my lectures, I have taught one doctrine, namely, the infinitude of the private man" (JMN VII, 342). Rather than denigrating Emerson's doctrine of inspiration, he allies it with ecstasy. As had Gray before him and as would David Robinson four decades later, this pivotal moment became the constitutive element in meaning. Pointing the way toward the later emphasis on Emerson's process, Matthiessen examines the restless dynamic that characterizes the poetry and the prose.

For Matthiessen, as for his contemporaries, that dynamic yielded art only when restlessness gave way to poise. Matthiessen writes, "In his most adequate account of expression [Emerson] recognized that it was not enough to proclaim the radiance of the vision he had had, but that he must compose a structure that would bring that radiance to a point of concentration. Organic wholeness was what he admired most" (28). Harking back to Foerster's work, Matthiessen also places himself well within the confines of a New Critical framework. There must be "structure" and "concentration." Matthiessen comments, "The ease with which he could abandon the details for the plan, in both life and art, is a symptom of why, in spite of all the scattered evidence of his close appreciation of poetry, he so generally failed to write sustained poems" (52–53).

Surveying Emerson's writing, Matthiessen finds few examples of excellence. Like his contemporaries, he maintains that Emerson was at his best when he "confined himself . . . to observing phenomena" (4).

Emerson's generalizations were the problem. When they entered a work, its "concentration" dissipated; the plan was abandoned and the whole fell into fragments. The one poem that did not succumb to this failure was a poem that had long been termed one of Emerson's best. Matthiessen's discussion of "Days" is one among many, but it stands apart for its close reading of the antecedent sources in the journals and its reference to the later prose rendition in "Works and Days." In effect, Matthiessen uses his discussion of the poem to dramatize Emerson's own dilemma of dualism: "his trust in the fullness of the moment and his sense that the moment eluded him" (63).

Matthiessen ends his discussion of Emerson by considering the stylistic elements of the prose. His debt to Firkins is clear and clearly acknowledged. At the same time, he provides a more narrative structure to his presentation than did Firkins. He notes Emerson's fascination with metaphor, charting its outcome in the proliferation of analogy in Emerson's writing. Commenting on the predominant imagery in the prose, he observes the preference for "images of flowing" (69). He attributes the aphoristic style to the governing principle of Emerson's thought: "Such intensification of the moment in literature would be the natural instrument of the man for whom the intensification of the moment was the meaning of life" (65). He calls attention to the use of an almost fictive "character" in the essays, paving the way for later work by such writers as Stephen Whicher and Leonard Neufeldt on the speakers within Emerson's prose.

While Emerson's limitations are never far from Matthiessen's view, he treats them as largely a matter understood without explanation. In many ways his project was far more modest than Vivian Hopkins' *Spires of Form: A Study of Emerson's Aesthetic Theory* (1951). Drawing upon essays, poems, lectures, journals, and letters, she sought to articulate Emerson's aesthetic theory and demonstrate that it was both more systematic and consistent than had been assumed. She divides her project into three parts, a study of the creative process, of the work itself, and of the audience's role in completing that work. As she notes, the latter element was crucial to Emerson's understanding of any creative work and yet had rarely been studied. An emphasis on process unites the three aspects of Emerson's aesthetic, a process embodied in Emerson's use of organicism. Well aware that the organic principle in art was fast becoming a meaningless cliche, she grounds it in concerns specific to Emerson. She connects it with correspondence, in this case between "organic and spiritual form" (65) and explores this connection from the vantage point of the artist, the art work and the observer. She also looks to the background of Emerson's ideas, charting their development through his reading of Bacon, Coleridge, Goethe, Reed and Oegger.

Examining Emerson's comments on aesthetic experience, Hopkins parallels the observer's and creator's roles. "'Sensibility' and 'perception' have the same meaning for the observer as for the creative artist; not merely a transference of images from retina to brain, but the *interpretation* of those objects by the receptive mind" (166). Whether artist or audience, the individual is involved in the process of "realizing" the work of art. "The observer's enjoyment is no mere addition to created beauty, but the very means of bringing it to life" (166). She meets the New Critics' criterion of "concentration" by judging the art through its power to focus the attention of the viewer. She too points to the importance of ecstasy, in this case creating a "union" of observer and creator through the "absolute mind" (199). Distinguishing this experience from a purely contemplative state, she argues that "such moments of illumination . . . provide the mind with a new power which it carries over into other experience" (204). Whether creator or observer, the individual leaves the experience with a new discipline, or structure.

Keenly aware of the common charges against Emerson, Hopkins opens the book with her own version of Emerson's reception. She argues that there is much more to Emerson's views on art than Henry James' 1872 experience would suggest. The failed visit to the Louvre, she asserts, is more a matter of Emerson's old age than of his vital interest and commitment to the creative process termed art. She charges Santayana with a similar simplification, with reducing Emerson's position to a direct response to Puritanism rather than an outgrowth of Emerson's encounter with Unitarianism and German idealism. She notes the twentieth century's distaste for Emerson's assumed moralism and seeks to assuage that bitterness with an emphasis on mysticism. She suggests that Babbitt's disappointment with Emerson stemmed from his need for the kind of absolute standards Emerson distrusted, and she finds Foerster's work of reclamation flawed by his need to defend Emerson and situate him within the neohumanist tradition.

She reminds her readers that Emerson was "in advance of his own time" in several ways, citing his "enjoyment of the human body as portrayed in sculpture" at a time when "the battle of the nude was still being fought in periodicals" (223). She credits Emerson with anticipating the twentieth-century interest in a psychological study of aesthetic experience (226). As would Carpenter and Whicher in 1953, as did Perry in 1931, she maintains that the modern-day pessimism need not be taken as an absolute standard of judgment. Speculating that Emerson could serve his old function of tonic yet again, she draws at-

tention both to self-reliance and to his "treatment of evil." Acknowledging the problematic elements within each, she nonetheless maintains that both provide a corrective balance to the present. She
concludes with a comment that marks the pressures on criticism as well
as the eventual world beyond them. Her study succeeds if it "has done
something to redeem Emerson's aesthetic thought from the charge of
vain dreaming, by showing its inherent system; if it has helped to save
his critical reputation from the opposite charges of Rousseauistic pan-
theism and arbitrary moralism." She writes in the service of "the right
reading of Emerson" (228–29). Part and parcel of an age that sought
clear, one might say "scientific" judgment of literary work, she defines
her project within the framework of definitive interpretation. Her final
description of that interpretation, however, points the way toward the
multiplicitous Emersons and interpretations of the late twentieth century. She comments, "Emerson's aesthetic theory is the reflection of his
mind: curious about the new in literature and art, often holding in deli-
cate balance ideas antagonistic to each other . . . not fixed, but flowing,
with the accent on becoming rather than being" (230). The criticism of
the 1970s and 1980s bears out this emphasis on the empirical, the
flowing, the becoming.

Hopkins was not alone in her interest in the dynamic within Emerson's aesthetic. Focused more closely on the writing itself, Sherman
Paul's *Emerson's Angle of Vision* (1952) directs attention to the mechanism by which Emerson bridged at least one of the dualisms of his
thought. His focus is the doctrine of correspondence. He writes, "For
[Emerson], correspondence covered all the ways by which man came
into relation with the world *outside* of himself, transformed the world
into himself, and expressed the insight of the *experience* in words and
character" (4). Defining Emerson as an "affirmer," Paul connects that
affirmation with Emerson's thoroughgoing rejection of an immediate
past. As had Firkins before him, Paul argues that Emerson's lack of
logic was a deliberate refusal. "Linear logic" was a "dead-end" for Emerson (17); it expressed "the despair of the times" (19). In response to
such despair, "Emerson felt called on to raise the vertical axis, to give
the universe its spiritual dimension, to reinstate its mystery and wonder
by giving scope to the mythic, symbolic, and religious components of
human experience" (22). Paul sees this "vertical axis" as Emerson's
means for "assert[ing] a multi-dimensional universe" and places the
"paradoxes and polarity of his thought" as part and parcel of the
"struggle to inform the life of the horizontal with the quality of the
vertical" (25).

Paul grounds his abstract geography of thought in a single dominant image of "vision." He located this vision in the yet more specific images of sight and seeing. He termed sight "the agency of correspondence with nature and of inspiration" (74). It provided Emerson with a perfect means for generating analogy. There were many types of seeing; the physical act was readily connected with its equivalents in perception. There was "proximate vision" and "distant vision" which Paul equates with "Democratic vision" (Whitman's "Democratic Vistas" is clearly a referent here as is the work of Ortega y Gasset). Through it, "synthesis and relatedness were achieved" or, in Gasset's words, "the point of view becomes the synopsis" (76). Paul looks at the "best focal distance" in Emerson's thought and sees it in "the unlimited extent" (80). Particular images carried powerful weight within this system. Emerson's use of the horizon, for example, was the apt representation of dualism held within unity: "if the finite limit of the horizon suggested the illimitable, its hazy fading in the distance promised the bipolar unity of the moment of inspiration" (80).

The focus on vision enabled Paul to address central images within Emerson's writing and pivotal interests within his thought. Though not the first to note Emerson's early interest in astronomy, he reminds his readers of its importance to Emerson's emerging definition of the scholar's role. He also gives the first sustained attention to Emerson's fascination with the eye. While critics before him suggested its importance — whether in terms of the life (Emerson's early problems with his eyes) or his writing — Paul gave the most extended discussion to date. He also opened the door for a number of essays in the 1960s that would take the eye as their focus. Kenneth Burke's study of Emersonian equivalence in his often reprinted "I, Eye, Ay" (1966) tropes upon the trope in its title. While the essay itself is about the process of transcendence, the equivalence of the title as well as a small discussion of the literally "starry-eyed" observer put the imagery of vision at the heart of Emerson's work.

Chief among those who looked directly at the "eyes" in Emerson's work was Tony Tanner. In "Emerson: The Unconquered Eye and The Enchanted Circle" (*The Reign of Wonder, Naivety and Reality in American Literature*, 1965), Tanner identifies the eye as the motivating image and seeing as the dominant narrative in Emerson's prose. Illustrating the Transcendentalists' belief in an "unmediated admiration and response" (20), Emerson praised a clarity of vision attainable only through close, attentive observation. Tanner notes that Emerson's ideal observer was most frequently cast as the child, the "innocent" eye unclouded by preconception (32–35). Interested as well in the effect on

Emerson's prose, Tanner examines the implications of an immediate, detailed immersion in seeing. The style privileges the part over the whole; individual perception over formal structure.

Ten years later in his essay, "R. W. Emerson: The Circles of the Eye," James Cox focused on the most noted of Emerson's metaphors, calling the "transparent eyeball" Emerson's "master metaphor." No simple statement of equivalence, this stridently configured eye "is an *action*, a statement of a change from being into seeing" (61). With Tanner, he equates Emersonian "seeing" with perpetual revision. Emerson's "bare common" is a richly evocative landscape, transforming the ordinary and the social into the visionary. Noting its importance to the reader's understanding of Emerson, Cox writes, "If we take Emerson, standing on the bare common, become an eye at the natural center of society to see and thereby recreate it, we have the essential Emerson" (66). Writing in the context of the early 1970s discomfort with the "imperial self" and its Emersonian connections, Cox uses the complexity of Emerson's metaphor to counter the current attack against Emerson.

That the "eye" remains both interesting and useful appears in the steady and continued attention the image generates: Richard Poirier's "Is there an I for An Eye" first published in *A World Elsewhere*, 1966; reprinted in Buell, 1993; Barbara Packer's "The Instructed Eye: Emerson's Cosmogony in 'Prospects'" in *Emerson's Nature: Origin, Growth, Meaning* (1979) and later in "The Riddle of the Sphinx" in *Emerson's Fall* (1982); David Porter's *Emerson and Literary Change* (1978); Carolyn Porter's *Seeing and Being: The Plight of the Participant Observer in Emerson, James, Adams and Faulkner*, 1981). Since Paul's discussion in the early 1950s, this interest in the eye remains a staple of the criticism.

Another 1950s staple of late-twentieth-century criticism is, of course, Stephen Whicher's *Freedom and Fate* (1953). Keenly aware of Emerson's precarious position in philosophical and literary inquiry, he devised an answer that fit neatly within modernism's own terms. Unlike previous critics who sought to show that Emerson could be made consonant with the demands of New Criticism, he took a different approach. He would not be concerned with the stylistic method of Emerson's expression nor would he create a system out of Emerson's thought. Instead he placed his discussion firmly at the center of modernist values. His emphasis was the life of the mind and the development of thought. While Emerson's final position made him "more irritating than helpful in our disastrous times" (172), he was nonetheless a poignantly representative man. The language Whicher chose for Emerson described the intellectuals of his own generation. Whicher writes, "His final optimism took him to a wise and balanced empiricism, a detached report on the human condition, and a genuinely humanist ethics. Yet it meant a defeat of his first unworldly protest against the world, a defeat that laid a shadow of promise unfulfilled across his later serenity" (171–72). So also might seem the 1930s from the vantage point of the 1950s.

Whicher was not alone in his attempt to reclaim Emerson for a New Critical age. One of its main charges centered on Emerson's lack of a so-called tragic vision. In the wake of the Second World War, that concern was increasingly figured as Emerson's unsatisfactory engagement with the problem of evil. Noting Emerson's description of Europe after the Napoleonic Wars, Miller comments, "He did, we must confess, look upon the desolation with what seems to us smugness, we who have seen Europe infinitely more burned and demoralized" (43). Carpenter settled on the side of this objection to Emerson, demoting Emerson's writing and attributing that demotion to Emerson's own inability to write in the tragic mode. Twenty years earlier, Bliss Perry acknowledged that absence as a fact, but critical of the emerging New Criticism itself, he encouraged his readers to value a different type of poetry. F. O. Matthiessen took up the issue as did Vivian Hopkins. In each case, the critic acknowledged Emerson's apparent inadequacy and then went on to show where Emerson allowed for a momentary encounter with the tragic. Matthiessen located this moment in the failure represented within "Days"; Hopkins reminded her readers that Emerson's aesthetic always held a place for the "ugly," that his treatment of evil was no simple matter of denial.

Whicher's Emerson was perhaps the most deeply rooted in Modernism's fascination with the tragic, and the success of Whicher's Emerson can in part be attributed to how carefully consonant this Emerson was with the experienced tragedy of the modern period. Bringing Emerson up to date for his readers, Whicher presented a decidedly modern man. Emerson was the disillusioned idealist for whom the great bulk of years was spent living out the disappointment of youth. The self-reliant individual, independently and creatively powerful, was a mirage.

Whicher's argument is singly-directed. As later critics would note, he heightened one element within Emerson's writing from the 1830s and diminished the rest. It was, however, a persuasive representation in which Whicher's powerful paraphrasing of Emerson's thought held a conviction of its own. Whicher carefully selects his quotations from Emerson. The quotations themselves are relatively short and seamlessly woven into Whicher's prose. He uses Emerson's words as a spring board for a discussion of ideas, in this case the development of an individualism that emphasized absolute freedom yet contained within it its own future concession of limitations.

That concession forms the second and shorter half of Whicher's book. He examines Emerson's return to skepticism but argues that it offered an inadequate resting place for Emerson's thought. Calling upon the "lords of life" named in the essay "Experience," Whicher connects the skeptic's approach with its fundamental limitation: "These [lords] he could not explain, but only observe and reconcile as he might. To call the roll of these guardians was as close as the skeptic could come to a philosophy of life" (115). This observer's method offered a new kind of "naturalistic self-reliance," a self-reliance "without the Transcendentalism" (119). Loss of that Transcendentalism, however, introduced a new problem: the individual's freedom was unmistakably limited and the best that could be made from such limitation was the last of many identities Emerson imagined for the self. Emerson sought to recoup his losses through his "final vocational hero-type, the Poet" (136). From Whicher's standpoint, the poet was the fitting emblem of the failed impossibility at the center or Emerson's thought. Entire self-dependence was an illusion. What he called the "dream of greatness" was just that: a dream. Emerson's figure of the poet, however, did its best to give that dream a type of permanence. Pointing out the division within the poet himself, Whicher describes Emerson's lasting fascination with the power of the moment: "The poet's life is not a poetic life, but an ascetic service of his thought. His reward, the reward he brings others, is not self-union, but a magic flare of imagination, without means and without issue, an intoxicating glimpse of the inaccessible ideal" (138).

Whicher's Emerson is a curious construct. Built upon a division between the "early" and the "late" Emerson, it plays fast and loose with chronology. Late Emerson begins early in Emerson's career. As later studies of "Experience" would show, some of the harshest statements about limitation date well back into the journals of the 1830s or even into the sermons of the late 1820s. The affirmation of self-reliance was never quite so absolute as Whicher argues. By the same token, Whicher's framework required him to set aside a startling amount of Emerson's writing. With the exception of "Fate" and "Illusions," *Essays, Second Series* marks the outward bound, and both of the essays from *The Conduct of Life* are presented as a kind of coda to "Experience." Little is said of the poetry and nothing, except by way of dismissal, of the antislavery lectures. Whicher's judgment that Emerson's intellectual development was essentially finished by 1847–48 severely truncates Emerson's active career. It also effectively shaped the focus of scholarly work for the next three decades.

For the academic within the American university, Whicher's vision spoke powerfully. Emerson's fate mirrored the common experience. While the staying power of Whicher's Emerson certainly demonstrates its resonance with American society, it also cannot be attributed solely to that. Whicher's division of Emerson's career carries with it the power of explanation. It makes sense of the tonal difference between essays like "Self-Reliance" and "Experience." It seamlessly weaves the life into the work, thus continuing the biographical bent of criticism but taking it in a new direction. By focusing on the "life of the mind," Whicher participated in the growing interest in psychological and intellectual development of literary figures, but he also brought attention to specific essays themselves. He did not quite break with the dominant tradition of quoting Emerson to the end, not of literary style, but to the greatness of paradox or complexity of ideas, and yet, he ostensibly found a way to combine both philosophy and literature. In *Freedom and Fate*, the writings are both means and end.

Whicher would himself compile an anthology (*Selections from Ralph Waldo Emerson: An Organic Anthology*, 1957) as an extension of his "inner life" approach. It is still seen as one of the best for teaching Emerson. Subtitled "An Organic Anthology" it focused on the writer's development. Interspersing selections from the journals with the essays and addresses, it follows the peculiar chronology Whicher created from Emerson's life. The Second Series essays "The Poet" and "Politics" are separated from their companion essay "Experience," which in turn is placed within a section entitled "skepticism" and also includes the essay "Montaigne." To mark the period from the mid-1840s to the Civil War, Whicher uses "Fate" and an excerpt from "Works and Days" (pointing the reader toward the poem "Days"). Nothing is included from *English Traits* and no mention, except by way of journal entries, of Emerson's antislavery lectures. "Thoreau" serves as the statement of the war years.

These selections reinforce the curious, but compelling, romance Whicher created for and from Emerson's intellectual life. His was a "modern tragedy" defined by a loss of agency, a sense of powerlessness, which for the late twentieth century spoke with all the rhetorical irony New Criticism demanded. Emerson's solution in acquiescence and optimism betrayed its own limitations. The most he could do was teach his audiences how to make the best of it, and even he did not understand how bad that pronoun without an antecedent could be.

What is curiously apparent in this retrospective view on Whicher is the number of concessions he made to those who found Emerson so painfully inadequate. Their name was legion. Their charges are the ones this chapter has in small measure shown. There are many more. Seymour Gross spoke from a mid-1950s perspective when he castigated Emerson's poetry for its numerous flaws ("Emerson and Poetry," 1955). With Matthiessen and Whicher, he would grant that "Days" was not only a "good" but an "excellent" poem, but he made clear that such excellence was the exception that proved the rule. He comments, "When Emerson left behind him the frantic leaps for superhuman truth and dealt rationally with experience, he managed to achieve such poetic excellence as 'Days.' But only then" (94). He questions the various studies of Emerson's poetic theory, suggesting that an "organic" principle, especially in the case of Emerson's thought, may well be "aesthetically impossible" (82). From Gross's perspective, the organic is suspect because it all too readily subordinates form to a study of development. The point, he argues, is the poem, not the process, and in Emerson's poetry, the form clearly faltered. What could be expected, he asks, from an individual who emphasized inspiration at the expense of composition.

Earlier critics, including Stuart Sherman and before him Joel Benton and Frank Sanborn, carefully argued that Emerson composed his writing; that the "doctrine of inspiration" was a powerful metaphor but not the actual fact of the writer's craft. With the publication of the *Journals and Miscellaneous Notebooks*, the *Topical Notebooks* and the *Poetry Notebooks*, later critics would have the means to show the truth of those earlier assertions, but mid-century criticism was caught in the discrepancy between the published work and the power of the current critical standard. Emerson's poems failed for want of internal consistency, and the same could be and was said of his ideas. Picking up where Winters left off, Gross comments, "This is the self-reliance of the dog, not the man. How or why the idiot and the ignorant boy are able to pierce the density of experience, when the rational dissector cannot, is beyond comprehension; in fact it is demonstrably false" (107).

Four years later, Newton Arvin sought to illustrate what was "demonstrably false" in the various ongoing attacks on Emerson. His 1959 essay published first in *The Hudson Review* opens with a short history of the criticism. Citing Hawthorne, Melville, James, Eliot, Lawrence, Yeats, he sums the problem by way of a question: "A writer who lacks the Vision of Evil, who has no great sense of wrong — how can he be read with respect, or perhaps read at all, in a time when we all seem agreed that anguish, inquietude, the experience of guilt, and the knowledge of the Abyss are the essential substance of which admissible literature is made" (38). The judgments against Emerson are many and powerful; they may well be taken as "not only a damaging but fatal indictment" (38). Arvin's argument hangs upon the "may well be taken": "may" but need not be; perhaps have been, but should not continue to be. Maintaining the importance of the charges, he nonetheless pointedly shows their limitations. The letters and journals are his greatest asset. He takes his title from one of Emerson's early letters to Mary Moody Emerson. Emerson wrote, "He has seen but half the Universe who never has been shown the house of Pain." This observation, he argues, was not simply the product of a single moment. The phrase reappears in Emerson's 1839 lecture and subsequent *Dial* essay, "The Tragic," and the sensibility it represents is part and parcel of Emerson's writing, even at its most celebratory. Unlike Whicher, he hears many different notes in the tone of the 1830s. "Even in this period," he writes, "and certainly later, there is another tone, an undertone, in his writings which we should listen to if we wish to sensitize ourselves to the complex harmony of his total thought" (43). Arvin allies this complexity with the continuous polarity within Emerson's work: regardless of the decade there was always the uneasy balance between the "powers of the human will" and "the forces in nature . . . hostile and even destructive" to that will (43).

Emerson's approach to that polarity becomes the focus of Arvin's discussion. Regardless of its perceived inadequacy for the late twentieth century's needs, it was nonetheless a firmly and carefully established position. Behind him lay the distinguished history of a particular philosophical tradition and Emerson's use of that tradition was careful and cogent. Reminding his readers that "our own guilt-ridden and anxious time" may blind individuals to the integrity of a different perspective (46), he places Emerson squarely within the Neoplatonic tradition. Emerson keeps good company with St. Augustine, and if the saint no longer speaks to the present, no one doubts the seriousness of his intellectual endeavor. Arvin suggests that we extend the same courtesy to the nineteenth-century sage. He also reminds his readers of Emerson's interest in Buddhist and Hindu philosophies and the confirmation they offered to his own views. He comments, "His controlling mode of thought, even in his later and more skeptical years, is a certain form of Optimism and *not* a form of the Tragic Sense, and what I should like to say now is that, however we may ourselves feel about this philosophy, it was one that rested not only on a deep personal experience but on a considered theory of Evil, and moreover that this was a theory by no means peculiar to Emerson, or original with him: on the contrary, it had a long and august tradition behind it in Western thought and analogies with the thought not only of Europe but of the East" (46). Bringing together numerous examples of Emerson's unblinking confrontations with the "odious facts" of savage nature and human savagery, he argues that Emerson's treatment of evil was always deliberate. If Emerson wrote "on the other side of Tragedy . . . he did not simply *find* himself there; if he had got beyond Tragedy, it was because he had *moved* beyond it" (49).

He in turn asks his readers to move beyond their assumptions. The perspective from the mid-twentieth century was a powerful one. The necessary pessimism engendered by the First and Second World Wars, followed by the Korean War, continued in the escalating tensions of the Cold War gave reason enough for damning any form of optimism, particularly with the deaths of six million Jews so palpably part of the conflict. No wonder that the "Tragic Sense" seemed the only reality; it was clearly the only viable reality for the present. At the same time, he sees danger in the present perspective. The complacency associated with Emerson's optimism may well be matched by a "complacency of pessimism" (48). Sounding a Baudelairean note — "we hug our negations, our doubts, our disbeliefs, to our chests" — he suggests that such an embrace all too easily becomes another intellectual self-indulgence. If the individual himself remains on "*this side* of Tragedy," he clearly participates in an unacceptable complacency, whether that state resulted from a jaunty optimism or an indulgent pessimism. Tellingly in his description of Emerson, he places him "on the other side." While Emerson's solution could not be the twentieth century's, Arvin maintains that the nineteenth-century thinker arrived there by unyielding intellectual labor (48–49).

Arvin suggests an equivalent labor for his audience. He calls for a thorough reexamination of Emerson and maintains that "thoroughness" will be judged by the extent of the work. The reader must look at the "whole" of Emerson's writings. Arvin's injunction was by no means new. Kern advocated reading Emerson in the essay not the excerpt; both Perry in the 1930s and Carpenter in the 1950s reminded their readers of the amount of Emerson that remained unpublished. Both Miller and Whicher drew upon some of that unpublished material using the early lectures in their discussions. Whicher was also centrally involved in the large project of publishing the unpublished Emerson, serving as one of the editors of the *Early Lectures*. The first of those volumes was published in 1959, the year of Arvin's essay, and if it ushered in a new era in Emerson criticism, it also can serve as a reminder of the other side of Emerson criticism in the period from 1930 to 1960.

While the 1930s are remembered for their flamboyant attacks on Emerson, they also witnessed three signal publishing events in the history of Emerson criticism. In 1938 Arthur McGiffert, Jr., published twenty-five of Emerson's one hundred and seventy-one sermons. The title of his work — *Young Emerson Speaks* — reveals its focus. The sermons, McGiffert remarks, are of "profound biographical interest" (xviii). They shed light on a time when the record of Emerson's life is sparse. McGiffert positions his edition as essential to understanding the development of a writer's work, and he thus heralds studies such as Matthiessen's and Whicher's. Although his emphasis is largely biographical, McGiffert does acknowledge that audiences will find other reasons to be interested in the sermons. In selecting the particular sermons for publication, he cites their religious and literary interest as well as the biographical elements they provide.

The effect of this volume was immediately apparent. A number of the sermons find their way into discussions of the late 1930s, early 1940s. Henry Nash Smith mentions the just-published sermons in his highly influential and often reprinted discussion of Emerson's vocational crisis ("Emerson's Problem of Vocation: A Note on the American Scholar, 1939). He calls attention to Sermon 143, which McGiffert titled "Find Your Calling" and cites it as evidence of Emerson's early struggle to free himself from clerical conventions. Both Paul and Whicher find it a useful point of reference.

A year after McGiffert's volume was published, another major addition to Emerson studies appeared with the six-volume edition of Emerson's letters. Edited by Ralph Rusk, the project was heralded as a masterpiece of editing. As with the sermons, the letters soon made their appearance in the critical literature. Like the journals, they were seen as a primary source for understanding the development of Emerson's thought, and in some cases, style. Agreement over their significance was divided, and the balance of judgment often weighed against them. Much of Emerson's correspondence had been published in various forms, and many reviewers saw the letters as simply more of the same. As with the sermons, they were considered to be primarily of biographical interest, and when Ralph Rusk's biography appeared in 1949, the importance of the letters in that capacity was clearly and firmly established.

What remained were lingering questions about the amount, content and quality of Emerson material still in manuscript. In his 1943 essay "The Emerson Canon," Henry A. Pochmann surveyed the landscape and suggested that the literary territory was by no means simple. When Arvin called for a reading of the "whole" Emerson fifteen years later, it was clear to Emerson scholars that the whole was increasingly massive and complex. Pochmann bluntly asserted that the present "canon" of 1943 was seriously suspect and questioned the decision to publish the six volumes of letters rather than a full edition of the journals. His discussion presciently raised the questions that would become the living matter for Emerson criticism at late century, and in his assessment, he also chronicled the textual difficulties that would face those who took as their province, if not the whole Emerson, the non-canonical parts.

Pochmann begins his discussion by citing the early century contribution to modern scholarship. The "carefully annotated" Centenary edition followed by the *Journals* "marked a new era of scholarly concern . . . [and] inaugurated a series of investigations that wrought a complete reinterpretation of the man and his significance" (476). With the completion of the *Journals*, however, it was assumed that the Emerson canon was "intact." Subsequent decades called that assumption into question. As Pochmann notes, Bliss Perry made "casual reference to omissions and condensations" in the printed edition of Emerson's journals. Five years later, Townsend Scudder directed a more serious charge against their selective nature. The questions, Pochmann comments, "became insistent. . . . How complete is the text of Emerson's writings? Upon what principles, and how intelligently, were the selections made? How faithfully, especially in the case of the journals, did the editors execute their task" (477). Calling for a complete reediting of the journals, he argues their absolute necessity to a full understanding of Emerson's work. Until that time, the commentary on Emerson would be unreliable. "Condemned to be provisional and tentative" (484), it would limit the progress of the field. Pochmann cites one example, drawing from his own experience. The stakes are high and clearly framed within the demands of the time. He writes, "The extreme importance of such deleted passages came to my attention when, following the leads of Professor Joseph Warren Beach's provocative article on 'Emerson and Evolution,' . . . I had the manuscript journals after 1849 searched for references to post-Kantian philosophers. The results revealed a score of passages omitted in the *Journals*." Such omissions, he claimed, were not a simple matter of benign absence. Their presence would show a far different Emerson than the one chastised by the current criticism. He asserts, "[These passages] supply . . . objective proof that Emerson's philosophy, far from being a haphazard affair of whim, rags and patches, and irreconcilable contrarieties, followed a course of consecutive development, traceable through four rather clearly defined epistemological phases." "This four-fold progression suggest[s] a complete reinterpretation of Emerson," but its possibility not only lies beyond the purview of his essay, it also awaits the full edition of the journals (483).

Pochmann's emphasis spoke for his times. The Emerson they needed was the systematic philosopher or aesthetician whose works would stand up to modern criteria of philosophical or literary unity. His emphasis on the importance of the journals, however, spoke to the future that Arvin would project. Neither imagined the extent of that project. Arvin's "whole" was far less ambitious than the amount of material available by century's end. Pochmann privileged certain manuscripts over others, diminishing the sermons and the letters, and not mentioning the lectures, in favor of the manuscripts he deemed most important.

The 1940s and the 1950s wavered over what the whole Emerson might include. Whicher's model suggested a compact unit, and yet he himself was involved in one of the many new editions that would mark the next period of criticism. As did Miller and Matthiessen, Whicher incorporated the then unpublished early lectures within his discussion of Emerson's development, suggesting their centrality to the project by the very persuasive nature of the quotations he selects. Part of the growing emphasis on the "textual" Emerson, Whicher's view firmly included the journals as well. Carpenter gave a more circumspect estimate. These manuscripts would never hold interest for the general reader, he claimed; they would only be pertinent to the specialized few. He did not foresee the "Emerson industry" of the 1980s, but he did say enough to whet his readers' appetites. In his words "much of genuine interest remains unpublished" (73). The next decades would prove his point. The story of the late twentieth century is the story of the editions.

Works Cited

Aaron, Daniel. *Men of Good Hope.* New York: Oxford University Press, 1951.

Allen, Gay Wilson. *American Prosody.* New York: American Book Company, 1935.

Anderson, Quentin. *The Imperial Self: An Essay in American Literary and Cultural History.* New York: Knopf, 1971.

Arvin, Newton. "The House of Pain and the Tragic Sense." *The Hudson Review* 12 (1959): 37–53.

Blair, Walter and Clarence Faust. "Emerson's Literary Method." *Modern Philology* 42 (1944): 79–95.

Burke, Kenneth. "I, Eye, Ay: Emerson's Early Essay on Nature: Thoughts on the Machinery of Transcendence." *Sewanee Review* 74 (1966): 875-95.

Calverton, V. F. *The Liberation of American Literature*. New York: Charles Scribner's Sons, 1932.

Carpenter, Frederic Ives. *Emerson and Asia*. Cambridge, MA: Harvard University Press, 1930.

———. *Emerson Handbook*. New York: Hendricks House, 1953.

Cox, James. "R. W. Emerson: The Circles of the Eye" in *Emerson: Prophecy, Metamorphosis, and Influence*. David Levin, editor. New York: Columbia University Press, 1975: 57–82.

"Emerson's Addresses." *Literary World* 5 (3 November 1849): 374–76.

Gross, Seymour. "Emerson and Poetry." *South Atlantic Quarterly* 54 (1955): 82–94.

Hazard, Lucy Lockwood. *The Frontier in American Literature*. New York: Thomas Y. Crowell Company, 1927.

Hicks, Granville. *The Great Tradition: An Interpretation of American Literature since the Civil War*. New York: International Publishers, 1933.

Hopkins, Vivian C. *Spires of Form: A Study of Emerson's Aesthetic Theory*. Cambridge, MA: Harvard University Press, 1951.

Kadison, Isabel. "Emerson Followed Webster." *Word Study* 20 (April 1945): 8.

Kern, Alexander. "Emerson and Economics." *New England Quarterly* 13 (December 1940): 678–96.

Mabbott, Thomas. "Emerson Rhymes." *Word Study* 20 (April 1945): 7–8.

Matthiessen, F. O. *American Renaissance: Art and Expression in the Age of Emerson and Whitman*. New York: Oxford University Press, 1941.

McEuen, Kathryn. "Emerson's Rhymes." *American Literature* 20 (1948): 31–42.

McGiffert, Arthur, Jr., editor. *Young Emerson Speaks*. Boston: Houghton Mifflin, 1938.

Miller, Perry. "Emersonian Genius and the American Democracy." *New England Quarterly* 26 (1953): 27–44.

Packer, Barbara. "The Instructed Eye: Emerson's Cosmogony in 'Prospects'" in *Emerson's "Nature"—Origin, Growth, Meaning*. Merton M. Sealts, Jr. and Alfred R. Ferguson, editors. Expanded Edition. Carbondale: University of Southern Illinois Press, 1979: 209–21.

Parrington, Vernon L. *Main Currents In American Thought: An Interpretation of American Literature*. 3 vols. New York: Harcourt, Brace and World, 1927–1930.

Paul, Sherman. *Emerson's Angle of Vision: Man and Nature in the American Experience*. Cambridge, MA: Harvard University Press, 1952.

Pochmann, H. A. "The Emerson Canon." *University of Toronto Quarterly* 12 (1943): 478–84.

Poirier, Richard. *A World Elsewhere: The Place of Style in American Literature.* New York: Oxford University Press, 1966.

Porter, Carolyn. *Seeing and Being: The Plight of the Participant Observer in Emerson, James, Adams and Faulkner.* Middletown, CT: Wesleyan University Press, 1981.

Porter, David. *Emerson and Literary Change.* Cambridge, MA: Harvard University Press, 1978.

Rusk, Ralph, editor. *The Letters of Ralph Waldo Emerson.* 6 vols. New York: Columbia University Press, 1939.

Scudder, Townsend. *The Lonely Wayfaring Man: Emerson and Some Englishmen.* New York: Oxford University Press, 1936.

Smith, Henry Nash. "Emerson's Problem of Vocation — A Note on 'The American Scholar.'" *The New England Quarterly* 22 (1939): 52–67.

Stratton, Clarence. "Emerson's Rhymes." *Word Study* 20 (December 1944): 3–4.

Tanner, Tony. *The Reign of Wonder, Naivety and Reality in American Literature.* New York: Cambridge University Press, 1965.

Whicher, Stephen. *Freedom and Fate: An Inner Life of Ralph Waldo Emerson.* Philadelphia: University of Pennsylvania Press, 1953.

———. *Selections from Ralph Waldo Emerson: An Organic Anthology.* Boston: Houghton Mifflin Company, 1957.

Winters, Yvor. "Jones Very and R. W. Emerson: Aspects of New England Mysticism" in *In Defense of Reason.* Chicago: The Swallow Press, 1937: 262–82.

———. "The Significance of *The Bridge*, by Hart Crane Or What Are We to Think of Professor X?" in *In Defense of Reason.* Chicago: The Swallow Press, 1937: 577–603.

Yeats, William Butler. *The Trembling of the Veil.* London: T. Werner Laurie, 1922.

6: Imagining a New Emerson: The Power of the Editions

AT THE BEGINNING of the essay "Experience," Emerson gives his reader a chilling image of an inescapable waking nightmare. In sentences that have long been familiar in the criticism he writes, "Where do we find ourselves? In a series, of which we do not know the extremes, and believe that it has none. We wake and find ourselves on a stair; there are stairs below us, which we seem to have ascended; there are stairs above us, many a one, which go upward and out of sight" (*Collected Works* 3: 27). The Emerson critic at the beginning of the twenty-first century might well take this image (or this series of images, if one prefers) as the emblem of the late-century scholarship. What Lawrence Buell termed the "annus mirabilis" of 1982 is now seen as only one moment, albeit a pivotal one, among many. The stairs above us continue and with the imminence of the bicentenary celebrations in 2003, the series shows no sign of ending.

Not simply one staircase, there are many, each with its own series of unknown extremes, often ascending in parallel. What remains for the twenty-first century is to connect these separate paths. In some cases, the work is already being done. In others, it is barely begun, both in terms of connecting recent work and in looking back to the "extremes" of which the particular essay or book is yet another stair. Or to change the rickety image of separate staircases connected by precariously supported bridges, another of Emerson's perennial favorites serves the criticism. We require the "primary figure . . . the highest emblem in the cipher of the world" (*Collected Works* 2: 179). The circle, if it does not reduce our interpretations to nothing, offers the promise of an open secret we can readily spend our lifetimes reading.

I begin with this play of Emersonian images to reflect a signal change in the criticism since 1960. This chapter locates that change squarely in the work that made such re-envisioning possible. The modern editions, heralded by the three volumes of the *Early Lectures* and the sixteen volumes of the *Journals and Miscellaneous Notebooks* (1960–82), offered readers far more by way of Emerson's process than had been seen in the published essays or *Journals*. The initial effect of these editions was a considered attention to Emerson's literary artistry. As an increasing number of volumes in JMN were made available, the work of cultural studies became viable for Emerson criticism. The self-styled "experimenter with no past at [his] back" was increasingly studied as a writer engaged vitally and contentiously with the specific reform issues of his times.

As the publication of the *Journals and Miscellaneous Notebooks* and the *Early Lectures* drew increasing attention to Emerson's method and practice of composition, the ideological focus of the criticism shifted away from the history of ideas and back to Emerson the literary artist. The impetus came not simply from this influx of texts. Intellectual history had reached a dead end in discussion of Emerson. At the twentieth century's end it would arise in a new form, but in the late 1950s, the case for Emerson's "ideas" had been pushed as far as it could go, and there were few critics who were able to see a future in the ideas associated with him. As Jonathan Bishop remarked in his still deeply influential *Emerson on the Soul* (1964), "The labor of intellectual history can make Emerson seem paraphrasable at the expense of making him uninteresting" (3).

Until the 1980s Emerson remained interesting primarily for his work as a literary artist. When his ideas came under discussion, the tone was pointedly critical. The charges against his (assumed) ideological positions were still vital. Descendants of the 1930's Marxists and also of New Criticism, these attacks targeted the ugly consequences of one particular model of individualism. In the midst and wake of the Vietnam War, the American "imperial self," to borrow Quentin Anderson's succinct phrase, loomed large, and the very old questions about self-reliance returned. The earliest reviewers faulted the concept for the seemingly unavoidable actions it would entail. The unrestrained self would willfully follow its every demand for gratification. The perspective of 1970 was in marked agreement: self-reliance was simply another phrase for self-aggrandizement. Emerson was a strange but powerful underwriter for the aggressive American policies abroad and at home.

While many have argued against Anderson's representation of Emerson's concept (the essays in *Emerson: Prophecy, Metamorphosis and Influence*, for example), such critiques of self-reliance continue predictably with the increase of American militarism. David Marr's *American Worlds Since Emerson* appeared in 1988 at the end of a decade that witnessed the invasion in Granada, U.S. military action in Haiti, and the continuation of covert operations in Central America. Foregrounding the "political meaning of Emersonian privatism," Marr tightly connects past and present. In his words, "Emersonian privatism, moralism, and anti-politicism are major elements in American social character. They belong, therefore, to the history of American politics and the eclipse of the political in the modern age" (4). To further that understanding Marr takes Emerson at his journal word. Noting Emerson's remark that he followed a single idea — "the infinitude of the private man" — Marr explores that concept, its idealized privatism and the "politically sanitized world" it engenders (37). In his 1990 essay "Emerson, Individualism, and the Ambiguities of Dissent," Sacvan Bercovitch claims Emerson's radicalism as a successful competitor to "the socialist types of radical consciousness then emerging in Europe" (Buell, 1993, 125). Success, however, is limited to the system which produced it. While he argues that Emersonian individualism is something other than "liberal co-optation," it is nonetheless a product of laissez-faire liberalism, and as such it is fundamentally contained within that system.

Though published into the next decade, Christopher Newfield's *The Emerson Effect* (1996) took shape in the 1980s and continues that decade's critique of American individualism in its focus on the deceptive harmony Emerson created between individual freedom and democratic society. Like Marr, Newfield is concerned with the influence of Emerson's ideas. Summing his argument, he writes, "My purpose is to work through the components of Emerson's ambivalent, influential weakening of democracy. . . .Individualism comes to include submission and democracy to include authoritarianism. Emerson's international fame as a major prophet of the self makes his development of a submissive kind of individualism particularly astonishing and culturally important" (6).

Worth noting in this connection are A. Bartlett Giamatti's words from his baccalaureate address in 1981 during his presidency at Yale ("Power, Politics, and a Sense of History"). He too examines the "devaluation of political life" in the United States (*The University and the Public Interest*, 172). He too finds that Emerson is a major player. Not part of the scholarly tradition represented by Marr and Newfield, Giamatti nonetheless speaks from within the academy, adopting a tone reminiscent of an earlier era. His words bring to mind Yvor Winters, but his remarks exceed even Winters's invective. Winters's focus remains literature. As much as he may have wanted his reader to look from the writing to the culture, he nonetheless restricted himself to the writing. Giamatti draws no such bounds in the scope of his remarks. The writing is the culture. "With extraordinary literary skills at a crucial moment in our nation's life, it is Emerson who freed our politics and our politicians from any sense of restraint by extolling self-generated, unaffiliated power as the best foot to place in the small of the back of the man in front of you, and who promoted shoving as the highest calling that abolitionist, moral New England could conceive" (174). Giamatti's position is an uncompromising rejection. "Emerson's views are those of a brazen adolescent, and we ought to be rid of them. The maturing of America will occur when we have absorbed, not rejected, our past" (177). Audience response can only be conjectured. Presumably the graduating Yale students were no longer the brazen adolescents they may once have been, but did they catch Giamatti in his own double standard: rejecting Emerson while championing a full absorption of the American past?

While the 1990s accomplished the unthinkable, redeeming Emerson not only as a philosopher, but a political philosopher, reclaiming individualism as a respectable concept, the 1960s pushed readers of Emerson to think in a different direction. The thrust was artfully crafted, and is in primary ways, the reason the next to last decade of the century could discover a route out of a previous dead-end. Central to the renewed focus on Emerson as literary artist is Bishop's 1964 book, *Emerson on the Soul*. It admirably succeeded in the program Bishop set for himself. Stepping aside from the Emerson decline, he advocated the "*literary* achievement." From the near past of the early 1960s he could write, "So far as Emerson is an artist in words, he still tends to be left out of the picture" (5). John Jay Chapman, William James (for better or worse), O. W. Firkins, and Stuart Sherman kept that Emerson in the picture, but their focus was clearly not what Bishop intended. Nor was the approach seen in writers like Matthiessen or Hopkins or Paul. From his perspective, their works remained firmly rooted in intellectual history: Matthiessen argued from specific notions of literary form, Hopkins generated an aesthetic theory, Paul worked from the doctrine of correspondence. In each case, the thought dominated the study of the expression.

Bishop himself would draw upon that approach. The first half of his book is divided into sections with ideas for their titles: "Science," "History," "Compensation," "Self-Reliance," "The Whole Soul," "The Vital Mind." His treatment differs, as does his emphasis. Moving away from the dominant thrust of the middle decades of the century, Bishop is not as interested in Emerson the reconciler as he is in Emerson the representor. Emerson designs his writing to represent and reproduce experience. This massive and palpable undertaking is the reason why intellectual history falls short in its interpretation. It is also why the word *soul* can escape its clichéd status. The word itself represents the full range "in the motions of life" (21): it comprises the intellect knowing, the organic life being, the mind comprehending. Bishop builds up the various faculties of the soul as Emerson describes them in his work. He then turns to the writing itself and matches each element with its own finely-crafted literary device. As Bishop himself notes, the equations can appear glib, but in Bishop's close readings, they nonetheless work. While many may disagree with his assessment of "the transparent eyeball" as "innocently absurd at best," "vapid" at worst (15), his beautiful elucidation of the bare common is now central to our reading of its more famous counterpart (11–15).

Beautiful is the apt word for Bishop's discussion. Not concerned with creating a system, he is intent upon displaying the elegance of Emerson's prose. A passage in his introduction speaks for this interest, and in retrospect, speaks for the scholarly activity that would follow his work. Bishop characterizes his approach as sustained attention to *how* one thinks and how one *says* what one thinks. Although the critics who anatomized the organic principle in reference to Emerson made some headway in that connection, they nonetheless subordinated the writing to the ideas. Bishop hopes to open a new method for thinking about Emerson's work. He comments, "most readers will be tantalizingly aware that the qualities of the Emersonian style are somehow close to the center of imaginative action for which they are searching" (5).

Bishop's central contribution may well lie in his discussion of metaphor. Unlike Matthiessen, he was willing to see Emerson's metaphors as something other than veiled analogies. He stepped away from the concept of correspondence, finding its mechanism problematic. With correspondence as the focus, Emerson's sentences themselves readily disappeared into a discussion of an idea. As part of his work to make the literary quality essential, Bishop presents metaphor as the individual's primary way of knowing. He writes, "The conclusion to which Emerson's results on both science and history would lead is that, without metaphor, no state of affairs is knowable at all" (65). Scientists and historians might well disagree, but from Bishop's vantage point, the only way to know something is through the fundamental comparison that says "is." Emerson, as Bishop reminds his reader and as 1990s critics explored, was fascinated by science precisely because of its potential for creating "true" equations between objects that may not have been previously connected. History internalized that connection.

When Bishop later turns to the writing itself, his section on metaphor writes the way toward the future. Furthering the emphasis on agency, he makes clear that the *is* within an Emersonian metaphor is always dynamic. Linking metaphor to metamorphosis (126), he observes the connection that would become the focus of discussion in the 1970s and 1980s. David Porter's study of Emerson's aesthetic theory, *Emerson and Literary Change* (1978) firmly located that aesthetic in process. Every stylistic device that Emerson used was put to work in order to highlight the making of meaning rather than the artifact of that making. Both Barbara Packer (*Emerson's Fall*, 1982) and Julie Ellison (*Emerson's Romantic Style*, 1984) make dynamism central to their arguments, but it is in Leonard Neufeldt's work that Emersonian metamorphosis found its chief expositor.

Before we turn to those critics, I turn back to Bishop's own prophecy for the future of Emerson studies. In all but one case he was a canny predictor. As he looked to the next generations of Emerson critics, he asked "What would it take to create a new Emerson, who could throw affirmative light upon the old" (219). With his colleagues of the 1950s, he wondered how Emerson's view of the moral sentiment and his belief in compensation could ever be anything but useless to the twentieth century. The concluding five years of the century began the project of reclaiming the irreclaimable. The results are pending in work such as Lee Rust Brown's *The Emerson Museum* (1997) and George Kateb's *The Inner Ocean* (1992) and *Emerson and Self-Reliance* (1995). While Bishop did not envision such attempts, he did prepare the way for them. He saw a "new" Emerson possible only if the critics could come up with a "convincing idiom." This is precisely the work done by critics such as Porter in the 1970s, Ellison in the 1980s, Brown in the 1990s, and Cavell in an ongoing project that covers the last three decades of the century. The varieties of literary theory and their philosophical foundations clearly have been key, not so much in the idiom they have created, but in the ways their methods opened Emerson's idiom for reinterpretation.

In addition to the new idiom, Bishop called for an approach entirely different from the one perfected by New Criticism. He questioned the hegemony of academic discourse, wondering whether its structures could ever yield more than an illusory success. He comments, "There is something at the heart of Emerson's message profoundly recalcitrant to the formulations of the discursive intelligence" (6). He acknowledges that the "most suggestive critical remarks" often had little to do with scholarly work: "What one wants, then, is not a criticism of Emerson but a continuation — or rather, a continuation that would make the criticism real" (220). While such continuation has not yet found its way fully into the literary criticism, one writer in particular has practiced this art of extension. Philosopher Stanley Cavell experiments with Emerson's form of thought, not only practicing an Emersonian style of thinking in his own prose but championing that style as "genuine" philosophy. In the 1970s, Cavell was a voice in the wilderness; in the 1990s, he was heard as an authority and no mere scribe.

In predicting the future, Bishop's clear vision was clouded in one signal area: the editions of Emerson's work. Acknowledging their importance, he nonetheless underestimated their significance. As had Carpenter before him, he assumed the difference would be a matter of degree, not kind. "This 'new' Emerson is not really so new," he commented, "if changes of emphasis are necessary, they are less profound than novelty might lead us to think" (7). Hoping to initiate an ongoing study of Emerson's literary achievement, he feared that the influx of new material would derail the project. As the criticism of the past forty years shows, such fears were not realized. In and of themselves, the newly published materials have received surprisingly little attention: there is only one book on Emerson's journal (Lawrence Rosenwald's *Emerson and the Art of the Diary*, 1988), only two on the sermons (Wesley T. Mott's *"The Strains of Eloquence": Emerson and His Sermons*, 1989 and Susan R. Roberson's *Emerson in His Sermons: A Man-Made Self*, 1995), one book which combines discussion of the sermons and early lectures (David Robinson's *Apostle of Culture: Emerson as Preacher and Lecturer*, 1982), and one on Emerson's reform writings (Len Gougeon's *Virtue's Hero: Emerson, Antislavery and Reform*, 1990).

Time is still a factor for full assessment of the "new" editions. What is no longer argued, however, is their importance for further study. Bishop's own work was clearly indebted to the journals and early lectures. He used the analog passages to show Emerson's conscious crafting of style, a technique that had been amply used by earlier critics (Matthiessen, Hopkins, Whicher) and would become the standard model for the discussion of Emerson's style. As Pochmann pointed out in 1943, such studies would necessarily be "provisional" as long as the journals were readily available only in their "selected" and "edited" version.

For many critics, the question of "newness" found a succinct answer in the different "Emersons" made available to a reading audience. The sermons and the antislavery writings offer an interpretation of Emerson that has rarely been popular and perhaps is tenable only in light of these writings. Working from complete texts, critics like Robinson (in both *Apostle of Culture*, but particularly his later *Emerson on the Conduct of Life*) and Gougeon, have given us a much more complex study of Emerson's role as an ethical thinker than was previously available.

If this Emerson is not new, then he is undeniably more complex. He is also a writer with a longer viable career than many early critics or reviewers would grant. And eventually, he may be a writer for whom the so-called canon finally expands. The essays of critical interest remain remarkably static: *Nature*, "The American Scholar," "Self-Reliance," "The Poet," "Experience." There have been a few notable inclusions ("Fate," "The Method of Nature," "Circles"), a few losses ("The Over-Soul," "Character"), but the Emerson deemed essential shows a disconcerting continuity given the various announced changes of approach during different moments of the twentieth century.

The small group of works in the Emerson canon is nowhere more apparent than in the scholarship on the poems. A handful of poems are held in critical esteem; most are dismissed (or unknown) and assumed to be yet more examples of the way Emerson failed his poetic theory in practice. Matthiessen's assessment has often been internalized within the criticism: "Days" is the best of Emerson's few good poems. It succeeds because its form is not marred by Emerson's interest in process.

An early exception to this assessment is the work of Carl Strauch. By the 1960s he had been working on Emerson's poetry for two decades. His 1946 doctoral thesis was a variorum edition of the poems. In the 1940s and 1950s, he pursued a virtual one-man operation on the poetry, working, as he said, to establish a clear critical context within which to grant the poems their rightful importance in the Emerson canon. His argument often privileged the ideas within Emerson's poetic oeuvre. In "Emerson and the Doctrine of Sympathy" (1967), for example, he places Emerson's fascination with a "mobile, ever-changing universe" within the context of Romanticism's dynamic order (152). He cites the poems in Emerson's 1847 volume as the single best examples of this fascination and turns to the "neglected masterpiece" ("Woodnotes") to prove his point. His focus is decidedly on the dominant ideas within the poems and less with the *how* that governs their expression. He clearly has in mind the larger context of Emerson criticism in which particular explications fall on deaf ears. Speaking of the "affirmations" in "Woodnotes," Strauch forwards his attempt to separate Emerson from those who dismiss him. "If this is a victory for the spirit," he writes, "it is not an easy optimism, not a flabby acquiescence, but a hard-won struggle in time and space" (174). Emerson's "optimism" is an "affirmation of a living universe" — a point that a much later critic working in a much different area (George Kateb, in the 1990s, on democratic individuality) would also find a useful reminder to his audience.

With his emphasis on Emerson's ideas, Strauch is closer to Matthiessen and Whicher than to Bishop. His Emerson is the "reconciler" rather than the "unsettler." It would take the work from the mid-1960s through the mid-1980s to again give power to that image, and in this case, an esteemed power rather than one to be carefully contained. Several works in the 1970s began building a strong case for this "new" Emerson, an Emerson that would include texts once dismissed. In the 1960s and 1970s, critics turned to the poems or to Emerson as a poet. Prompted largely by the renewed interest in Emerson as a writer, they frequently defined themselves within the new project outlined by

Bishop. The focus targeted method: in some cases, Emerson's; in others, the reader's. The question of *how* we read Emerson became and indeed remains foremost in the criticism. The mid-century question of *whether* to read Emerson at all slowly receded into the background and late-twentieth-century critics were (almost) free to choose a frame for their work different from the once obligatory apology.

To that end, the critics of the 1970s and 1980s clearly did their work well. The task was not simple. As Hyatt Waggoner notes in his *Emerson as Poet* (1974), "Emerson has long been a problem for modern readers. Should we read him at all" (53). The key word in Waggoner's sentences may well be "modern," for it is clear that whatever is meant by postmodernism, the time period it describes has changed the fundamental question about Emerson from whether to read his work to what approach(es) will best serve its interpretation. Waggoner's discussion is clearly one step toward that transformed problem.

He notes the difficulty for the particular time. The established methods yield little. To accomplish his goal of "trying to get Emerson's verse read again freshly," he must separate his readers from both "Victorian" and "New Critical assumptions" (partly the former, largely the latter). He seeks a new method and promises his reader something that will "bear as little resemblance to traditional judicial criticisms as I can manage" (110). If other critics have delivered more ably on that kind of promise, Waggoner nonetheless establishes two clear guides for reconsidering the poetry. Both are steeped in literary tradition, making clear that Emerson's poetry is important precisely within that context. In contrast to Matthiessen's lament that "excellent" poetry cannot be written in the absence of a "living tradition to draw upon and modify," Waggoner argues for a shift in focus. He does not want Emerson simply to be seen as a precursor but to be fully connected into the poetic tradition for which he was largely responsible. As he commented in his *American Poets* (1968), "Emerson is our nineteenth-century poet most in need today of being rediscovered" (90). Noting the difficulty of the task, he flags the New Critical assumptions: "Is there a way of seeing that will make it seem that irony is not the only honest poetic stance" (93).

For his study of Emerson's poetry, Waggoner limits himself to two revisionary approaches. He begins by surveying the critical response to Emerson's poems, pointing out its limitations. The terms used to analyze Emerson's poetry have been for the most part inappropriate. Waggoner encourages his readers to abandon their familiar interpretive methods. Emerson's poems require an approach commensurate with their conception. They are best seen as "illuminations," not "compositions" (51). He allies such illumination with a prophetic stance and connects its expression with a specific form. He identifies the poems as a continuation in the "Ancient, Medieval, and Renaissance literary and philosophic tradition of paradoxy" (110).

Waggoner encourages his readers to suspend the standards of conventional criticism and develop a model that changes the critic's role as "judge and arbiter" (109). He echoes Bishop's thoughts about where the "best" insights occur, and suggests a different kind of reading where the reader's identification with the text is not carefully edited out. His own discussion, however, is still firmly rooted within the "judge and arbiter" model as he works to discover what are the "best" Emerson poems and why and whether the "best" poetry finally does occur in the prose.

Four years later, Ralph Yoder's *The Orphic Poet in America* makes no apology for Emerson's poetry. Yoder isolates the singular power of the Orpheus myth for its nineteenth-century American audience: Orpheus tamed the wilderness. "The rocks and trees and wild beasts arranged themselves in order around this central man" (xiii). Examining Emerson's engagement with and redefinition of the "orphic poet," Yoder charts its culmination in a particular aesthetic. It celebrates the attainable felicity found within the ordinary ("the titmouse dimension") without sacrificing "the primary fable of a poet-hero" (93).

While some critics looked primarily to Bishop for their model, others acknowledged both Whicher and Bishop. As Yoder noted in his essay "Emerson's Dialectic" (1969), Whicher's anatomy of Emerson's "inner life" freed the criticism from a dead end of logic. While much of the effort of the 1930s to the 1950s had been devoted to creating a system for Emerson's work, Yoder maintains that not only were such attempts doomed to collapse, but they could say very little about Emerson's writing. With Bishop, he championed the literary achievement and identified Emerson's "rhetoric" as the necessary topic. As with many critics of the time, the word became a shorthand for "literary effects . . . insofar as they can be distinguished from subject, argument, and conclusion" (314). Later critics would continue this work in an ongoing subgenre within the criticism. Not surprisingly, these studies are firmly comparative, looking to Emerson's sources and analogues. Foremost among them are Alan Hodder's *Emerson's Rhetoric of Revelation* (1989, a study of *Nature* in light of the apocalyptic language of the Bible) and Richard O'Keefe's *Mythic Archetypes in Ralph Waldo Emerson: A Blakean Reading* (1995, a study of "dialectical organization" through the governing form of both Blake's and Emerson's literary method: the use of archetype and myth to create immanence).

In his desire to separate "literary effects," from "subject, argument, conclusion," Yoder participated in the 1960s reclamation of Emerson.

He was artist, not philosopher; argument was the least interesting part of his writing and invariably dead-ended the reader who chose that for his focus. The style, however, was a different matter. Yoder locates its interest in a potentially difficult place. The style is characterized by a term that sounds like philosophy — "dialectical momentum" — but Yoder carefully distinguishes this momentum from a "dialectical logic" (318, 315). He uses Emerson's fascination with polarity as the source for the structures of the essay. His description of the common rhetorical strategy in Emerson's essays became the standard summary. Yoder writes, "They all assert a basic dichotomy and develop a balance between its opposite or extreme terms. This equilibrium gradually disintegrates, and a single theme or thesis emerges, often indirectly by image and suggestion rather than by direct statement. The theme or thesis expresses doubt or moral ambiguity in nature. It builds up assertive power until suddenly it is dashed away by a climactic turn in the essay, almost always indicated by a contrastive conjunction ('But,' 'yet,' 'whilst'). The antithesis introduced by the turn is an expression of unity and hope, and leads into Emerson's peroration" (325).

Critics had long noted the element of polarity in Emerson's writing and discussed the tension between Emerson's opposing statements, but the earlier discussions invariably became an argument from logic or a lament over lost unity. Yoder took a relatively new direction: to understand Emerson's written style, careful attention to its performed aspects were necessary. Yoder terms this "dramatic presentation" but does not place that "presentation" back into its lyceum or church origin.

One of Yoder's contemporaries did precisely that. A. M. Baumgartner called upon the older definition of rhetoric — the one which included sermon-writing and on which Emerson cut the teeth of his prose — and argues its importance in the formation of Emerson's style ("'The Lyceum is My Pulpit': Homiletics in Emerson's Early Lectures," 1963). Addressing the question of logic within the writings, Baumgartner notes that the Unitarian ministry and its teachers never put a premium upon it. He cites Blair's *Rhetoric* for its distrust of traditional logic and quotes Henry Ware, Jr.'s teaching notes from Harvard Divinity School. Ware instructed his students to adopt a style of "indirect directness" (485). While Baumgartner acknowledges the difference between sermon and lecture, he also reminds his readers that the line was readily blurred.

He also places his study of Emerson's style firmly in the context of the new editions. His essay opens with a project-defining sentence: "The publication of the first volume of Emerson's early lectures evidenced the need for a reevaluation of his later works" (477). Chief among the writers pursuing this work in the 1960s and early 1970s were Robert Spiller, Merton Sealts, Ralph LaRosa, and Lawrence Buell. Spiller and Sealts were both involved in the editorial process: Spiller for the lectures, Sealts for JMN. In his 1962 essay "From Lecture to Essay: Emerson's Method of Composition," Spiller takes the long-established formula and applies it according to the evidence of the manuscripts. In the process he dismantles the old image of Emerson's compositional "method," still firmly ensconced in the "common wisdom." In 1868, James Russell Lowell noted, "It was as if, after vainly trying to get his paragraphs into sequence and order, he had at last tried the desperate expedient of *shuffling* them" ("Emerson the Lecturer," 379). The description led easily into dismissive asides, often presented as if the observation itself were self-sufficient: Emerson did not so much compose his essays as assemble them from random, though topically related, parts. Spiller systematically shows how different the popular image was from the written reality of Emerson's texts.

Sealts directed his attention to a different aspect of Emerson's style, focusing on one of, if not *the*, prime figure within Emerson's addresses and lectures ("Emerson on the Scholar, 1833–1837," 1970). Returning to many of the questions raised by Henry Nash Smith in his 1939 essay, Sealts offers a detailed chronicle of how Emerson's image of the scholar underwent continual revision in the years between 1833 and 1837, the years that describe the arc from the first lyceum lectures to the Phi Beta Kappa address at Harvard. Sealts targets Emerson's interest in natural history as a signal element in this ongoing revision: Emerson was repeatedly examining what it meant to be a naturalist whose subject was "man." Central to this natural history project was Emerson's insistence on originality. Sealts distances this originality from nationalism, in part a comment back against the early fifties work of Aaron and Miller on genius and democracy, in part a comment for his own present.

The question of *originality* was often a sticking point in the criticism, and the material provided by the journals and lectures offered critics new possibilities for that topic. From the moment of the earliest reviews, originality held significant space in the readers' minds. It was largely a yes or no question, and in consequence, a decidedly polemical one. In its various versions, the question played out in a perfectly balanced, perfectly loaded form: was Emerson original, or was he an imitation of Carlyle or of German idealism or of Neoplatonism. The shift away from this two-sided question can be seen in Ralph LaRosa's essay "Emerson's Search for Literary Form: The Early Journals" (1971). Undeniably arguing for Emerson's originality, LaRosa nonetheless shifts the ground of the discussion by putting a particular literary form at the cen-

ter of the topic: the small form of the pithy moral statement, the senten-
tia. Tracing the verbal record of Emerson's thoughts on originality,
LaRosa pursues a double-edged interest. He describes the inherent tensions between subject and expression: Emerson reflects on originality in
a journal that also identifies itself as a commonplace book. At the same
time, the sentence is also the most flexible form for undertaking experiments in original thought. LaRosa begins his discussion by referring his
reader forward to Emerson's late essay "Quotation and Originality." It
was an essay and a set of topics to which future critics would turn as the
influence of deconstruction handily called into question the stability of
texts.

For the particular moment of the early 1970s, the question of origin
followed a different path. Lawrence Buell's immensely important *Literary
Transcendentalism* appeared in 1973 and offered another defining moment for the future of Emerson studies. Following Bishop's lead, Buell
turned to the literary dimension of the Transcendentalists. Taking on the
difficult task of nonfiction, a form for which few critical methods had been
developed, Buell emphasized the importance of such work. He writes,
"The student of nonfictional literature must be prepared to show why the
thought of an Emerson . . . leads irresistibly to strongly poetic or rhetorical forms of expression rather than to a relatively unadorned argument of
exposition" (13). Examining the stylistic conventions that governed the
Transcendentalists' writings, he includes Emerson as a powerful voice in
that group, but only one voice among many.

In his several chapters on the background of the "Transcendentalist
aesthetic," Buell laid the groundwork for a particular type of study that
would become increasingly important. Unitarianism had long been the
poor relation in Emerson studies. The early twentieth century's fixation
on Puritanism doubly marginalized Unitarianism. It appeared, if at all,
as a flawed byway, the dead-end of eighteenth-century rationalism.
Looking at the writings of the Boston Unitarians, Buell offered a different picture. Whatever their rising or falling force in American society,
their rhetorical techniques were anything but impoverished; their sermons displayed a rich play of literary devices. These were "literary performances" and the congregations' interest could be measured by a
theology that was heading ever closer to an aesthetic. Buell notes,
"there is a strong tendency in Unitarian preaching when dealing with
biblical and doctrinal subjects not to confront the issues directly but to
substitute one's own poetic imagery" (109). Baumgartner's quote from
Ware is precisely to the point: Harvard's teaching ministers advised the
preaching ministers to inspire their listeners' religious sentiment through
the highly literary practice of "indirect directness."

Buell enumerates a series of techniques well known to readers of Emerson: redefinition of key words, an "accretive" method that relies on the "device of multiple statement or illustration" (124), the use of paradox and analogy, of list-like phrases that yield a kind of catalogue rhetoric and the "free and creative use" of quotation. Buell locates these strategies in the Unitarian practice of scriptural and doctrinal interpretation. As he notes, it is a small step to Emerson: "Their [the Unitarian ministers'] approach to the Bible was a near anticipation of the Emersonian habit of interpreting its supernatural element metaphorically" (114).

In addition to his discussion of the Unitarian background, Buell continues the conversation on a Transcendental aesthetic. Metaphor functions as argument in Emerson's prose: Buell's discussion adds another powerful voice to the growing chorus on "metamorphosis." In Emerson's world, "the feeling of inspiration was linked with the image-making power" (154). Image invariably highlights process.

Buell notes the difficulty of placing activity at the center of an aesthetic: "Emerson's fascination with metamorphosis . . . runs him into difficulty on the question of literary form, as his critics have always been quick to point out" (156). Joining Yoder, he sees the primary impetus in Emerson's essays as "dialectic" and, like Yoder, is careful to distinguish this dialectic from argumentative logic. The dialectic is stylistic, a way of giving flux a literary formulation. As he had argued in an earlier essay, "Reading Emerson for the Structures: The Coherence of the Essays" (1972), there is far more order in an Emerson essay than is assumed. There is not, however, the kind of dialectical unity sought by earlier critics. Instead, a wide-ranging repertoire of structures represented the active imagination and encouraged its further activity. Buell writes, "[Emerson's] use of structure . . . furnishes the essays with the same combination of abandonment and unity that he observed in nature" (68). A far cry from the organic unity of New Criticism, it had more in common with the growing interest in open-endedness.

Buell ends his 1972 essay with an imperative and an injunction. Comparing Thoreau and Emerson scholarship, he finds that the latter lags far behind the former in the study of the writer's work as *writer*. Buell writes, "[Emerson's] achievement in the area of form has been underrated" (69). He points to the "journals, miscellaneous notebooks, and lectures" as the material which will make that necessary, but habitually overlooked, work possible. "We may expect," he writes, "a general reappraisal of Emerson as an artist of wholes as well as parts." He then offers those future critics a piece of advice. "Such a reappraisal," he comments, "however, should not be apologetic, should not make the mistake of seizing upon the ordering elements in Emerson's prose as if they were the sole thing which saves his essays from disaster. We must also accept the validity, at least for him, of the open-ended kind of discourse Emerson was attempting."

As the studies of style continued, it was clear that such open-endedness would continue to rise in value. The work Buell looked forward to has been done in part — with a significant emphasis on the part. In terms of stylistic studies, the late 1970s and early 1980s gave far more attention to Emerson as an "artist of parts" than to the "artist of wholes." With the famed lubricity of an Emerson sentence, a focus on the whole invariably veered away from the literary expression and back to the ideas with which Emerson so creatively worked.

The artist of the parts remained a markedly rich area of inquiry well into the 1980s. With greater accuracy, it could be said that critics studied Emerson as the artist of process. The clear focus in the criticism of this period readily emerges from its immediate predecessors. It is implied in Buell's description of lectures and sermons as "literary performances," in the dynamic tension Waggoner finds in Emerson's paradoxes, in LaRosa's comments about literary experimentation. The invitation extended by Bishop in the early 1960s, accepted in the 1970s, remained open for the 1980s. Bishop observed the metamorphic quality of Emerson's metaphor. Later critics turned that observation into full-scale studies.

In *Emerson and Literary Change* (1978), David Porter could well have had Bishop in mind when he championed a new idiom for the discussion of Emerson's writing. He also comes the closest to Buell's comment on the "artist of the whole," for Porter takes as his project the entirety of Emerson's published work: poetic theory, poems and essays. Questioning the established wisdom about the discrepancy between theory and practice, he notes that "the contrary actually seems to be true," that Emerson's "practice . . . bore out in a remarkably consistent way the theory he proposed." Unlike the familiar assertions that Emerson could never keep his attention focused on form, Porter maintains that "Emerson not only was concerned theoretically with form, but that he was intimately engaged with the minute elements" of its practice. In Emerson, Porter sees an eminent craftsman whose skill was honed in the practice of various expressions. He recognized the distance between this Emerson and the versions of earlier criticism: "This is a new view of Emerson, showing that the totality of his work — theory and practice — was a consistent and self-generating passage toward a new calculation of the way language might grip experience without tyrannizing it" (137).

To make this new Emerson convincing, Porter concedes the old. With other critics of Emerson's poetry, he acknowledges its so-called defects, and relentlessly pursues these perceived flaws. He locates them in a familiar place. The poems cannot bear the weight of the ideas behind them. Porter places this squarely on Emerson's understanding of poetry itself: "In Emerson's conception, a poem was a transfer of knowledge, where a reader is not expected to feel his life in manifold new ways but rather to locate himself intellectually" (23). Employing the familiar turn of the early days of deconstruction, Porter sees the systemic flaw as coincident with the systemic strength. Studying the structures of Emerson's thought, Porter terms conversion its central element (46). This emphasis on change was a powerful motive behind writing, yet also a potential barrier to the written. He comments, "The metamorphosis involved a world of elements. Basically it transformed ignorance to understanding, but its analogues were also the change from the inarticulate to the articulate and from confusing flux to intelligible fixity" (46). All too often, Porter argues, that "intelligible fixity" fell prey to itself. It did not, however, always fall. Porter's opening chapters bring the reader up short against his or her own limited expectations. We look for subjective life in a poem, expecting it to stand on its own, as no one's or no thought's representative. Emerson's understanding was markedly different. Porter maintains that Emerson systematically "sacrificed" the "particulars of any given poem" in the service of the "symmetrical, dramatic, and moral whole" that composed his aesthetic. Based on the image of seeing, of which the transparent eyeball is the central fact, this aesthetic was centered in process. If we see the process, we see the poetry. Porter makes clear that the process is no simple repetition. Emerson's own study of the imagination, his fear of losing imaginative power, his interest in the ongoing generation of poets and artists played a complex set of variations on what others have seen as a unidimensional theme.

The achievement of the 1980s can be figured in similar terms. Critics took the long-observed aspect of Emerson's interest in metamorphosis and his long-noted fascination with polarity and turned those observations into a method for reading Emerson. The focus was change, flux, permutation: the conclusions reflect the mercurial nature of the topic.

In Emerson's shape-shifting language, many critics found the incipient pragmatism of his work. Discussing Emerson's other problem of vocation, Glen M. Johnson turns to the aesthetic difficulty raised by the growing pressures of professionalism in American culture ("Emerson on 'Making' in Literature: His Problem of Professionalism, 1836–1841,"

1982). Not only did Emerson "need to discover a cultural role for him-self," but he simultaneously "need[ed] to develop a theory of creation consistent with the demands of writing for a vocation" (*Centenary*, 65). Johnson argues that Emerson's shift from a sole focus on "art by inspiration" to art deliberately made provided a theory not only consis-tent but eminently usable. The lecture and essay writer's work was liter-ally cut out for him. David Hill also puts the emphasis on a usable aes-thetic, showing in his discussion of "Experience" a persuasive linkage among its recalcitrant sections ("Emerson's Eumenides: Textual Evi-dence and the Interpretation of 'Experience,'" 1982). He writes, "The 'lords of life' in 'Experience' are neither logical steps toward a developed assertion nor a series of merely casually assembled pieces of fine writing. Instead they are steps toward a usable self, contributions toward the artfully constructed voice which closes the essay" (*Centenary*, 109).

While Barbara Packer's *Emerson's Fall* (1982) does not generally place itself in the growing interest in Emerson's pragmatic side, it does suggest just how closely connected were use and art. Reminding her readers of the project of reform that Emerson took upon himself, she calls attention to its many-sided nature. Emerson sought nothing less than to "reinvigorate" a dead (or at least) dying language. Behind this creeping death lay the stark issue of the individual's ability to experience something other than a rote repetition of conventional behaviors. To succeed where the available forms of literature were failing, Emerson generated a shifting pattern for his thought. Packer locates this pattern in his studies of "the fall": humanity was evidently not where it began. Tracing the path from the origin to the present became Emerson's ca-reer-long project, and tracing turned out to be no simple matter. To effect the essential reinvigoration, he also needed to articulate the apt form of expression for the varied experiences of falling away from origin. Although she ends Emerson's period of "greatest power and productivity" (xi) sooner than would many critics today (with *Representative Men*), she also provides a model by which that career could be extended. The fa-bles do not end with *Representative Men*: they are refigured for *English Traits*, for the antislavery writings, for *The Conduct of Life*.

Her shorthand for each of the four fables works well to evoke the whole she draws from them: "the interlocking fables of *contraction* and *dislocation*," the "law of *ossification*" with its application to society, "*reflection* or self-consciousness" and its attendant focus on the "vicis-situdes of the inner life" (x–xi). While her debt to Whicher is clear, so also is her movement beyond him. His version of acquiescence be-comes her exploration of Emerson's creative regenerations. Emerson, she maintains, was a writer restlessly interested in origins. Citing his experience in the Jardin des Plantes, she notes his own version of the naturalists' observation. In the naturalist's eye, the world was both utterly familiar (if not familial) and strangely alien. There was a curious blend of "kinship and estrangement." Packer frames Emerson's guiding problem: "We need a theory of origins that can explain both how nature came to resemble us and why it presently holds itself aloof from us — is permeated with human meaning, yet not subject to human will" (43). Examining Emerson's reading in the 1830s together with his growing fascination with sight, light and its embodiment within the eye, she turns to the mechanism by which both theory and explanation were possible. Fable provides the mediating force between "the contradictory demands of the Reason and the Understanding, between the truths of Eternity and the hard facts of Time" (59).

The uncertainty in the practical terms of the late 1830s drove Emerson into yet another version of the fall. Given the large economic crisis of 1837 and the ongoing "crisis" in American literature over its assumed nonexistence, Emerson turned increasingly to images of perpetual alternation between extremes. Paralleling Emerson's observations on the alternating states in human consciousness with the alternating cycle of prosperity and collapse, she writes, "The single thing that had previously restrained Emerson from preaching a full reliance on the inner life — its disturbing alternation between states of ecstasy and desolation . . . is shown to be at least no worse than the boom-and-bust cycles inherent in the structure of capitalism, and in one respect better: spiritual capital, unlike the tangible kind, returns eventually of its own accord" (97). Packer sees that spiritual capital realized in the new myth that emerges from the addresses and essays of this period. She notes Emerson's increasing attention to the social world. As a naturalist of society he faced a new problem: "the universal human preference for the familiar, the customary, the traditional" (132). For this problem, he developed a new myth and one with greater urgency. Packer terms it the fable of "ossification" and discusses "The Protest," "Circles," and "Self-Reliance" as Emerson's scheme for redemption from that particularly noxious fall into custom.

Packer's final focus turns to the best known and most direct statement of man's fall, the passage from "Experience" where the individual's self-conscious perception is termed "The Fall of Man." As Packer notes, such an equation was by no means original with Emerson; it readily refigured thoughts from Romanticism. Packer singles out a difference in Emerson's tone. "What is strikingly new about 'Experience,'" she writes, "is the voice that is heard in its opening paragraph, a voice neither powerful nor ruthless, but instead full of bewilderment, exhaustion, and despair" (151). Packer extends this discussion into Emerson's poetic theory. Unlike Porter, she finds form a problematic approach. From her view, Emerson undeniably developed an ecstatic theory of poetry, largely motivated by the mind's tendency to harden into particular patterns of thought. Bringing the fables into their fullest use, she identifies the self-consciousness associated with reflection as the primary cause of ossification. Hence Emerson's emphasis on abandonment, enthusiasm, whim.

Packer's work offers a significant revision of an earlier sticking point in Emerson criticism. The long debate over the role of inspiration and the power of imagination had been pursued with much energy but often ended in a kind of exhausted frustration. If the poetic theory were indeed a theory of inspiration based on the unpredictable powers of the imagination, then there was little to say about either Emerson's theory or practice. Packer's emphasis on the *use* of ecstasy and its fundamentally unpredictable nature offers a different approach. If poetry represented vision, it would never succeed in a blindered system. Rather than resolving ecstatic moments into a unified system, she freed the moment to become its own focus.

Something similar could be said of those working on the concept of metamorphosis. Leonard Neufeldt examined Emerson's often mentioned but rarely studied interest in science. As did Packer, Neufeldt ties this study to Emerson's reading of Newton. Through this reading, Emerson formulated his working metaphors. In this case, however, it is the Newton of the *Principia* rather than the *Opticks*. Neufeldt describes a law of permutation that governs Emerson's thought and applies this, not to Emerson's sentences but to his speakers. Neufeldt harks back to a suggestion Whicher made in the introduction to his *Selections from Ralph Waldo Emerson*. There, Whicher argued that the speakers in the essays were the wisest place to focus the study of Emersonian style. While Whicher's reason spoke to the New Critical concerns of his day (by focusing on the speakers, the essays displayed the dramatic quality that might let them in the back door of literature), Neufeldt turns to the number and variety of these speakers for their role in voicing the law of metamorphosis.

Neufeldt's interest in the speaker was clearly an interest with a long foreground — it can be seen in the discussion of Emerson's problem of vocation; it forms part of the discussion of Emersonian heroes — but it finds a new, primarily stylistic focus in the 1980s. Baumgartner, Buell and Packer earlier called attention to the "voiced style" of Emerson's prose, and Porter debated the viability of the poetic speaker in those terms. In the early 1980s David Hill and Richard Francis approached the fragmentary nature of "Experience" by focusing on the speakers within that essay. Gertrude Reif Hughes extended this into a type of "ventriloquism" in Emerson's writings (*Emerson's Demanding Optimism*, 1984). Julie Ellison (*Emerson's Romantic Style*, 1984) abstracted the speaker's persona into an "intellectual voice" whose tone is a composite of the author's prior reading.

Less concerned with process in itself, Ellison shifts attention away from the origin of poetry to the creation of criticism. Emerson's methods of composition, she argues, reflect his definition and redefinition of the critical enterprise. With Packer and Neufeldt, she urges critics to take Emerson's reading more seriously, and she offers one means to that end. By examining his theories of reading, critics finally discard the old unexamined assumptions about Emerson's eclecticism. Influence centers her study. In her context, the phrase "Quotation and Originality" means both the Emerson essay and the constitutive polarity of Emerson's work.

While the influence of Harold Bloom is clearly evident, and openly acknowledged by Ellison elsewhere, she takes Bloom a step further into the dynamics of Emersonian composition. An influence that begins as enabling ("He invokes the muses of the ancients to inspire him, and the great authors enter him in his acts of imitation") invariably provokes a crisis that shatters both the writing-reader and the works by which he is inspired. Ellison then notes the possible defensive reactions: "He can accept the plenitude of earlier works and turn them against each other." But when the individual becomes aware of his defensive moves, he suffers a disorienting loss of vision. Distinctions blur: self and other, reader and text, present and past are rendered meaningless. Any claim of identity is itself short-lived: the reader turned writer attempts his masterpiece, discovers that he has not written a "work of epic stature," and the process of emulation begins again (152–53).

Ellison reminds her readers that repetition is a precarious position for Emerson, and as the critical history shows, many readers cited repetition as one of Emerson's cardinal flaws. Ellison hopes to put a different spin on an old concept, linking it to the style itself. She turns to the shaping elements within Emerson's prose to explore the function of repetition. Noting Emerson's greater interest in the moments that comprise a cycle rather than in the cycle itself, she narrows this further to focus on the spaces between these moments. She writes, "This is the sublime and/or ironic turn celebrated by Emerson as 'transition' and 'metamorphosis.'" These very transitions are the embodiment of the power Emerson valued — not the power of "dominance itself" but the "ability always to break out of either a dominant or a subordinate stance" (153). To accomplish this outbreak within a world of repeated patterns, Emerson encouraged a subtle but effective sleight of mind. Repetition must be forgotten; transition becomes the means to that end.

Approaches as divergent as Ellison's and Sealts's or Porter's and Packer's occupied common ground in one key aspect: discussion of Emerson's style was impossible without the *Journals and Miscellaneous Notebooks and the Early Lectures.* A comparable claim would be made for the other neglected writings of Emerson: first the sermons, then the antislavery lectures. In each case the Emersons once dismissed by the criticism became increasingly important to the essential Emerson. In turn, these works would question such essentialism. If there was a real Emerson, his name was legion.

Emerson's sermons had long been one of the poorest among the many poor relations of Emerson studies. They were generally dismissed as work Emerson and his readers were all too happy to reject. The biographical element in the criticism clearly held sway, with the old nineteenth-century plot in full force. Emerson's resignation from Boston's Second Church was seen as a clear rejection of Unitarianism together with its written products. Whatever doubt may have lingered in Emerson's mind, so the argument went, it was fully dispelled by the Divinity School Address in 1838. The sermons were the one place a critic did not need to go. Few responded to Kenneth Walter Cameron's 1956 call for their considered study.

Nineteenth-century assessments were no help, for their praise struck the mid-twentieth century as further reason to reject Emerson's pulpit efforts. Although Elizabeth Palmer Peabody called for an edition of the sermons in 1884, no publication occurred (with the single exception of "The Lord's Supper," Emerson's resignation sermon) until McGiffert's collection in 1938. As we have seen, most critics then assumed we had had enough of the sermons: what they showed in terms of Emerson's developing ideas could be seen from within the confines of these twenty-five supposedly representative pieces. Interest did not entirely disappear, however. Any discussion of Emerson's problem of vocation invariably led back to "Find Your Calling," the sermon first mentioned by Smith. Buell's focus on the Unitarian stylistic antecedents of American Transcendentalism suggested how much more complex was the story than Emerson's assumed rejection of Unitarianism, and his discussion of some few of Emerson's sermons reinforced that conclusion.

Another decade would pass, however, before the sermons became their own topic of discussion. David Robinson's *Apostle of Culture* (1982) persuasively illustrated how fundamentally and creatively indebted Emerson was to his Unitarian background. In a careful dismantling of the various straw men of Unitarianism, Robinson demonstrated the powerful models Emerson found for both thought and expression. Unitarianism was a religion integrally bound to eloquence: the most forceful idea was also the most beautiful. It was also a religion whose eloquence was largely spent on the concept that Emerson would revise into self-reliance. Robinson locates the Emersonian principle in William Ellery Channing's idea of self-culture.

Robinson does not stop with the sermons but continues his discussion of Emerson well into his lecturing career. He calls attention to the thought-provoking connections both in subject and style. The transparency of the sermonic "Genuine Man" lays the groundwork for later, more famous embodiments of transparency. The structure of *Nature* is compared to the well-known, but now forgotten, devotional literature of the period. In all, Robinson argues for a greater continuity in Emerson's career than had yet been presented.

Robinson's work comes the closest to Bishop's vision of a study of the whole, not the parts. While *Apostle of Culture* frequently engages the element of flux in Emerson's early work, two of Robinson's essays from the early 1980s focus specifically on that element. In his 1980 essay "Emerson's Natural Theology and the Paris Naturalists: Toward a Theory of Animated Nature," Robinson examines Emerson's fascination with science, and the prospect it held for him as he rethought his relationship to the moral law. Both his experience at the Jardin des Plantes and his reading in science offered him "a dynamic concept of nature" (80) which he incorporated in his science lectures on "Natural History."

The theory of animated nature is again Robinson's focus in an article written for the centenary of Emerson's death. This time, however, the text is Emerson's 1841 lecture "The Method of Nature." Placing himself within the group of critics whose concern is metamorphosis, Robinson turns to one of its pivotal aspects. In the Emersonian system, change occurs by way of ecstasy. In the context of Nature's method, such a process has profound consequences. As Robinson notes, "Emerson's position here [that "nature" exists "to a universal and not to a particular end"] marks a significant departure from his earlier interpretations of nature, although it is a departure that had been in preparation for some time. By denying that nature can be thought of as a line, or as a movement from one fixed point to another, he denies a teleological interpretation of nature which places man at the center of its design" (84). Robinson shows how powerful a concept ecstasy would prove, not simply in decentering the individual but in Emerson's own poetic theory. The "redundancy or excess of life" that Emerson associated with ecstasy in nature in turn mirrored the human experience of a powerful influx from a divine source. It created art and it also freed the individual from the tyranny of the completed work of art.

Assessing the shifts in Emerson's emphasis, Robinson identifies "The Method of Nature" as a defining text. It demonstrates "the process by which Emerson came to place heavier and heavier stress on momentary illumination, as opposed to purposeful self-culture, as the means of affirming the value of the soul" (91). When Robinson turned again to that aspect within Emerson's work, he traced the dynamic throughout Emerson's career. In *Emerson and the Conduct of Life: Pragmatism and Ethical Purpose in the Later Work* (1993), Robinson illuminates the continuity across the varying essays. The unifying force emerges from Emerson's varied interpretation of "ecstatic moments." This is no matter of repetition, but a concerted effort toward pragmatism. In his increasing "ethical commitment," Emerson developed a practicable method for living the moments between illumination.

Robinson's work has been both catalyst for and representative of much of the scholarly work in the 1980s and 1990s. With Robinson, Wesley Mott focused attention on the sermons, examining their agreement with and departure from the Unitarian discourse of Emerson's young adulthood. Mary Cayton's *Emerson's Emergence* (1989) delineates the first twenty years of Emerson's career by highlighting its development during the waning days of Federalism in Unitarian Boston. She examines Emerson's development into the "first philosopher of the mass culture of American capitalism" (241) and also the "first to grapple seriously with some of [commercial capitalism's] essential contradictions" (240). Susan Roberson also took the "early" Emerson as her province and the sermons as her text. Where Mott focused on Emerson's revisionary versions of Jesus, Roberson looked closely at the effect of Ellen Tucker Emerson's death upon Emerson's self-definition within and through his sermons.

Robinson links the Emerson of the sermons with the "ethically committed" Emerson of the 1850s and 1860s. The periods share much in common, both in Emerson's own definition of his work and in the way that work has been viewed. The primary texts in each area were nearly invisible in the criticism. Both the sermons and the antislavery lectures did not see the light of full publication until recently. The sermons, under the general editorship of Albert von Frank, appeared between 1989 and 1992. The antislavery writings, edited by Len Gougeon and Joel Myerson, were published in 1995. In each case, the publication was preceded by significant books. Len Gougeon's *Virtue's Hero* (1991) did for the study of Emerson's antislavery activity what

Robinson's *Apostle of Culture* had done for the sermons. In many ways, Gougeon's work was even more daunting than Robinson's.

The received interpretation excused Emerson's earliest work by citing immaturity (i.e., the young man soon grew up and realized his poor fit with established religious thought), but later Emerson was branded for his position on social reform and social accountability. In this case, the entries in Emerson's journals were often of little help, showing as they did Emerson's conflicted thoughts on race. Gougeon's strength lies in his systematic attention to a different set of events in Emerson's life. He traces the long line of commitment to antislavery work in Emerson's family as well as among his close colleagues and friends. In his discussion of Emerson's own early antislavery activities, he shows the power of reception to shape future commentary. The conservative version of Emerson put forth in the 1880s by Oliver Wendell Holmes was virtually taken for truth, and thus Emerson's willingness to open his church to speakers sympathetic to the antislavery movement or his protest of the Cherokee removal became the dead facts biography failed to bring to life.

As with Robinson's work on the sermons, Gougeon is not the sole critic involved in the larger project of reevaluation. Linck Johnson's "Reforming the Reformers: Emerson, Thoreau, and the Sunday Lectures at Amory Hall, Boston" (1991) locates both Emerson's and Thoreau's early advocacy of individualism within the Amory Hall lecture series of 1844. Speaking to an audience that valued "association" as a plausible means to substantive reform, Emerson designed "New England Reformers" for a dual purpose: it both justified his position on the self's singular work and called his listeners to a different center of reform. "Abstract theories" would invariably prove futile; only the "lessons of nature and experience" and their own clear association with "change and metamorphosis" would serve as apt guides (258, 257). Johnson suggests that Emerson himself learned those lessons well. Ten years after "New England Reformers," Emerson "embraced the position of the reformers," singling out the importance of "cooperation" (280).

Johnson's attention to the authorizing forces of nature and experience speaks directly to the ongoing reevaluation of Emerson's political engagement. One of the many "new" Emersons at the end of the twentieth century, this rediscovered figure is the individual whose work in the 1850s virtually disappeared from the written record. Reclamation takes several forms. Among the most recent is a collection of essays on Emerson's career-long struggle to define an ethically defensible approach to social reform (*The Emerson Dilemma: Essays on Emerson and Social Reform*, T. Gregory Garvey, editor, forthcoming in 2001). The opening section addresses the psychological motivations behind Emerson's early reform activities (in a section entitled "Emerson's Other Inner Life" in response to and correction of Whicher's phrase). Subsequent sections trace the development of Emerson's attitudes toward and involvement within the debates over women's rights and abolition. The volume concludes with essays on Emerson's critique of "American civilization" through the 1862 essay of the same name and his ongoing legacy for political theorists of democracy. Editor Greg Garvey reminds his readers that a dual image ("Emerson the Transcendentalist and Emerson the reformer") still governs the criticism: "Emerson is portrayed as a philosopher of independence, spiritual autonomy, and psychological power, and he is represented as an ardent family man and a reformer zealous enough to help finance John Brown's guerrilla war in Kansas" (xxi). The essays in this collection negotiate that dualism by examining "how Emerson's reform activism emerges out of his transcendentalism" (xi).

Critics such as Thomas Gustafson (*Representative Words: Politics, Literature and the American Language*, 1992) and Eduardo Cadava (*Emerson and The Climates of History*, 1997) firmly ground Emerson's language of reform in his ongoing examination of nature. Closely related are the eye-opening contextualizations which carefully reconstruct the web of related events in which Emerson's words appeared. Johnson's work on the Amory Hall lectures is an obvious example as is Barbara Ryan's examination of Emerson's attempted domestic and social experiments and their effect on Emerson's increasingly involved opposition to slavery ("Emerson's 'Domestic and Social Experiments': Service, Slavery and the Unhired Man," 1994). As Ryan notes, by 1839 Emerson acknowledged the unnerving connection between domestic service and Southern slavery. Only after seeing the impossibility of reforming the relations between employer and wage servant did Emerson speak out directly against slavery. With different focus but similar intent, Sallee Engstrom explores the effect of Emerson's New York state lectures of the 1850s on his increasingly powerful voice against slavery (*The Infinitude of the Private Man: Emerson's Presence in Western New York, 1851–1861*, 1997).

Foremost among the contextual approach is Albert von Frank's *The Trials of Anthony Burns: Freedom and Slavery in Emerson's Boston* (1998). Here is the strongest presentation of Emerson's power within the antislavery movement. In a tour de force re-creation of the year 1854, von Frank gives palpable presence to the Boston past. This is not any Boston, but one that von Frank calls "Emerson's." Illuminating the effect of Emerson's rhetorical strategies, von Frank examines Emerson's various addresses *and* illustrates how profoundly influential they were on the individuals most actively involved in the antislavery movement. The old charges against Emerson's idealism fail when read against the actions of Thomas Wentworth Higginson, Bronson Alcott, Theodore Parker, Moncure Conway, and Henry David Thoreau. Von Frank comments, "Emerson was a force in antislavery because of his idealism, not in spite of it" (327). Noting the eminently practical nature of this idealism, he identifies the governing differences in antislavery strategy as divided by gender. Emerson's appeal to abstract principle "admittedly . . . looks cold. To a great extent, this view of things appealed to male heroism but failed to move women. . . . Yet as a practical matter, it was not the women who needed convincing. If something were to be done about slavery, it was men's minds, not women's hearts, that had to be renovated, because power lay with the former" (333).

In connection with "practical power," another multi-faceted group of critics approached Emerson's political engagement from a largely theoretical point of view. Giving less attention to the actual events of Emerson's reform activities, they concentrate on the revealing play of language within and between Emerson's essays. That this "play" prompts (or can or should) serious work is their contention. Whether the focus is on indeterminacy as in Richard Poirier's work or on process as in Stanley Cavell's or democratic individuality as in George Kateb's, Emerson emerges as an incisive voice, anatomizing the problems within society and offering a means toward their amendment. That process is the province of the next chapter.

Works Cited

Baumgartner, A. M. "'The Lyceum is My Pulpit': Homiletics in Emerson's Early Lectures." *American Literature* 34 (1963): 477–86.

Bishop, Jonathan. *Emerson on the Soul.* Cambridge, MA: Harvard University Press, 1964.

Buell, Lawrence. *Literary Transcendentalism: Style and Vision in the American Renaissance.* Ithaca: Cornell University Press, 1973.

———. "Reading Emerson for the Structures: The Coherence of the Essays." *Quarterly Journal of Speech* 58 (1972): 58–69.

Cadava, Eduardo. *Emerson and the Climates of History.* Stanford: Stanford University Press, 1997.

Cayton, Mary Kupiec. *Emerson's Emergence: Self and Society in the Transformation of New England, 1800–1845.* Chapel Hill: University of North Carolina Press, 1989.

Ellison, Julie. *Emerson's Romantic Style*. Princeton: Princeton University Press, 1984.

Engstrom, Sallee Fox. *The Infinitude of the Private Man: Emerson's Presence in Western New York, 1851–1861*. New York: Peter Lang, 1997.

Garvey, T. Gregory, editor. *The Emerson Dilemma: Essays on Emerson and Social Reform*. Athens: University of Georgia Press, 2001.

Giamatti, A. Bartlett. "Power, Politics and a Sense of History." Yale Baccalaureate Address, 1981 printed in *The University and the Public Interest*. New York: Atheneum, 1981: 166–79.

Gougeon, Len. *Virtue's Hero: Emerson, Antislavery and Reform*. Athens: University of Georgia Press, 1990.

Gustafson, Thomas. *Representative Words: Politics, Literature and the American Language, 1775–1865*. New York: Cambridge University Press, 1992.

Hill, David. "Emerson's Eumenides: Textual Evidence and the Interpretation of 'Experience'" in *Emerson Centenary Essays*. Joel Myerson, editor. Carbondale: Southern Illinois University Press, 1982: 107–21.

Hodder, Alan D. *Emerson's Rhetoric of Revelation*. University Park: The Pennsylvania State University Press, 1989.

Hughes, Gertrude Reif. *Emerson's Demanding Optimism*. Baton Rouge: Louisiana State University Press, 1984.

Johnson, Glen M. "Emerson on 'Making' in Literature: His Problem of Professionalism, 1836–1841" in *Emerson Centenary Essays*. Joel Myerson, editor. Carbondale: Southern Illinois University Press, 1982: 65–73.

Johnson, Linck C. "Reforming the Reformers: Emerson, Thoreau and the Sunday Lectures at Amory Hall, Boston." *ESQ: A Journal of the American Renaissance* 37 (1991): 235–89.

LaRosa, Ralph C. "Emerson's Search for Literary Form: The Early Journals." *Modern Prose* 69 (1971): 25–35.

Levin, David, editor. *Emerson: Prophecy, Metamorphosis, and Influence*. New York: Columbia University Press, 1975.

Lowell, James Russell. "Emerson the Lecturer." 1868. Reprinted in *My Study Windows*. Boston: J. R. Osgood, 1871: 375–84.

Marr, David. *American Worlds Since Emerson*. Amherst: University of Massachusetts Press, 1988.

Mott, Wesley T. *"The Strains of Eloquence": Emerson and His Sermons*. University Park: Pennsylvania State University Press, 1989.

Neufeldt, Leonard. *The House of Emerson*. Lincoln: University of Nebraska Press, 1982.

———. "The Science of Power: Emerson's Views on Science and Technology." *Journal of the History of Ideas* 38 (1977): 329–44.

Newfield, Christopher. *The Emerson Effect: Individualism and Submission in America.* Chicago: University of Chicago Press, 1996.

O'Keefe, Richard. *Mythic Archetypes in Ralph Waldo Emerson: A Blakean Reading.* Kent, Ohio: Kent State University Press, 1995.

Packer, B. L. *Emerson's Fall: A New Interpretation of the Major Essays.* New York: Continuum Publishing Company, 1982.

Porter, David. *Emerson and Literary Change.* Cambridge, MA: Harvard University Press, 1978.

Roberson, Susan R. *Emerson in His Sermons: A Man-Made Self.* Columbia: University of Missouri Press, 1995.

Robinson, David. *Apostle of Culture: Emerson as Preacher and Lecturer.* Philadelphia: University of Pennsylvania Press, 1982.

———. *Emerson and the Conduct of Life: Pragmatism and Ethical Purpose in the Later Work.* New York: Cambridge University Press, 1993.

———. "'The Method of Nature' and Emerson's Period of Crisis" in *Emerson Centenary Essays.* Joel Myerson, editor. Carbondale: Southern Illinois University Press, 1982: 74–92.

Rosenwald, Lawrence. *Emerson and the Art of the Diary.* Oxford: Oxford University Press, 1988.

Ryan, Barbara. "Emerson's 'Domestic and Social Experiments': Service, Slavery and the Unhired Man." *American Literature* 66 (1994): 485–508.

Sealts, Merton M. Jr. "Emerson on the Scholar, 1833–37." *PMLA* 85 (1970): 185–95.

Spiller, Robert. "From Lecture to Essay: Emerson's Method of Composition." *The Literary Criterion* 5: 3 (1962): 28–38.

Strauch, Carl. "Emerson and the Doctrine of Sympathy." *Studies in Romanticism* 6 (1967): 152–74.

Von Frank, Albert. *The Trials of Anthony Burns: Freedom and Slavery in Emerson's Boston.* Cambridge, MA: Harvard University Press, 1998.

Waggoner, Hyatt. *American Poets from the Puritans to the Present.* Boston: Houghton Mifflin, 1968.

———. *Emerson as Poet.* Princeton: Princeton University Press, 1974.

Yoder, Ralph A. *Emerson and The Orphic Poet in America.* Berkeley: University of California Press, 1978.

———. "Emerson's Dialectic." *Criticism* 11 (1969): 313–28.

7: The Philosophers' Stone: Emerson Between Centuries

WITH THE BICENTENARY in clear sight, a number of new Emersons replaced the old image of reconciler and idealist. Jonathan Bishop's question from the 1960s — "What would it take to create a new Emerson, who could throw affirmative light upon the old" (219) — received (seemingly) definitive answers and in precisely the way Bishop envisioned. Critics developed a number of "convincing idioms," and the emergent Emerson was defined by a group of affiliations earlier readers all but rejected. The common parlance of the critical vocabulary reminded the readers that as new as any particular Emerson apparently was, it was by no means, novel. Reclamation, redemption, resurrection: the language of the times bespoke a kind of Emersonian originality. Here were thoughts, differently assembled, yielding insight where a blind, or blindered, dismissal once operated. At the turn of the twenty-first century, Emerson was scientist, philosopher, pragmatist, ethicist and above all, a writer whose prose emerged from relationship.

Approaches balanced between the contextual and the philosophical. The theory wars seemed a province of the past, and the new territory suggested that old enemies could become Emersonian friends. A common element united once disparate approaches. No matter what the theoretical persuasion, there was agreement about Emerson's full involvement in the multi-faceted dimensions of the physical world. Whether that world was inflected as power, physical forces or domestic exchange, the ordinary material of everyday life was at the center of Emerson's written representations. Where philosophical and literary study had once been keenly separate, the 1990s saw their possible union. Stanley Cavell predicted their merger in a process approaching transfiguration. Not surprisingly, Emerson stood to profit by that venture and, as the language suggests, such claims were rightly unsettling. Had the criticism succeeded in incorporating experimentation into Emerson's ethical commitment. Could a late-twentieth-century consciousness put those terms together?

While biographical study often works mercilessly against the interpretation of Emerson's writing, one area not only promised a different result but actually succeeded in transforming Emerson biography itself. As Robert Richardson noted, he could not write the intellectual biography he originally imagined because Emerson's ideas were so deeply entwined within his relationships. Through their contextual studies of Emerson in the midst of these varied relationships, late-twentieth-century scholars made eminently clear that ethics and experimentation were essentially linked within Emerson's work. This was arguably the newest Emerson of all, for the old image of self-isolated thinker lingers even in the most contemporary studies of written influence. The lived relationships, however, and their rich textual density tell a different story.

Perhaps the widest vein in Emerson criticism since the mid-1980s, this area promises a foreseeable future of continued interest and excellence. While such studies range broadly in focus, they hold in common a similar approach. The emphasis is contextual: what were the circumstances in which Emerson wrote his particular words? Sharing with new historicism the interest in our access to the past, it places greater emphasis upon the writings themselves. Whether Wes Mott's study of the sermons (*The Strains of Eloquence*, 1989), Phyllis Cole's of the Emerson household ("'Men and Women Conversing': The Emersons in 1837," 1997), or David Robinson's of Thoreau's response to one of Emerson's questions ("Thoreau's 'Ktaadn' and the Quest for Experience," 1997), the emphasis is direct verbal exchange. This is intertextuality in its most practical and powerful dimension: the critics study the ongoing debates that brought Emerson into close conversation with those around him. Emerging from these studies is a far richer understanding of the world of which Emerson was a part and, as Robert Richardson's 1995 biography illustrated, a far less isolated Emerson.

Work on Mary Moody Emerson is a clear example. In her essay "The Advantage of Loneliness: Mary Moody Emerson's Almanacks, 1802–55" (1982), Phyllis Cole provided one of the first substantial considerations of Mary Moody Emerson's influence. She there argued that importance through her writings. The *Almanacks* articulated "an idealization of the solitary self [that] was radical for both its gender and its time: indeed a significant anticipation of the self-reliance that Mary's nephew Waldo Emerson would articulate as the primarily masculine romantic vision of the next generation" (3). As David Robinson's work also made clear, critics in the early 1980s were ready to revisit questions of origin. Whether the self-culture of Unitarianism or the solitary self formulated by a single, familially powerful individual, Emerson's ideas were reexamined for their responsive connections with others.

The Mary Moody Emerson connection slowly moved from the margin to the center. Part of the post-sixties interest in psychobiography and Erik Erikson's delineation of young adult development,

Evelyn Barish saw Mary Moody Emerson as the single most important influence for the young Emerson. Intersecting as well with the Bloomian model of anxiety, Barish's *Emerson: The Roots of Prophecy* (1989) takes its point of departure from Emerson's "unmourned" father, but with Cole, she underscores the centrality of Mary Moody Emerson. From her, and not from his male forebears, Emerson learned "to interrogate the Arminian self-assurance and complacency that dominated upper-class Unitarian thought" (38). Barish locates Mary Moody Emerson's influence in the particular tone of her expression: "she was a naysayer, a would-be prophet, and an uncompromising intellectual — the first of these types he encountered. To know him, one must know her" (38).

It took decades for that assertion, now become nearly a commonplace in the criticism, to become credible, let alone persuasive. Notwithstanding Emerson's acknowledgement of her importance, the criticism rarely found more than a sensational place for Emerson's aunt. She was the eccentric, the New England old maid whose mercurial personality formed a set piece within the various early biographies. Rarely was she seen as an influence on Emerson's intellectual development. If given any serious attention at all, Mary Moody Emerson was generally characterized as the voice of Calvinism which Emerson would confront and (depending upon the critic) more or less successfully reject. Her role was deemed minor, though necessary. It emerged as a product of the early century's embattlement over America's Puritanical element.

What remains to be studied is the distinct interpretive tradition fostered by women in the late nineteenth and early twentieth centuries. Dismissed by the critical tradition as merely appreciative writing, these works have gone largely unnoticed. They nonetheless give a canny interpretation of Emerson's role as an underwriter of reform, but their voices were silenced in the general misogyny of the era. This is hardly surprising given the number of offhand remarks made against women in the early twentieth century. When Emerson was seen as a kind of quack medicine for "fat women" (Mencken's words) or a commodity for schoolgirl consumption, there was little chance that women writing about him would fare differently.

The textual revolutions inaugurated by *The Journals and Miscellaneous Notebooks* and *The Early Lectures*, however, laid the groundwork for the consideration of other texts within Emerson studies, and the work within feminist criticism reinforced the importance of such work. In keeping with the recovery and reprinting of texts by women writers, many of the influential figures within the Emerson circle could finally be read. Although feminist criticism itself has not yet exerted the direct influence on Emerson studies predicted for it back in 1984 by Lawrence

Buell, it nonetheless fostered the growing interest in the women writers of the Transcendentalist movement and their counterparts within Unitarian Boston. The last twenty years of the century saw the completion of several editions: the complete letters of Margaret Fuller, letters and journals of Louisa May Alcott, letters of Elizabeth Palmer Peabody, Caroline Sturgis Tappan, Caroline Healey Dall, Elizabeth Hoar, sermon notes of Anna Tilden Gannett, as well as the Mary Moody Emerson letters.

With the publication of Mary Moody Emerson's *Selected Letters* (1993, Nancy Simmons, editor), readers first gained access to a major portion (the *Almanacks* remain unpublished) of the writings that proved so important to Emerson's intellectual development. As Simmons notes in her introduction, "Here we find a woman negotiating her freedom beyond marriage, practicing a vocation that is closest to theology, and transforming the minor genre of letter writing into a major vehicle for free discussion" (xxix). The audience for that discussion was often Waldo Emerson, and the correspondence with his aunt profoundly affected his intellectual development. "Stimulated by this dialogue, Mary Emerson raised the epistolary conversation to an art form, drawing out the best in her companion, provoking him to self-expression and then taking back the theme and weaving it into her own vision of divine order. This process — a mutual stimulation and fertilization of ideas — was one that both Mary and Waldo recognized and enjoyed. On it they built their relationship" (127–28). Phyllis Cole's 1998 biography *Mary Moody Emerson and the Origins of Transcendentalism* makes the power of that relationship patently clear. From Aunt Mary, Emerson learned both subject and style. The two were virtually inseparable because Aunt Mary's interest in prophecy required a visionary stance and produced a corresponding voice.

The extent of Emerson's texts — and their responsive nature — has made readers increasingly aware of the complex issue of influence. The word cuts both ways: critics variously study Emerson as influenced *by* or influence *upon*. This emphasis is by no means new. It appeared for years in the number of works defined by the "and" in their subject: Emerson and Thoreau, Emerson and Whitman, Emerson and Dickinson. As the simple conjunction suggests, a static balance structured this work; the received understanding of one or the other figure was the dominant force. The old genre of source study underwent a vital transformation in the late twentieth century, offering readers a more richly-textured understanding of how a writer uses his or her reading.

Fueled in part by the Bloomian model, but also drawing upon reader-response as well as reception theory, these late-century influence studies present themselves as "empirical" — firmly grounded in the cultural context and firmly centered in the close reading of texts within that context. Notable among these is Gustaaf Van Cromphout's *Emerson's Modernity and the Example of Goethe* (1990). It is surprisingly, the first book-length study of Goethe's influence on Emerson. Robin Grey explores the Miltonic influence on Emerson's style and self-styling in *The Complicity of Imagination: The American Renaissance, Contests of Authority and Seventeenth-Century English Culture* (1997). Lee Rust Brown's *The Emerson Museum* (1997) reexamines Coleridge's influence as part of a larger project of defining an "American" Romanticism. Recent work suggests that the two approaches once deemed mutually exclusive may in fact work together within the same text. Brown's book, for example, firmly places itself in the language of theory and involves careful evocation of the actual encounters of Emerson in the Jardin des Plantes.

Nowhere is this slow merging of two fields more prominent than in the gradual closure of the century long gap between philosophical and literary studies. Critics — whether in departments of philosophy or English — who study Emerson's relation to American pragmatism face the complex questions of influence as well as the longstanding assumptions that Emerson was no philosopher and that pragmatism was no philosophy. As Russell Goodman noted in 1987, "Emerson's position in American literature is secure, but his position in American philosophy is not. His thought plays a minor role in many histories and surveys of American philosophy, perhaps because it has no obvious connection with the major American movement of pragmatism" ("Freedom in the Philosophy of Ralph Waldo Emerson," 5). Two years later, Cornel West illustrated how difficult that double reclamation would be.

In *The American Evasion of Philosophy: A Genealogy of Pragmatism* (1989), West views Emerson as the powerful shaping force of the evasion he identifies with American pragmatism. The evasion is seen most clearly in Emerson's refusal of two types of authority: authority claimed by developing a "professional, i.e., scientific respectability" and authority grounded in a careful "search for foundations" (36). Instead, Emerson's "interpretation of power, provocations and personality" (35) established both the double-face of American pragmatism ("rhetorically supporting American expansionism yet morally contesting its consequences," 39) and the way in which constituencies are created. Faulting this way as politically impotent (35–41), West suggests one of American pragmatism's limitations. Divided within itself, its practice yielded little in social change.

For Sacvan Bercovitch in his 1990 "Emerson, Individualism and the Ambiguities of Dissent," division is central to Emerson's thought. He locates that division within the difference between the ideologies of American laissez-faire individualism and European anti-bourgeois individuality, a distinction that continues to bear fruit in discussions of Emerson's individualism. Bercovitch argues that Emerson provided a potent voice of dissent, successfully (for Bercovitch only through *Essays, First Series*) navigating the tension between the two vastly different approaches to the individual. He writes, "The appeal of Emersonian dissent lies in an extraordinary conjunction of forces: its capacity to absorb the radical communitarian visions it renounces, and its capacity to be nourished by the liberal structures it resists. It demonstrates the capacities of culture to shape the subversive in its own image, and *thereby*, within limits, to be shaped in turn by the radicalism it seeks to contain" (Buell, 1993, 126). While Bercovitch highlights resistance, he also sees an inevitable collapse back into the term that is consistently more powerful within the United States. "Emersonian individualism comes down to us as a distinctive type of radical thought," but it remains dependent upon the "systemic individualism" it opposes (125).

Accompanying this study of experience and its theorizers are the studies of Emerson's engagement with various philosophical traditions. Here again, major revision marks the work. Beginning with Stanley Cavell's "Thinking of Emerson" (1979), "Being Odd, Getting Even (1985) and *In Quest of the Ordinary: Lines of Skepticism and Romanticism* (1988), it became increasingly clear that Emerson's engagement with philosophical questions was much more informed than it was assumed to be. Russell Goodman squarely placed Emerson within the development of American philosophy through his study of Emerson's importance for both John Dewey and William James (*American Philosophy and the Romantic Tradition*, 1990). Working from within the disciplines of literary study, David Van Leer argued that the "private vocabulary" of Emerson's essays could be translated into "the more public one of traditional philosophy" (*Emerson's Epistemology: The Argument of the Essays*, 1986: xii). Where Van Leer emphasizes epistemology, he carefully frames its relation to expression: "epistemology is best seen as not a philosophical discipline but a literary genre. Like the lyric or the epic, epistemology tends to deal with certain questions (about the logical structure of the mind) while avoiding other topics (like history or society)" (17). Emerson's "unsystematic style" reflects his "critical attitude toward epistemology" (17). Having discussed *Nature*, lectures from the 1830s and "Self-Reliance," Van Leer comments, "once again, Emerson builds his argument not to an absolute statement about the nature of reality but to a careful distinction between frames of reference" (141). For Van Leer, Emerson faced his greatest challenge in skepticism; it "effectively calls a halt to any epistemological enterprise" (184). John Michael takes that vexed dynamic as his focus on skepticism and its vital life within Emerson's early work (*Emerson and Skepticism: The Cipher of the World*, 1988). David Jacobson's *Emerson's Pragmatic Vision* (1993), David Robinson's *Emerson and the Conduct of Life* (1993), Eduardo Cadava's *The Climates of History* (1997), and Gustaaf Van Cromphout's *Emerson's Ethics* (1999) extend this study of Emerson's philosophical positions, offering a much more complicated system within Emerson's thought. Allied with the comparable work in Emerson's literary experimentation, these studies create an Emerson that both fields find eminently useful. Jacobson argues that philosophical interpretation of the writings is necessary if we are to understand the real development of Emerson's thought (2). He cites "The Method of Nature" as the defining moment of development and links that definition to Emerson's well-crafted practice of life in which the everyday became the philosophical. Van Cromphout offers a decidedly different and more tightly built structure within which to understand Emerson's engagement with the ordinary. Suggesting that neither Whicher nor Porte should have the last word on Emerson's moral thought ("obvious and uninteresting, in his moral thought," 2), he provides a study of a remarkably understudied area. While many have written about Emerson as a moralist, "no book has examined his ethics as such" (2). Van Cromphout defines that as his project.

David Robinson's *Emerson and the Conduct of Life* examines a particular dynamic within Emerson's ethics. Taking Giles Gunn's definition of pragmatism as his starting point ("a method for performing work in a world without absolutes," 3), Robinson rereads the essays from the 1830s to the 1860s to show Emerson's extension of "ecstatic" moments into "ethical" ones. Focusing on the "structured encounters with skepticism," Robinson illustrates their deep engagement with a world of reform and relation. As the frequency of ecstatic moments lessened, Emerson made "self-culture into a doctrine of social criticism and political dissent" (41). Encouraging readers to expand their canon of Emerson essays, he calls attention to "Compensation" and "Friendship." Both place their readers fully in a world of relations.

Robinson firmly grounds his discussion in the ongoing criticism of Emerson's supposed position on social reform. His arguments respond to Sacvan Bercovitch's 1990 assertions that Emerson's writing after the mid-1840s loses the productive ambiguity of the earlier work. He uses Whicher's familiar frame of a two-part career defined by "acquiescence" to argue a different interpretation: "Whicher's explanation has obscured a full sense of Emerson's enormous creative achievement in the late 1840s and 1850s. The break "Experience" signals is better understood as the movement toward an ethical pragmatism, a growing insistence that the ideal must be experienced in and through the world of fact, time, and social relations" (71).

As do Jacobson and Robinson, Eduardo Cadava turns to "The Method of Nature" in *Emerson and the Climates of History*. The essay provides the critics with the most succinct statement of Emerson's life-long project: the transfer of Nature into writing. Cadava focuses on language itself. He chooses his texts precisely: a sentence from the journals, the opening paragraph of *Nature*, two Civil War poems ("Boston Hymn" and "Voluntaries"). Cadava uses each passage to examine the transformative power of language. When the vocabularies of history, politics and nature are joined, what kind of discourse results? His Emerson, like Jacobson's, Robinson's, Michael's and Goodman's, is deeply committed to the "praxis of thought" (201) in a clearly defined world of relations.

That world provides the possible meeting ground for once markedly different approaches, as Cadava's and Robinson's books suggest. Cadava's work parallels the contextual work of Cole, von Frank and Robinson. Both approaches privilege the everyday, but with a decidedly different emphasis. The texture of allusive texts informs the one; the texture of lived experience, the other. It remains for the twenty-first century to weave together these complementary explorations of the "ordinary." Whether the focus is on Emerson the ethicist, the perfectionist, the antislavery lecturer, or the political observer, the old horror of Emersonian individualism has been transformed into the (re)new(ed) blessing of a philosophically respectable engagement in political life and thought. Contextual and theoretical approaches bring the reader to the same central questions: how did Emerson shape his concept of power? How did his engagement in the physical circumstances of his daily life inform that concept? What matter lies behind and moves within the writings and their insistent attention to the moment?

One answer appears in recent studies on Emerson and science. Once considered a superficial interest, Emerson's fascination with the scientific developments of his day has now been heralded for its substantive engagement. As Eric Wilson comments in a review essay of books published in the 1990s, "These new scientific texts are crucial for viewing Emerson as a Nietzschean, pragmatic, worldly thinker, for each presents him as fully engaged in understanding and utilizing physical power — biological life, electromagnetic energy, astronomical and geological forces. They illustrate that Emerson's *gai science* was indeed a science of nature (*physis*, *bios*) and not merely a leap to spirit" ("From Metaphysical Poverty to Practical Power," 314). Wilson's essay is part of a collection on Emerson and Nietzsche, a connection, Wilson argues, that can best be understood by examining Emerson's ongoing study of power as it is displayed in the physical world.

Until the 1990s, Emerson's interest in science received only intermittent attention over the many years of the critical history. The late nineteenth and early twentieth centuries often read Emerson within the context of evolution. Later critics increasingly distanced themselves from that position, seeing in it a misreading of the Darwinian concept. Joseph Warren Beach gives the most considered version of this disassembling of a nineteenth-century connection. In "Emerson and Evolution" (1934), he argues for a careful reconsideration of Emerson's reading and its reemergence in his writing. He traces the course of Emerson's scientific readings to show how and when Emerson passed beyond a belief in the non-evolutionary graduated scale of being. He as firmly shows where Emerson's conceptual development ended: "he never rightly understood the implications of evolution" (495). Ending his essay by referring to Emerson's "ethical system," he terms it "provincial" (496). Dependent upon idealism, it "read ethical meanings into nature . . . [but] never stopped to inquire where man got these ethical concepts" (496). From Beach's perspective, Emerson stopped short. Hindered by idealism, he and his fellow Transcendentalists failed to "develop the possibilities of naturalism" (497).

A more consistent strand within the critical history was provided by Harry Hayden Clark's essay "Emerson and Science" (1931) in which he argued the importance of Emerson's interest in astronomy. That interest would remain a thread within the criticism for the next several decades. McGiffert included Emerson's sermon on astronomy in the 1938 collection. In 1975, Gay Wilson Allen asked his readers to take "A New Look at Emerson and Science" (the title of his essay for a volume honoring the contribution of Harry Hayden Clark). Allen argued that Clark's work had not been fully assimilated into Emerson criticism and reminded his readers that the most influential reading for Emerson during the 1830s was his extensive reading in contemporary science. He shows the extent of that interest, expanding the field from astronomy to include geology and chemistry and maintains that Emerson's central ideas were grounded most firmly in science. He comments, "the two most basic concepts in his philosophy, . . . were 'compensation' and 'polarity,' both derived from scientific 'laws.'" He then identifies science as the source of one of Emerson's most powerful metaphors:

"'circularity' . . . translated into poetic metaphors the principle of 'conservation of energy'" (75). That translation of science into poetry appears in Porter's study as well as Packer's and Neufeldt's careful examination of Emerson's reading of Newton. While maintaining that Goethe and Coleridge were more powerful influences, David Robinson nonetheless called for a closer study of "Emerson's involvement with science in this period" ("Emerson's Natural Theology and the Paris Naturalists: Toward a Theory of Animated Nature," 1980: 70). He remarks, "there is still much to be said about the contribution of pure science to the pattern of his development" (70). Robinson's focus on the Natural History lectures places the scientist (rendered as naturalist) as one more of Emerson's heroic figures and locates this heroism in the naturalist's clear sight of nature's "dynamism" (80).

Lee Rust Brown (*The Emerson Museum*, 1997), Laura Dassow Walls ("The Anatomy of Truth: Emerson's Poetic Science," 1997) and Eric Wilson (*Emerson's Sublime Science*, 1999) accept Robinson's challenge and argue the importance of another seemingly new Emerson: the romantic scientist. As Wilson notes, the failure to consider seriously Emerson's involvement in the sciences of his day profoundly limits the understanding of his work. *Nature* looks very different when read through the lens of the revolutionary developments in early-nineteenth-century science. No "song of innocence" to the later "Experience," it is designed to "cause uncertainty and insecurity" (16). Wilson's focus is electromagnetism with its argument that "the world is a vast field of force, matter emerging in condensations of electrical energy" (45). One of the new sciences of the day, electromagnetism provided Emerson with a powerful model for his own writing, a model that the church failed to give. From Emerson's perspective, the new science was "sublime" because it developed vigorously plausible connections between matter and spirit, poetry and science, the mental and the physical. It also underwrote a particular aesthetic, creating a "sublime" manner of expression. Part and parcel of these examinations of Emerson's science is a clear emphasis on Emerson's style. Wilson associates this style with Emerson's translation of electromagnetic complexity into a "charged" language where tropes productively "shock" their readers. Taking three figures in the first three chapters of *Nature* (the transparent eyeball is central among them), Wilson argues that Emerson's "building of discourse" is less architectural than electrical.

For Brown, the governing concept is transparency; the motivating scientific force is the French naturalists. Observing their classification system in the Jardin des Plantes, Emerson saw its wide-ranging implications for expression. Brown returns to the moment in Emerson's life that both Matthiessen and Whicher brought forward as pivotal. Brown comments, "The real subject of the Museum was not raw nature but rather was the specimen form of the classification, a form at once practical and ideal, and most clearly communicated through transparent media of display. Classification, as it appeared in the Museum, was a technical form that converted everything, not only biological individuals but also the displays representing them, into new instances of itself" (119). This conversion applied equally to the matter of verbal composition. "Emerson beheld the figure of transparency nested within the compositional paradigm at the Jardin des Plantes. Reviewing the fragmentary corpus of his journals, he saw that transparency could be nested there as well." Drawing upon Alfred Fergusson's comments as editor of JMN IV, Brown remarks that Emerson's journals change from that moment of observation. "The journals before this time had been more fully devoted to extended meditations on specific issues; but after October 1833 the journals show a decided turn to the aphorism, a less limited range of subjects, a far greater willingness to experiment with radical statements and thoughts that could not be completed. Emerson could abandon the demands of closure in particular entries because he felt the whole enterprise to be fully methodical" (119–20).

Like Brown, Laura Dassow Walls sees natural history as the grounding force of her argument. In "The Anatomy of Truth: Emerson's Poetic Science" (1997), she profiles Emerson's fascination with various scientists, and in particular with John Herschel and Georges Cuvier. Herschel's reconfiguration of natural law and Cuvier's search for a unifying principle appealed to Emerson in his search for a convincing formulation of dynamic equilibrium. Reminding readers that Emerson "drew not just his vocabulary but his organizing ideas from science" (429), Walls revisits and virtually rewrites our understanding of organicism. Exploring its meaning for modernism as well as its place in Emerson's thought, she clearly distinguishes her interpretation of organic unity from her predecessors. Suggesting a different definition, she stresses its connection with a phenomenon she terms "gnomicism." Its features are central to Emerson's unifying law of relation. Under the rubric of gnomicism fall epigrammatic sayings "compact to the point of self-evidence" and figures both "gnomonic" and "nomian," identified by their self-replicating extension (the circle added around the circle) and essentially "giv[ing] the law or 'nomos' to themselves" (434–35). Emerson's was a "gnomic science" readily apparent in its stylistic equivalent and fundamentally grounded in his unwavering understanding of law as necessary and causal. She reminds her readers that this position was the still largely unaccepted newcomer to the science of the 1830s. The established view held that law was simply a matter of empirical observation.

Disputing that empiricism, Emerson turned to the gnomonic elements he found constitutive and thus representative of existence. Walls argues that the self-similarity in the gnomonic figure provided Emerson with precisely the evidence he needed. She comments, "Here is just what Emerson said he most wanted of science: that it give not mere details but declare 'the relation between things and thoughts'" (439). Here as well was the paradigm-breaking moment in which Emerson participated so powerfully. Walls writes, "Emerson draws science and literature into one united enterprise through the notion of 'action' in the world, action that has the power to dissolve and reshape the world not just conceptually but actually, according to human will. Emerson is theorizing man as a force of nature because he is one of the first intellectuals of his age to comprehend that man is indeed altering, even remaking, nature itself" (429).

Walls' depiction — "theorizing man as a force" — speaks directly to another growing area within Emerson studies. The combined force of "power" and "influence" is brought to bear in a singular connection that has long been noted but more often than not carefully dismantled or summarily dismissed. Nietzsche is the central figure. At a (relatively) safe distance from the charges of Nazism that Carpenter confronted in the 1950s, Nietzsche's writings ground much of the recent work in critical theory. His use of fragments, his close attention to the constructedness of meaning, his distrust of language and his relentless anatomy of power make him a thought-provoking figure as late-twentieth-century critics examine the power plays that shaped their world.

As impossible as it would have seemed from the perspective of Carpenter and his contemporaries, Nietzsche has been a powerful force in the "recuperation" of Emerson both for philosophic and literary study. No figure has been more influential in this recuperation than Stanley Cavell. As he notes, his interest in Emerson originated from his interest in Nietzsche. Once he began pursuing the connection, he found one of the major projects of his career. That interest, in turn, opened the way for a thoroughgoing consideration of the complex relation through which Emerson and Nietzsche could be read. George Stack's 1992 *Nietzsche and Emerson: An Elective Affinity* was the first book-length study on Emerson to discuss the connection itself as the central subject rather than a subsidiary one. In the process, Emerson looks much less idealist and much more the thinker firmly grounded in the effects of the physical world. Michael Lopez, long a proponent of "de-transcendentalizing Emerson, uses Nietzsche to understand Emerson's philosophy of power (*Emerson and Power*, 1996). The study firmly associates its philosophical implications with the literary critical world (and certainly questions the "idealizing" internalized in those divisions).

Lopez demonstrates the centrality of Nietzsche to a contemporary reevaluation of Emerson; that argument is given full weight in *Emerson/ Nietzsche*, the 1997 double issue of *Emerson Society Quarterly*. Bringing together the work of ten scholars, it forcefully shows the power in pursuing the under-studied, consistently marginalized connection. Ralph Bauer gives an eminently useful survey of this marginalized tradition in his description of the various Emerson-Nietzsche studies pursued in Europe and more often than not contentiously, then summarily, dismissed. The politics of influence is the underlying force, and as the fate of the Emerson-Nietzsche connection makes clear, a culture is bound by its dominant ideology. To acknowledge and legitimate the Emerson-Nietzsche connection meant acknowledging and legitimating the profound connection between United States and German cultures — something the twentieth century of the two world wars could not imagine, let alone allow. And yet, as Herwig Friedl argues, Emerson and Nietzsche stand behind the paradigm shift that would finally take effect in the late twentieth century.

In his introduction to the special issue, Lopez succinctly describes the long-standing resistance to Emerson-Nietzsche in any combination. Noting Vance Crummett's assessment ("the oversight may be due 'less to ignorance of Emerson's influence and more to the violence this acknowledgement does to stereotypical images of both figures'"), Lopez reminds his readers how Emerson and Nietzsche both labored under particular "reputations" (14). Only "our willingness to read Nietzsche in light of Emerson, and Emerson in light of Nietzsche" (15) will enable the twenty-first century to free itself from the dead-ending of Emerson as a second-rate thinker who fell prey to his own idealism. By "recovering their essential connection," critics "disentangle both thinkers from their legends" and in the process, create an alternative to the old Emerson image of the "idealist or utopian thinker" (15, 18). As Joseph Kronick argues, affirmation has been confused with idealism, but in its emphasis on "becoming," Emerson's thought was not so much an idealizing process (separating, including) as a mimetic one (incorporating, substantiating, 242–50).

The essays in the volume make eminently clear that the powerful new Emerson emerging at the end of the twentieth century was a case of the repressed returning. The very concern over the explosive qualities of Emerson's thought are here put to practice in exploding the old verities about Emerson's fundamental serenity. Heirs to the work on metamorphosis in the 1970s and 1980s, these critics argue Emerson's centrality to modern philosophical thinkers — whether the form is ethics (areteic vs Christian in Gustaaf Van Cromphout or pragmatist in James Albrecht), political systems (Russell Goodman and James Conant on the concept of "representativeness") or environmental concerns (Graham Parkes on Emerson and Nietzsche as philosophers of nature).

As the extent of this interest in Nietzsche demonstrates, Emerson criticism now encompasses a much larger range than a previous generation would have thought possible or desirable. The "Emerson that counts" is no longer exclusively the literary artist (Bishop et al) or the struggling intellect (Whicher et al) or the longstanding "friend and aider of those who would live in the spirit" (Arnold et al) or those who attacked the materialist bent of that aid (et al). We may well be in the place Robert Burkholder anticipated, where multiple Emersons no longer compete for the title of real or essential. Nowhere is this more apparent than in the work of Stanley Cavell, Richard Poirier and George Kateb. Though the three write from markedly different vantage points, they all place Emerson squarely within an ongoing philosophical debate.

In the development of his own thinking, Cavell embodies this profound shift in Emerson perception and reception. As dismissive of Emerson as his times would have made him, he initially found the well-known faults within Emerson's writing. In the first edition of *The Senses of Walden* (1972), Emerson is notably the poor second half of the Emerson-Thoreau duo. Cavell faulted Emerson for softening the harsh reality in which the individual lived. In contrast, Thoreau advocated an unrelenting confrontation that brought the individual "face to face with a fact."

Cavell's own thinking however, underwent a significant change as seen in the expanded edition of *The Senses of Walden* (1981). In the additional essays, "Thinking of Emerson" and "An Emerson Mood," Cavell revisits his earlier assessment that Emerson failed to critique Kant's *Critique of Pure Reason*. Crediting Emerson with developing an epistemology of moods long before Heidegger, Cavell argues that Emerson not so much misread Kant as disputed him, calling into question the very categories Kant posited as fundamental. Seeing this changed interpretation of Emerson as a revolution in his own thinking, Cavell remarks on the old denial once so persuasively articulated by Matthew Arnold. He notes, "But immediately, to imagine that Emerson could challenge the basis of the argument of the *Critique of Pure Reason*, I would have to imagine him to be a philosopher . . . we ought no longer to be as sure as Arnold was that the great philosophical writer is one who builds a system" ("Thinking of Emerson" first published in *New Literary*

History, 1979: 170). As Cavell comments, twentieth-century philosophy called into question the very definition of philosophy as system-building. For those who followed Heidegger or Wittgenstein, philosophy was less a product than a process, more a mode of thought that what that thought constructed.

Concerned by the rise of skepticism in the post-sixties and the fall in active political engagement, Cavell set out to reclaim moral thinking as a credible project in philosophy. It was eminently practical, potentially revolutionary, and not simply by definition conservative. The individual was also part and parcel of this recuperation. Cavell clearly identified his project as "redemptive" and as clearly argued that such a project was unassailably philosophical. The key player in Cavell's project has been Emerson, and while the work has often gone against the grain of current American thinking, it nonetheless succeeded in persuading many writers of Emerson's absolute centrality. Summing his work in 1995, Cavell describes his always ongoing philosophical project: "to re-appropriate Emerson . . . as a philosophical writer" ("Emerson's Constitutional Amending: Reading 'Fate,'" 12). Cavell's work answers and argues against a long line of thinkers from the 1920s to the 1990s (Calverton to Anderson to Bercovitch, et al). In contrast to the "imperial self" with no place for a true "other," Cavell posits a fully aware individual engaged in the fundamentally moral and political work of mutual intelligibility.

Emersonian thinking becomes the model of that mutual intelligibility. For Cavell, Emerson's emphasis on continual movement provides the powerfully productive safeguard against the charges that Emerson's individualism was inherently elitist. He posits a constitutive dynamic: Emerson's ideas on the self lead invariably to a creative tension between the attained and unattained but attainable self. This concept demands tension because it demands an unwavering attention to the "why" of any individual behavior. It also demands a careful consideration of the common appeal to principle. Is the individual compliant with some ideal of justice because of an unexamined conformity or does she chart her course through her own subjective perception? Reclaiming intuition as philosophically and politically credible, Cavell argues that such subjectivity is essential if the individual is to act with full awareness. He terms this use of intuition "reflective judgment" and grounds it in his interpretation of Emersonian Perfectionism.

The term itself requires Cavellian thinking of its readers: the initial late-twentieth-century response is an immediate, conditioned dismissal. Calling all such conditions into question, Cavell asked his readers to re-examine their thought and also their perception of Emerson. Since his reevaluation of Emerson in the mid-1970s, Cavell continues to explore Emerson's fundamental contributions to philosophy — its mode of thinking and its mode of expression. While separable, the works overlap, and Cavell makes a point of the ongoing dialogue that occurs across his own writings. In the case of *This New Yet Unapproachable America* (1989) and *Conditions Handsome and Unhandsome* (1990), work for each volume was virtually contemporaneous. Both take their titles from the same Emerson essay; both make that essay central to their exploration of the means and ends of philosophical thinking. "Experience," the test-case essay for literary critics of the 1980s, was likewise the key to Cavell's philosophical project.

If "Thinking of Emerson" marked the territory of Emerson's considered engagement with the process of thought, then "Finding as Founding" extended that boundary to include philosophy's origin. Focusing on "Experience", Cavell describes Emerson's essay as a piece "constituted by its quest for its topics" (*This New Yet Unapproachable America*, 90). Against those who found Emerson's writings weakly philosophical, Cavell uses this essay to show philosophical work in progress. Cavell's essay fittingly began its life as a lecture, a lecture all the more fitting for being part of the Frederic Ives Carpenter lectures at the University of Chicago. Confronting the common question of the dead child's role in the essay, Cavell hazards a definition of philosophy built from Emerson's essay: "Since in the figure of Waldo the power of passiveness, say passion, is shown as mourning, Waldo means: Philosophy begins in loss, in finding yourself at a loss. . . . Philosophy that does not so begin is so much talk. . . . Loss is *as such* not to be overcome, it is interminable, for every new finding may incur a new loss. . . . Then philosophy ends in a recovery from a terminable loss. Philosophy that does not end so, but seeks to find itself before or beyond that, is to that extent so much talk" (114). Emerson's success may well strike the reader as failure: the individual who assumes a different response to and place for loss is blind to the revolution Emerson posits. Every end is momentary; philosophy itself is a process of finding one's way, not of founding a way.

Establishing philosophy's origin in loss, Cavell examines the grief pregnant in Emerson's essay. The terms are Cavell's. Attracted to the numerous references to children and birth, he represents "Experience" as an essay that asks the multi-faceted question "Can we reach Waldo"? In concert with other critics who similarly explore Waldo's death (most notably Sharon Cameron's 1986 "Representing Grief: Emerson's 'Experience'" and Julie Ellison's 1999 "Tears for Emerson: *Essays, Second Series*"), he argues the non-negotiable character of loss. "If [Emer-

writing is his body in which he can bury Waldo, and the likes of you and me are accordingly, under certain conditions, given to discover him as if he were a new America" (107), then finding indeed proves to be a new founding. The reader, in effect, realizes Waldo's presence, and yet if we simply play that realization back into a biographical remark on Emerson's individual experience, we lose the authentic moment of philosophy as finding.

Cavell raises a different question of "experience" in *Conditions Handsome and Unhandsome*. The essays in this volume may well be read as the complement to "Finding as Founding" in *This New Yet Unapproachable America*. With his topic defined as Emersonian perfectionism, Cavell establishes its practicable dimension on the grounds of proximity. Using a concept of "nextness," he extends this place of relation to define the individual and his considered actions. We exist simultaneously in two dimensions of perception: "the self's always having been attained and its always having to be attained" (xxi). Avoiding a collapse back into nineteenth-century language about character, Cavell disrupts the old idea of continuum: "*Each* state of the self is, so to speak, final," he writes, but not the "last" (3). Arguing that such thinking about the self is precisely what squares democracy with perfectionism, he brings "representative" status to every individual. Clearly the forerunner of George Kateb's democratic individuality, he establishes the individual's power of self-critique as an intimate power with social force. It also foregrounds Cavell's use of Emerson to explore the moral urgency that can legitimately be associated with the "ordinary" (see also, "Being Odd, Getting Even"). The full implication remains to be studied.

While "Experience" figured importantly in *Conditions Handsome and Unhandsome*, "Self-Reliance" was an equally evocative presence. Using three sentences from the essay — "The virtue in most request is conformity. Self-reliance is its aversion. . . . Every word they say chagrins us" — Cavell explores the mode of thinking he describes as necessary, a mode he associates essentially with Emerson. Borrowing Emerson's word "aversion," Cavell places "aversive thinking" at the center of Emerson's writing. In *Conditions Handsome and Unhandsome*, its emphasis is transfiguration, demonstrated most provokingly in the equation Cavell creates between Emerson's "way of writing" and his "relation to the reader" (56). Using Emerson's comment from the opening paragraph of "Self-Reliance" — "In every work of genius we recognize our own rejected thoughts: they come back to us with a certain alienated majesty" — Cavell asserts that Emerson deploys his own words to function as the reader's rejected thoughts. They return to the reader as if they were his

or her own. Cavell than raises the stakes by introducing friendship —
potentially erotic — into this world of rejecting and returning. Folding
the various terms together, he writes, "Since his aversion is a *continual
turning away* from society, it is thereby a continual turning *toward* it.
Toward and away; it is a motion of seduction — such as philosophy will
contain. It is in response to this seduction from our seductions (con-
formities, heteronomies) that the friend (discovered or constructed)
represents the standpoint of perfection" (59).

In *Conditions Handsome and Unhandsome* perfectionism is the
frame of reference for aversive thinking. In Cavell's various essays on
Emerson's "Fate," the emphasis shifts to the structural questions of
freedom raised in and by Emerson's writings. For Cavell, "Fate" is the
third of his key Emerson essays. It punctuates his discussion in "Genteel Responses to Kant? In Emerson's 'Fate' and in Coleridge's *Biographia Literaria*" (1983), "Being Odd, Getting Even" (1986) and
"Emerson's Constitutional Amending: Reading 'Fate'"(1995).

In the last of these, Cavell addresses philosophy's and society's general failure to deliver on their promises (that philosophy yields a continuous expression of freedom, that a democratic society yields a
continuous emergence of individuals). Incorporating the concept of
pain, he suggests that we are better advised to bear the painful thought
than mourn it. Allying this choice with one of Emerson's most recalcitrant and also most provoking essays for the late twentieth century, he
argues that Emerson's "Fate" is a skillful silence spoken directly against
the slavery it supposedly overlooks. Where von Frank argues Emerson's
antislavery effectiveness through his direct influence on the leading
members within the movement and through his direct work in the
1850s as a speaker against slavery, Cavell focuses alone on the method
behind the words. Through his "aversive thinking," Emerson makes
emancipation fundamentally possible. Cavell writes, "human freedom,
as the opposition to fate, is not merely called for by philosophical writing but is instanced or enacted by that writing: the Emersonian sentence is philosophical in showing within itself its aversion to (turning
away in turning toward) the standing conformation of its words, as
though human thinking is not so much to be expressed by language as
resurrected with it" (31).

Cavell accomplishes this resurrection in part by affiliating Emerson
with the philosophers who follow him — initially Nietzsche but also
Heidegger and Wittgenstein. Emerson's aversive thinking becomes the
integrating ground where the split philosophy of the twentieth century
(divided between Wittgenstein and Heidegger) can meet. It is also the
place where skepticism is cannily met by Emersonian transfigurations —

of the ordinary (as in Wittgenstein: skepticism is not conclusion but condition) and of the categories which structure our knowledge. Cavell writes, "in calling for philosophy Emerson is not comprehensible as asking for guardianship by a particular profession within what we call universities. I assume what will become 'philosophy itself' may not be distinguishable from literature — that is to say, from what literature will become" (*Conditions Handsome and Unhandsome*, 62).

Cavell calls this formulation his "romanticism." Richard Poirier might term it healthy skepticism of a different order. Poirier's books of the late 1980s and early 1990s (*The Renewal of American Literature: Emersonian Reflections*, 1987; *Poetry and Pragmatism*, 1992) exemplified his own productive skepticism toward existing categories, particularly those involved in the enterprise of literary criticism. Not unlike Bishop's observation that the practitioners of "discursive language" rarely produce the best insight, Poirier takes this one step further to suggest that Emerson's writing is itself inimical to the critical project. He allies Emerson with a continuous unsettling of meaning; interpretation, on the contrary, works on the premise of fixing the meaning in a particular place. Even the theories that abandon the traditional understanding of a text or an author or a meaning implicitly participate in the assumption of the critics' powerfully determinative role. While the language differs (and reflects a more significant difference than Poirier may well allow), the underlying project does not. If the earlier interpreters of texts thought of themselves as discovering or illuminating the text's inherent meaning, later critics adopt an analogous role. They produce meaning. Though Poirier's own method is clearly sympathetic to poststructuralism and as clearly critical of the neo-neohumanism of the early 1980s (the cultural literacy projects forwarded by Allan Bloom and E. D. Hirsch), he is careful to distance himself from any "school."

While he eschews categorization, it is also clear that his thoughts on Emerson reflect the common concerns of the time. He too is fascinated by the Emerson of flux; the journals are signally important, giving the clearest indication of how central was Emerson's interest in metamorphosis. For Poirier the key word is "transition" and the key element within Emerson's writing is the trope. As he reminds his reader, troping means turning. Emerson's essays do precisely that. They never settle but are always moving, via their metaphors, into a different place. His aphorisms work to similar effect. Poirier writes, "There is something peculiarly unsettling about his aphoristic bravado, as if the aphorisms are meant to transcend the occasion of their utterance and of our reading" (69). While critics often attempt to settle the sentences back into their context, Poirier advises us to take Emerson at his word. Earlier critics often cited Emerson's dialectic as the means to achieve a certain balance. This was clearly the Emerson of the 1930s to the 1950s who was presented by Perry and Carpenter, Paul and Hopkins as the "reconciler." The unstable dualisms of Emerson's thought found their meaning in the hard-won balance he created among them.

Poirier suggests that such balance was always more the product of the critic than of the Emerson essay in question. In its place he sets forth the outlines of an Emerson that had become increasingly familiar through the work of Porter and Ellison. Describing Emerson's style, he presents his own theory that style in Emerson always served an ulterior, perhaps ultimate, motive. He writes,

> Emerson has a predilection for what he calls "abandonment". . . . The word helps explain his tendency to move out of any rhetorical position he has just occupied into another one, as if in hot pursuit of a truth elusive of more orderly verbal and syntactic inquiry. He sometimes gets almost audibly exasperated with any reader who might be satisfied only with what he has just said; he seems uncomfortable even with such concessions as he makes to the propriety of sentences and paragraphs, with their implicit commitment to ideas of duration, sequence, and logical progression. Obviously I am not describing what dreary criticism likes to call "verbal strategies." (74–75)

Poirier's distrust of and disdain for certain kinds of criticism is all too apparent, but his comments on process are suggestive. Reading Emerson's work will always (or should) signal exploration. The project is larger than a single text, or a single literary oeuvre: it involves an ongoing confrontation with the limits of language itself.

Poirier makes Emerson chief among the voices who successfully engage with those limits and their implications. He suggests readers turn back from their Foucault and their Nietzsche to the thinker who first articulated the concerns of the fatally trapped human consciousness. He comments, "He was ready to teach us, long before Foucault, that if we intend ever to resist our social and cultural fate, then we must first see it for what it is, and that its form, ultimately, is the language we use in learning to know ourselves. Language is also, however, the place wherein we can most effectively register our dissent from our fate by means of troping, punning, parodistic echoings, and by letting vernacular idioms play against revered terminologies. . . . Language is the only way to get around the obstruction of language, and in his management of this paradox Emerson shows why he is now and always essential" (72).

To move his reader from the essential Emerson to Emerson *as* essential, he centers his discussion on an Emersonian model of genius. Far removed from the democratic element of Perry Miller's argument, this genius has little to do with its representative or individual nature. While Poirier grants that it is an "aspect of individualism" (75), he clearly distances it from any individual's possession. From Emerson's writing, Poirier argues, "genius" emerges as "an activity, an influx, a movement." It is, in short, a "phenomenon of energy," and as such will never inhere in any of its artifacts. Reminding the reader yet again of the implied clash between Emerson and the critics, he contrasts Emerson's insistence on unimpeded energy with criticism's need for "products of genius" (i.e., works of literature). Emerson, Poirier claims, offers an entirely different use for literature. He quotes a passage from "Intellect" in which Emerson compares the act of reading to Jacob's wrestling with the angel. Even this, Poirier suggests is relatively mild in comparison with Emerson's journal reflection about the "function of criticism and the existence of literature." Emerson had written, "Criticism must be transcendental, that is, must consider literature ephemeral & easily entertain the supposition of its entire disappearance" (88). As Poirier is quick to point out, Emerson is again an uncanny predictor of the very issues addressed by critical theory. He writes, "Here, as everywhere, Emerson means to detextualize, to dehistoricize, to unauthorize 'genius,' leaving in place only an activity, and a barely traceable one at that" (88). Poirier will not, however, limit his comments to the humanists; his words are for all critics who retain an investment in the authorship and individual value of their work. They, too, are implicated in the work that stands inimically opposed to Emerson's call for relentless exploration. Criticism, finally, is only as good as the struggle it perpetuates. It can be judged by its own understanding as "ephemera"; it too must disappear in the constant struggle of language against itself.

The formulation is grim, but the effect is quite otherwise. Poirier challenges the reader: direct participation is the only accurate experience of genius that individuals may claim. Moving back and forth between words from William James and words from Emerson, Poirier centers attention upon process. Citing James's comments in *Pragmatism* about truth "happening" to an idea, he extends this exercise in "valid-ation" to the reader. He writes, "Literature is supremely the place where this process goes on, a process in which, ideally, the reader and writer become indistinguishable as partners in the enterprise of 'genius'" (44).

The pragmatic turn in Emerson's thought has thus taken center stage in recent criticism from both the literary and philosophical perspectives. In part this reclamation owes its power to the renewed interest and increasing respect for American pragmatism. Long the poor relation in the family of philosophical inquiry, the philosophy associated with William James and Charles Sanders Peirce fares differently since the 1980s. In place of the soft philosophy they were assumed to have fathered, their thought is now associated with a greater flexibility and a presciently keen sense of the intersection between human experience and the thought recorded about that experience.

Examining the appropriations of Emerson's thought in the works of William James and W. E. B. DuBois, Charles Mitchell discusses the shifting fate of Emerson's individual in *Individualism and its Discontents: Appropriations of Emerson, 1880–1950* (1997). An incisive reader of the Emerson reputation, he makes clear how that reputation intersects with the American dilemma of individualism. Mitchell concludes his study by juxtaposing comments of Quentin Anderson and George Kateb. Anderson framed individualism within the perspective of economic life: he saw Emersonian self-reliance played out in capitalist exploitation and alienation. Kateb writes from within the perspective of political systems: the individualism of American democracy ideally incorporates the strictures Emerson built into self-reliance. Worth noting, although Mitchell does not, are the very different Americas within which Anderson (1971) and Kateb wrote (1995). Mitchell places himself clearly with Kateb. Bringing together both ends of the twentieth century he writes, "At its base, as William James so clearly saw, Emersonian individualism is an ethical claim. It imposes responsibilities far more than it undermines them. As Kateb observed, the real task then is not to replace individualism but to rehabilitate it" (192).

That rehabilitation is largely the project of Kateb's *Emerson and Self-Reliance* (1995). In its immediate past are several forceful voices that speak the opposite conclusion. Christopher Newfield notes the effective submission associated with Emersonian individualism and David Marr isolates its apolitical privatism. Cary Wolfe's critique yields the most uncompromising position. In the abstract for *The Limits of American Literary Ideology in Emerson and Pound* (1993) he writes, "any form of individualism modeled on the logic and structure of private property will always reproduce the very contradictions and alienations that it set out to criticize and remedy." Set within the context of a study of Ezra Pound, Wolfe's argument examines the ideological kinship between American Romanticism and Modernism. Both Pound and Emerson predicated their individualism upon a similar dual and divided premise: "the pinnacle of selfhood" is achieved only upon condition of the individual's disappearance and the individual is conceived as "inalienable property." The first guarantees the writer's radical effect while the second as surely grounds him in "Lockean liberalism" and all its attendant contradictions (6–7). The "ethical idealism" Emerson developed invariably collapsed under the weight of these contradictions. With Marr and Bercovitch, and in sharp contrast to George Kateb, Wolfe find's Emerson's individualism "politically disabling" (10).

There is little hint of apology in Kateb's tone though he is clearly aware of the past treatment of Emerson. For example, he sees Nietzsche as a useful means for overcoming the customary condescension toward Emerson, but at the same time, pays little heed to what other critics of Emerson have said. His study is forwarded by Emerson's own words and his own. It is the study of a concept, and as such, it focuses on the complex elements of which it is composed. Dividing self-reliance into two dimensions — mental and active — he suggests their close connection and the clear subordination of one to the other. There is finally no contest between the two, though both are essential. Mental self-reliance saves individualism from becoming the living nightmare of the imperial self. It is defined by its impersonality and characterized by a flexible style of thought in which "contrast and antagonism" can be readily allowed (62–3, 70). In contrast to the limitation imposed by action (an action by definition "chooses and excludes," 135), mental self-reliance is defined by its openness. In his discussion of Emerson's uneasiness with the idealist position, he examines an internal proof for the existence of the other. He writes, "Reality is not my mind imposing itself as it pleases; if my mind is self-reliant, its task is to open up reality by being open to reality. If there is no reality independent of what my mind thinks about it, there could be no need for those other powers, those interpretative powers by which one seeks to know one's own experience and the world at large, and to know by observation, retrospection, and contemplation" (47). Essential to that knowledge of (or about) experience is the mind's own capacity to distance itself from its personal involvement. It can disengage by tolerating a high level of contrasting or contradictory ideas. Emerson's method is designed to effect that action within the reader.

One of the few critics in the twentieth century who reads Emerson sympathetically on the issue of action, Kateb echoes Emerson's position. He writes, "Emerson's effort to claim superiority for thinking over doing can come to mean that thinking is actually the highest kind of doing, rather than the intellectually secular completion of worldly doing" (71). Allowing Emerson his position, he also acknowledges its nineteenth-century underpinnings. The moral law of Emerson's system virtually holds no place in ours. And yet, Kateb again confronts the internal evidence to suggest that Emerson's position is not simply still relevant but absolutely essential. In his conclusion he turns to the twentieth century's experience with evil and frames this experience within a discussion of innocence. Is innocence even still possible? He answers an emphatic "yes." He sees it as essential to "finding self-reliance a genuine ideal," but he makes it clear that innocence must bear a quite particular meaning in the twenty-first century. He writes, "I do not say that Emerson's theory is inherently innocent, innocent at birth, hopelessly innocent even in its own time. I wonder rather whether it has become innocent. What I mean is that if slavery was an exceptional phenomenon, an aberrant system of atrocity, the political events of this century — beginning with World War I — have established atrocity as the norm. There has been deliberate infliction of suffering on a large scale and as a matter of policy and there is a quantity of material misery that is scarcely imaginable even to us today — leave aside what Emerson or people in his times could have conceived. On the one hand, mass wars, extermination camps, the gulag; on the other hand, millions and millions of human beings living in inhuman conditions. The extent of capitalist misery, the sort that enraged and incited Marx and others, is dwarfed by the misery of the immensely overpopulated globe of the twentieth century. How, in the face of these horrors, can Emerson's vision of life be compelling?" (198). The question sounds like a rhetorical one with a single obvious answer. Emerson can no longer be compelling just as it is no longer defensible to be innocent.

Kateb risks the opposite answer. He owns the difficulty: "The prevalence of evil in the world, then, denies the self-reliant mind permission to absolve and affirm the world" (200). He says there may be "no answer to this line of argument," yet he sees different evidence in everyday experience. Individuals do (and must) "absolve and affirm the world"; such behavior is not fundamentally "self-serving and culpable" (201). He reminds his audience that Emerson himself practiced an "interrupted self-reliance" and that this may finally be the right model. In the end, he offers a wager not unlike Pascal's, though in this case, it is life itself that is at stake. He suggests that Emerson's optimism was a cogent strategy: "Emerson may be said to limit the scope of his attention [to evil] in order to allow himself to affirm life." Kateb suggests the reason why such a limitation is necessary. He asks, "Given the amount of terrible evils in the world, what we can do is ask ourselves whether we would wish that human existence cease," and then answers, "I cannot think that anyone would have the right to countenance such a prospect." He concludes by stating that the individual's best position is to "want" life rather than simply giving it a begrudging acceptance. Clearly harking back to his comments on the "impersonality" of Emersonian self-reliance, he suggests we learn that attribute:

Not beauty, not sublimity even, is sufficient either to affirm or to absolve the world. But each supplies some part of the reason we could give in saying why we have no right to countenance the end of human existence as the reward for its perpetration of evil . . . instructed by Emerson we can learn to behold the world's beauty and sublimity and also learn to find them where we had not been expecting them — in antagonism and contrast. Driven to ask whether and why we want human existence to go on, we put on a more experienced innocence (201–02).

With many of the thinkers of the last decades of the twentieth century, Kateb adopts a kind of pragmatic element that holds tightly to an underlying idealism. This is not the Platonic doctrine of the primary reality in absolute forms, but an urgent belief that the world need not be as bad as it is. Emerson posed that question in 1844 and offered a still unsettling response: "in the solitude to which every man is always returning, he has a sanity and revelations, which in his passage into new worlds he will carry with him. Never mind the ridicule, never mind the defeat: up again old heart! — it seems to say, — there is victory yet for all justice; and the true romance which the world exists to realize, will be the transformation of genius into practical power" (*Collected Works* 3: 49). I leave to the readers their own multiple assessments of the particular circle inscribed within this "true romance." The self-isolated thinker of earlier generations has become the highly relational one. This "new Emerson" is the twentieth century's contribution to the twenty-first.

Works Cited

Albrecht, James. "'The Sun Were Insipid, If the Universe Were Not Opaque': The Ethics of Action, Power, and Belief in Emerson, Nietzsche, and James." *ESQ: A Journal of the American Renaissance* 43 (1997): 113–58.

Allen, Gay Wilson. "A New Look at Emerson and Science" in *Literature and Ideas in America: Essays in Memory of Harry Hayden Clark*. Robert Falk, editor. Athens: Ohio University Press, 1975: 58–78.

Barish, Evelyn. *Emerson: The Roots of Prophecy*. Princeton: Princeton University Press, 1989.

Beach, Joseph Warren. "Emerson and Evolution." *University of Toronto Quarterly* 3 (1934): 474–97.

Bercovitch, Sacvan. "Emerson, Individualism and the Ambiguities of Dissent." *Southern Atlantic Quarterly* 89: 3 (1990): 623–62.

Bishop, Jonathan. *Emerson on the Soul.* Cambridge, MA: Harvard University Press, 1964.

Brown, Lee Rust. *The Emerson Museum: Practical Romanticism and the Pursuit of the Whole.* Cambridge, MA: Harvard University Press, 1997.

Cadava, Eduardo. *Emerson and the Climates of History.* Stanford: Stanford University Press, 1997.

Cameron, Sharon. "Representing Grief: Emerson's 'Experience.'" *Representations* 15 (Summer 1986): 15–41.

Cavell, Stanley. "Being Odd, Getting Even: Threats to Individuality" in *Reconstructing Individualism: Autonomy, Individuality, and the Self in Western Thought.* Thomas C. Heller, editor. Stanford: Stanford University Press, 1986: 278–312.

———. *Conditions Handsome and Unhandsome: The Constitution of Emersonian Perfectionism.* Chicago: University of Chicago Press, 1990.

———. "Genteel Responses to Kant? In Emerson's 'Fate' and Coleridge's *Biographia Literaria.*" *Raritan* 3 (Fall 1983): 34–61.

———. *In Quest of the Ordinary: Lines of Skepticism and Romanticism.* Chicago: University of Chicago Press, 1988.

———. *Philosophical Passages: Wittgenstein, Emerson, Austin, Derrida.* Cambridge, MA: Blackwell, 1995.

———. *The Senses of Walden.* New York: Viking Press, 1972.

———. *The Senses of Walden: An Expanded Edition.* Includes "Thinking of Emerson" and "An Emerson Mood." San Francisco: North Point Press, 1981.

———. "Thinking of Emerson." *New Literary History* 11: 1 (Autumn 1979): 167–76.

———. *This New Yet Unapproachable America: Lectures After Emerson After Wittgenstein.* Albuquerque: Living Batch Press, 1989.

Clark, Harry Hayden. "Emerson and Science." *Philological Quarterly* 10 (1931): 225–60.

Cole, Phyllis. "The Advantage of Loneliness: Mary Moody Emerson's Almanacks, 1802–1855" in *Emerson: Prospect and Retrospect.* Joel Porte, editor. Cambridge, MA: Harvard University Press, 1982: 1–32.

———. *Mary Moody Emerson and the Origins of Transcendentalism.* New York: Oxford University Press, 1998.

———. "'Men and Women Conversing': The Emersons in 1837" in *Emersonian Circles: Essays in Honor of Joel Myerson.* Wesley T. Mott and Robert E. Burkholder, editors. Rochester: University of Rochester Press, 1997: 127–59.

Conant, James. "Emerson as Educator." *ESQ: A Journal of the American Renaissance* 43 (1997): 181–206.

Ellison, Julie. "Tears for Emerson: *Essays, Second Series*" in *The Cambridge Companion to Ralph Waldo Emerson*. Joel Porte and Saundra Morris, editors. New York: Cambridge University Press, 1999: 140–62.

Goodman, Russell. "Freedom in the Philosophy of Ralph Waldo Emerson." *Tulane Studies in Philosophy* 35 (1987): 5–10.

———. *American Philosophy and the Romantic Tradition*. New York: Cambridge University Press, 1990.

———. "Moral Perfectionism and Democracy: Emerson, Nietzsche, Cavell." *ESQ: A Journal of the American Renaissance* 43 (1997): 159–80.

Grey, Robin. *The Complicity of Imagination: The American Renaissance, Contests of Authority, and Seventeenth-Century English Culture*. New York: Cambridge University Press, 1997.

Jacobson, David. *Emerson's Pragmatic Vision: The Dance of the Eye*. University Park: Pennsylvania State University Press, 1993.

Kateb, George. *Emerson and Self-Reliance*. Modernity and Public Thought, vol. 8. Thousand Oaks, CA: Sage Publishing, 1995.

Kronick, Joseph. "Repetition and Mimesis from Nietzsche to Emerson; or, How the World Became a Fable." *ESQ: A Journal of the American Renaissance* 43 (1997): 241–66.

Lopez, Michael. *Emerson and Power: Creative Antagonism in the Nineteenth Century*. DeKalb: Northern Illinois University Press, 1996.

———, editor. *Emerson/Nietzsche*. *ESQ: A Journal of the American Renaissance* 43 (1997).

Marr, David. *American Worlds Since Emerson*. Amherst: University of Massachusetts Press, 1988.

Michael, John. *Emerson and Skepticism: The Cipher of the World*. Baltimore, MD.: The Johns Hopkins University Press, 1988.

Mitchell, Charles. *Individualism and Its Discontents: Appropriations of Emerson, 1880–1950*. Amherst: University of Massachusetts Press, 1997.

Mott, Wesley T. *"The Strains of Eloquence": Emerson and His Sermons*. University Park: Pennsylvania State University Press, 1989.

Poirier, Richard. *The Renewal of Literature: Emersonian Reflections*. New York: Random House, 1987.

———. *Poetry and Pragmatism*. Cambridge, MA: Harvard University Press, 1992.

Robinson, David. "Thoreau's 'Ktaadn' and the Quest for Experience" in *Emersonian Circles: Essays in Honor of Joel Myerson*. Wesley T. Mott and Robert E. Burkholder, editors. Rochester: University of Rochester Press, 1997: 261–70.

————. "Emerson's Natural Theology and the Paris Naturalists: Toward a Theory of Animated Nature." *Journal of the History of Ideas* 41 (1980): 69–88.

————. *Emerson and the Conduct of Life: Pragmatism and Ethical Purpose in the Later Work.* New York: Cambridge University Press, 1993.

Simmons, Nancy Craig, editor. *The Selected Letters of Mary Moody Emerson.* Athens: University of Georgia Press, 1993.

Stack, George. *Nietzsche and Emerson: An Elective Affinity.* Athens: Ohio University Press, 1992.

Van Cromphout, Gustaaf. "Areteic Ethics: Emerson and Nietzsche on Pity, Friendship, and Love." *ESQ: A Journal of the American Renaissance* 43 (1997): 95–112.

————. *Emerson's Ethics.* Columbia: University of Missouri Press, 1999.

————. *Emerson's Modernity and the Example of Goethe.* Columbia: University of Missouri Press, 1990.

Van Leer, David. *Emerson's Epistemology: The Argument of the Essays.* New York: Cambridge University Press, 1986.

Walls, Laura Dassow. "The Anatomy of Truth: Emerson's Poetic Science." *Configurations* 5: 3 (1997): 425–62.

West, Cornel. *The American Evasion of Philosophy: A Genealogy of Pragmatism.* Madison, WI.: University of Wisconsin Press, 1989.

Wilson, Eric. *Emerson's Sublime Science.* New York: St. Martin's Press, 1999.

————. "From Metaphysical Poverty to Practical Power: Emerson's Embrace of the Physical World." *ESQ: A Journal of the American Renaissance* 43 (1997): 295–321.

Wolfe, Cary. *The Limits of American Literary Ideology in Emerson and Pound.* New York: Cambridge University Press, 1993.

Editions

Texts

THE PUBLISHING HISTORY of Emerson's writings is complex. In addition to the first publication of each volume of Emerson essays or poems, there were various nineteenth-century editions of the collected works as well as of individual essays and essay collections. These nineteenth-century editions were superseded by Edward Waldo Emerson's Centenary Edition (published in 1903–04 to coincide with the hundred-year anniversary of Emerson's birth). The later volumes of this edition (6–12) remain standard in Emerson criticism but are being superseded by Harvard's *Collected Works*.

In addition to the essays and poems Emerson published in his lifetime, the late nineteenth and early twentieth centuries produced a number of volumes of previously unpublished work, primarily correspondence and journals. The last area of Emerson's writings to sustain interest were the sermons, with a selection of twenty-five published in 1938. In each case, modern editions have now superseded the earlier editions.

As a brief overview of the publishing history, the first part of the *Works Cited* is divided into two sections. The first lists original publication of the Emerson texts that have proved most significant in Emerson criticism. The second part gives today's standard editions for Emerson studies.

First Editions

Nature. Boston: James Monroe and Company, 1836.

Essays [First Series]. Boston: James Monroe and Company, 1841.

Essays, Second Series. Boston: James Monroe and Company, 1844.

Poems. Boston: James Monroe and Company, 1847.

Nature; Addresses and Lectures. Boston: James Monroe and Company, 1849.

Representative Men. Boston: Phillips, Sampson and Company, 1850.

English Traits. Boston: Phillips, Sampson and Company, 1856.

The Conduct of Life. Boston: Ticknor and Fields, 1860.

May-Day and Other Pieces. Boston: Ticknor and Fields, 1867.

Society and Solitude. Boston: Fields, Osgood and Company, 1870.

Letters and Social Aims. James R. Osgood and Company, 1876.

The Correspondence of Thomas Carlyle and Ralph Waldo Emerson, 1834–1872. 2 vols. Charles Eliot Norton, editor. Boston: James R. Osgood and Company, 1883.

Miscellanies. Boston: Houghton, Mifflin and Company, 1884.

Lectures and Biographical Sketches. Boston: Houghton, Mifflin and Company, 1884.

Natural History of Intellect and Other Papers. Boston: Houghton, Mifflin and Company, 1893.

Journals 10 vols. Edward Waldo Emerson, editor. Boston: Houghton Mifflin, 1910–14.

Young Emerson Speaks. Arthur McGiffert, Jr., editor. Boston: Houghton Mifflin, 1938.

Standard Editions

The Complete Works of Ralph Waldo Emerson. Centenary Edition. Edward Waldo Emerson, editor. 12 vols. Boston: Houghton Mifflin, 1903–04.

The Letters of Ralph Waldo Emerson. Ralph Rusk and Eleanor Tilton, editors. 10 vols. New York: Columbia University Press, 1939–94.

The Early Lectures of Ralph Waldo Emerson. Stephen E. Whicher, Robert E. Spiller and Wallace E. Williams, editors. 3 vols. Cambridge, MA: The Belknap Press of Harvard University, 1959–72.

The Journals and Miscellaneous Notebooks of Ralph Waldo Emerson. William H. Gilman et al., editors. 16 vols. Cambridge, MA: Harvard University Press, 1960–82.

The Correspondence of Emerson and Carlyle. Joseph Slater, editor. New York: Columbia University Press, 1964.

The Collected Works of Ralph Waldo Emerson. Robert E. Spiller et al., editors. 5 vols. to date. Cambridge, MA: Harvard University Press, 1971–.

The Poetry Notebooks of Ralph Waldo Emerson. Ralph H. Orth et al., editors. Columbia: University of Missouri Press, 1986.

Complete Sermons of Ralph Waldo Emerson. Albert J. von Frank et al., editors. 4 vols. Columbia: University of Missouri Press, 1989–92.

The Topical Notebooks of Ralph Waldo Emerson. Ralph H. Orth et al., editors. 3 vols. Columbia: University of Missouri Press, 1990–94.

Emerson's Antislavery Writings. Len Gougeon and Joel Myerson, editors. New Haven: Yale University Press, 1995.

Chronological List of Works Consulted

Bowen, Francis. "Transcendentalism." *The Christian Examiner* 21 (January 1837): 371–85.

Channing, William Henry. "Emerson's *Phi Beta Kappa Oration*." *Boston Quarterly Review* 1 (January 1838): 106–20.

Clarke, James Freeman. "R. W. Emerson and the New School." *Western Messenger* 6 (November 1838): 37–47.

Davis, G. T. "Review of Divinity School Address." Boston *Morning Post* (31 August 1838): 1.

Gilman, Samuel. "Ralph Waldo Emerson." *Southern Rose* 7 (24 November 1838): 100–106.

Norton, Andrews. "The New School in Literature and Religion." Boston *Daily Advertiser* (27 August 1838): 2.

Parsons, Theophilus. "The New School and Its Opponents." Boston *Daily Advertiser* (30 August 1838): 2.

Peabody, Elizabeth Palmer. "Nature — A Prose Poem." *United States Magazine and Democratic Review* 1 (February 1838): 319–21.

Brownson, Orestes. "Emerson's Essays." *Boston Quarterly Review* 4 (July 1841): 291–308.

Review of *Essays. Athenaeum* 730 (23 October 1841): 803–4.

Heraud, John A. "Emerson's Essays." *Monthly Magazine*, 3rd series, 5 (November 1841): 484–505.

Fuller, Margaret. "Emerson's Essays." New York *Daily Tribune* (7 December 1844): 1.

A Disciple. "Emerson's Essays." *United States Magazine, and Democratic Review* 16 (June 1845): 589–602.

Hedge, Frederic Henry. "Writings of R. W. Emerson." *Christian Examiner* 38 (January 1845): 87–108.

Bartol, Cyrus A. "Poetry and Imagination." *Christian Examiner* 42 (March 1847): 250–71.

Bowen, Francis. "Nine New Poets." *North American Review* 64 (April 1847): 402–34.

Review of *Poems. Critic* n.s. 5 (2 January 1847): 9–11.

"Emerson's Poems." New York *Daily Tribune*. (9 January 1847): 1.

Review of *Poems. Athenaeum* 1006 (6 February 1847): 144–46.

Review of *Poems. Literary World* 1 (3 April 1847): 197–99.

Review of *Essays, Lectures, and Orations. Critic* n.s. 6 (18 December 1847): 386–87.

Lowell, James Russell. *A Fable for Critics.* New York: G. P. Putnam, 1848.

"Emerson's Addresses." *Literary World* 5 (3 November 1849): 374–76.

B., L. W. "Ralph Waldo Emerson." *Yale Literary Magazine* 5 (March 1850): 203–06.

Review of *Essays, Essays, Second Series,* and *Nature; Addresses, and Lectures. Knickerbocker* 35 (March 1850): 254–63.

Review of *Representative Men. Critic.* n.s. 9 (1 February 1850): 59–91.

Review of *Representative Men. Literary World* 6 (9 February 1850): 123–24.

Parker, Theodore. "The Writings of Ralph Waldo Emerson." *Massachusetts Quarterly Review* 3 (March 1850): 200–255.

Review of *English Traits. Harper's New Monthly Magazine* 13 (October 1856): 694–96.

Maccall, William. "The Conduct of Life." *Critic* n.s. 21 (22 December 1860): 778–79.

Lowell, James Russell. Review of *The Conduct of Life. Atlantic Monthly* 7 (February 1861): 254–55.

Review of *The Conduct of Life. Athenaeum* 1929 (15 December 1860): 824–26.

Review of *The Conduct of Life. Knickerbocker* 57 (February 1861): 217–18.

Review of *The Conduct of Life. Westminster Review* 75 (April 1861): 588–90.

Howells, William Dean. Review of *May-Day and Other Pieces. Atlantic Monthly* 20 (1867): 376–78.

Norton, Charles Eliot. "*May-Day and Other Pieces.*" *North American Review* 105 (July 1867): 325–37.

Wasson, David A. Review of *May-Day and Other Pieces. Radical* 2 (August 1867): 760–62.

Lowell, James Russell. "Emerson the Lecturer." 1868. Reprinted in *My Study Windows.* Boston: J. R. Osgood, 1871: 375–84.

Burroughs, John. "Emerson's New Volume." *Appleton's Journal* 3 (28 May 1870): 609–11.

Harte, Bret. Review of *Society and Solitude. Overland Monthly* 5 (October 1870): 386–87.

Frothingham, Octavius Brooks. *Transcendentalism in New England: A History.* New York: G. P. Putnam's Sons, 1876.

Lathrop, George Parsons. "*Letters and Social Aims.*" *Atlantic Monthly* 38 (August 1876): 240–41.

Review of *Letters and Social Aims. Athenaeum* 2516 (15 January 1876): 81.

Cooke, George Willis. "Emerson's Literary Methods." Boston *Literary World* 11 (22 May 1880): 181.

"Emerson" [Special birthday section]. *Literary World* 11 (22 May 1880): 174–85.

Hedge, Frederic Henry. "Emerson the Philosopher and the Poet." Boston *Literary World* 11 (22 May 1880): 176–77.

Higginson, Thomas Wentworth. "Emerson as the Founder of a Literature." Boston *Literary World* 11 (22 May 1880): 175–76.

Whipple, E. P., et al. "Tribute." *Literary World* 11 (22 May 1880): 182–83.

Whitman, Walt. "Emerson's Books (The Shadows of Them)." Boston *Literary World* 11 (22 May 1880): 177–78.

Cooke, George Willis. *Ralph Waldo Emerson: His Life, His Writings, and Philosophy.* Boston: Houghton, Mifflin and Company, 1881. Expanded edition, 1892.

Conway, Moncure Daniel. *Emerson At Home and Abroad.* Boston: Houghton, Mifflin and Company, 1882.

Harris, William Torrey. "Ralph Waldo Emerson." *Atlantic Monthly Magazine* 50 (August 1882): 238–52.

Huntington, Frederic Dan. "Ralph Waldo Emerson." *Independent* 34 (18, 25 May 1882): 1–2, 1–2.

Ireland, Alexander. *Ralph Waldo Emerson: His Life, His Genius, and Writings, a Biographical Sketch, to Which Are Added Personal Recollections of His Visits to England, Extracts from Unpublished Letters, and Miscellaneous Characteristic Records.* London: Simpkin, Marshall, 1882.

Benton, Joel E. *Emerson as a Poet.* New York: M. F. Mansfield and A. Wessels, 1883.

Harris, William Torrey. "The Dialectical Unity of Emerson's Prose." *Journal of Speculative Philosophy* 18 (1884): 195–202.

Holmes, Oliver Wendell. *Ralph Waldo Emerson.* Boston: Houghton, Mifflin and Company, 1884.

Arnold, Matthew. "Emerson" in *Discourses in America.* London: Macmillan, 1885: 138–207.

Harris, William Torrey. "Emerson's Philosophy of Nature" in *The Genius and Character of Emerson: Lectures at the Concord School of Philosophy.* Franklin B. Sanborn, editor. Boston: J. R. Osgood, 1885: 339–64.

Hawthorne, Julian. "Emerson as an American" in *The Genius and Character of Emerson: Lectures at the Concord School of Philosophy*. Franklin B. Sanborn, editor. Boston: J. R. Osgood, 1885: 68–91.

Sanborn, Franklin B. "Emerson among the Poets" in *The Genius and Character of Emerson: Lectures at the Concord School of Philosophy*. Franklin B. Sanborn, editor. Boston: J. R. Osgood, 1885: 173–214.

———, editor. *The Genius and Character of Emerson: Lectures at the Concord School of Philosophy*. Boston: J. R. Osgood, 1885.

Stedman, Edmund Clarence. *Poets of America*. Boston: Houghton, Mifflin and Company, 1885.

Santayana, George. "The Optimism of Ralph Waldo Emerson." Bowdoin Prize submission, 1886. Published in *George Santayana's America*. James Ballowe, editor. Urbana: University of Illinois Press, 1967: 71–84.

Cabot, James Elliot. *A Memoir of Ralph Waldo Emerson*. 2 vols. New York: Macmillan and Company, 1887.

Garnett, Richard. *The Life of Ralph Waldo Emerson*. London: W. Scott, T. Whittaker, 1888.

Gosse, Edmund. "Has America Produced a Poet?" *Forum* 6 (1888): 176–86.

Emerson, Edward Waldo. *Emerson in Concord: A Memoir*. Boston: Houghton, Mifflin and Company, 1889.

Kernahan, Coulson. "A Half-Made Poet." *London Quarterly Review* 73 (1889): 27–35.

Richardson, Charles. "Emerson as Poet" in *American Literature, 1607–1885*. Vol. 2. New York: Putnams, 1889: 137–71.

Robertson, John M. *Modern Humanists: Sociological Studies of Carlyle, Mill, Emerson, Arnold, Ruskin, and Spencer with an Epilogue on Social Reconstruction*. London: Swan Sonnenschein, 1891.

Stearns, Frank. "Emerson as Poet." *Unitarian Review* 36 (1891): 259–70.

Hale, Edward Everett. *Ralph Waldo Emerson*. Boston: J. Stillman Smith, 1893.

Chapman, John Jay. "Emerson, or Sixty Years After." *Atlantic Monthly* 79 (January and February 1897): 27–41; 222–40. Reprinted in *Emerson, and Other Essays*. New York: Charles Scribner's Sons, 1898.

Pleasant Hours with American Authors. Philadelphia: American Book and Bible House, 1898.

Tappan, Eva March, editor. *Select Essays and Poems of Ralph Waldo Emerson*. Boston: Allyn and Bacon, 1898.

Malloy, Charles. "The Poems of Emerson." *The Coming Age* 1–4 (January 1899–August 1900).

Santayana, George. "Emerson" in *Interpretations of Poetry and Religion*. New York: Charles Scribner's Sons, 1900.

Wendell, Barrett. "Ralph Waldo Emerson" in *A Literary History of America*. New York: Scribners, 1900: 311–27.

Anon. "The Emasculation of Emerson." *Ethical Record* 4 (1903): 189–91.

The Centenary of the Birth of Ralph Waldo Emerson. Boston: Riverside Press, 1903.

Dewey, John. "Emerson — The Philosopher of Democracy." *International Journal of Ethics* XIII: 4 (July 1903): 405–13.

Emerson, Edward Waldo. Speech at the Concord Centenary Celebration in *The Centenary of the Birth of Ralph Waldo Emerson*. Boston: Riverside Press, 1903: 119–27.

Hazard, Caroline. Speech at the Concord Centenary Celebration in *The Centenary of the Birth of Ralph Waldo Emerson*. Boston: Riverside Press, 1903: 99–103.

Higginson, Thomas Wentworth. Address at the Concord Centenary Celebration in *The Centenary of the Birth of Ralph Waldo Emerson*. Boston: Riverside Press, 1903: 58–66.

James, William. Address at the Concord Centenary Celebration in *The Centenary of the Birth of Ralph Waldo Emerson*. Boston: Riverside Press, 1903: 67–77.

Norton, Charles Eliot. Address at the Concord Centenary Celebration in *The Centenary of the Birth of Ralph Waldo Emerson*. Boston: Riverside Press, 1903: 45–57.

Sanborn, Frank. *The Personality of Emerson*. Boston: Charles E. Goodspeed, 1903.

Santayana, George. "Emerson's Poems Proclaim the Divinity of Nature, with Freedom as his Profoundest Ideal." "Special Emerson Supplement." Boston *Daily Advertiser* (23 May 1903). Reprinted in *George Santayana's America*. James Ballowe, editor. Urbana: University of Illinois Press, 1967: 85–96.

Storey, Moorfield. Speech at the Concord Centenary Celebration in *The Centenary of the Birth of Ralph Waldo Emerson*. Boston: Riverside Press, 1903: 104–10.

Cary, Elisabeth Luther. *Emerson: Poet and Thinker*. New York: G. P. Putnam's Sons, 1904.

Malloy, Charles. "The Poems of Emerson." *The Arena* 31–33 (February 1904–March 1905).

More, Paul Elmer. "The Influence of Emerson" in *Shelburne Essays*, First Series. Boston: Houghton, Mifflin and Company, 1904: 71–84.

Carman, Bliss. "Emerson" in *The Poetry of Life*. Boston: L. C. Page, 1905: 151–58.

Peck, Harvey Whitfield. "Emerson's 'Brahma'; or, the Poet-Philosopher in the Presence of the Deity." *Arena* 33 (April 1905): 375–76.

Dugard, Marie. *Ralph Waldo Emerson, sa vie et son oeuvre.* Paris: A. Colin, 1907.

Woodberry, George Edward. *Ralph Waldo Emerson.* New York: Macmillan Company, 1907.

Babbitt, Irving. *Masters of Modern French Criticism.* Boston: Houghton Mifflin, 1912.

Perry, Bliss. *The Heart of Emerson's Essays.* Boston: Houghton Mifflin, 1914.

Firkins, O. W. *Ralph Waldo Emerson.* Boston: Houghton, Mifflin and Company, 1915.

Gray, Henry David. *Emerson: A Statement of New England Transcendentalism as Expressed in the Philosophy of Its Chief Exponent.* Stanford: Stanford University Press, 1917.

More, Paul Elmer. "Emerson" in *The Cambridge History of American Literature.* William Peterfield Trent, et al., editors. 3 vols. New York: Macmillan, 1917: 349–62.

Eliot, T. S. "American Literature" (review of the *Cambridge History of American Literature* vol. 2). *Athenaeum* 4643 (25 April 1919): 236–37.

Mencken, H. L. "An Unheeded Law-Giver" in *Prejudices,* First Series. New York: Alfred A. Knopf, 1919: 191–94.

Moravsky, Maria. "The Idol of Compensation." *The Nation* 108: 2817 (28 June 1919): 1004–05.

Ives, Charles. *Essays Before a Sonata.* New York: Knickerbocker Press, 1920.

Mencken, H. L. "The National Letters" in *Prejudices,* Second Series. New York: Alfred A. Knopf, 1920: 9–101.

Crothers, Samuel McChord. *Emerson: How To Know Him.* Indianapolis: Bobbs-Merrill Company, 1921.

Sherman, Stuart P. "The Emersonian Liberation" in *Americans.* New York: Charles Scribner's Sons, 1922.

———, editor. *Essays and Poems of Emerson.* 1921.

Yeats, William Butler. *The Trembling of the Veil.* London: T. Werner Laurie, 1922.

Foerster, Norman. "Emerson on the Organic Principle of Art." PMLA 41 (1926): 193–208.

Perry, Bliss. *The Heart of Emerson's Journals.* Boston: Houghton Mifflin, 1926.

———, editor. *Selections from the Prose Works of Ralph Waldo Emerson.* Boston: Houghton, Mifflin, 1926.

Parrington, Vernon L. *Main Currents In American Thought: An Interpretation of American Literature.* 3 vols. New York: Harcourt, Brace and World, 1927–1930.

Brooks, Van Wyck. *Emerson and Others.* New York: E. P. Dutton and Company, 1927.

Hazard, Lucy Lockwood. *The Frontier in American Literature.* New York: Thomas Y. Crowell Company, 1927.

Warren, Robert Penn. "Hawthorne, Anderson and Frost." *New Republic* 54 (1928): 399–401.

Carpenter, Frederic Ives. "Points of Comparison between Emerson and William James." *New England Quarterly* 2 (1929): 458–74.

Kreymborg, Alfred. *Our Singing Strength: An Outline of American Poetry, 1620–1930.* New York: Coward-McCann, 1929.

Adams, James Truslow. "Emerson Re-Read." *Atlantic Monthly* 146 (1930): 484–92.

Carpenter, Frederic Ives. *Emerson and Asia.* Cambridge: Harvard University Press, 1930.

Firkins, O. W. "Has Emerson a Future?" *Modern Language Notes* 45 (1930): 491–500.

Clark, Harry Hayden. "Emerson and Science." *Philological Quarterly* 10 (1931): 225–60.

Marchand, Ernest. "Emerson and the Frontier." *American Literature* 3 (1931): 149–74.

Perry, Bliss. *Emerson Today.* Princeton: Princeton University Press, 1931.

Brooks, Van Wyck. *The Life of Emerson.* New York: E. P. Dutton and Company, 1932.

Calverton, V. F. *The Liberation of American Literature.* New York: Charles Scribner's Sons, 1932.

Christy, Arthur. *The Orient in American Transcendentalism: A Study of Emerson, Thoreau and Alcott.* New York: Columbia University Press, 1932.

Lewisohn, Ludwig. *Expression in America.* New York: Harpers, 1932.

Hicks, Granville. *The Great Tradition: An Interpretation of American Literature since the Civil War.* New York: International Publishers, 1933.

Rusk, Ralph. Review of *The Life of Emerson* by Van Wyck Brooks. *American Literature* 5:1 (March 1933): 70–72.

Beach, Joseph Warren. "Emerson and Evolution." *University of Toronto Quarterly* 3 (1934): 474–97.

Allen, Gay Wilson. *American Prosody.* New York: American Book Company, 1935.

Dillaway, Newton. *Prophet of America: Emerson and the Problems of To-Day.* Boston: Little, Brown, and Company, 1936.

Scudder, Townsend. *The Lonely Wayfaring Man: Emerson and Some Englishmen.* New York: Oxford University Press, 1936.

Tate, Allen. *Reactionary Essays.* New York: Scribners, 1936.

Winters, Yvor. "Jones Very and R. W. Emerson: Aspects of New England Mysticism" in *In Defense of Reason.* Chicago: The Swallow Press, 1937: 262–82.

Winters, Yvor. "The Significance of *The Bridge,* by Hart Crane Or What Are We to Think of Professor X?" in *In Defense of Reason.* Chicago: The Swallow Press, 1937: 577–603.

Wright, Frank Lloyd and Baker Brownell. *Architecture and Modern Life.* New York: Harper and Brothers, 1937.

Tolles, Frederick B. "Emerson and Quakerism." *American Literature* 10 (1938): 142–65.

Carpenter, Frederic. "William James and Emerson." *American Literature* 11 (1939): 39–57.

Smith, Henry Nash. "Emerson's Problem of Vocation — A Note on 'The American Scholar.'" *The New England Quarterly* 22 (1939): 52–67.

Kern, Alexander. "Emerson and Economics." *New England Quarterly* 13 (December 1940): 678–96.

Miller, Perry. "From Edwards to Emerson." *New England Quarterly* 13 (1940): 589–617.

Matthiessen, F. O. *American Renaissance: Art and Expression in the Age of Emerson and Whitman.* New York: Oxford University Press, 1941.

Young, Charles Lowell. *Emerson's Montaigne.* New York: The Macmillan Company, 1941.

Pochmann, H. A. "The Emerson Canon." *University of Toronto Quarterly* 12 (1943): 478–84.

Blair, Walter and Clarence Faust. "Emerson's Literary Method." *Modern Philology* 42 (1944): 79–95.

Santayana, George. *Persons and Places.* New York: Charles Scribners Sons, 1944.

Stratton, Clarence. "Emerson's Rhymes." *Word Study* 20 (December 1944): 3–4.

Kadison, Isabel. "Emerson Followed Webster." *Word Study* 20 (April 1945): 8.

Mabbott, Thomas. "Emerson Rhymes." *Word Study* 20 (April 1945): 7–8.

McEuen, Kathryn. "Emerson's Rhymes." *American Literature* 20 (1948): 31–42.

Rusk, Ralph. *The Life of Ralph Waldo Emerson.* New York: Scribners, 1949.

Aaron, Daniel. *Men of Good Hope.* New York: Oxford University Press, 1951.

Hopkins, Vivian C. *Spires of Form: A Study of Emerson's Aesthetic Theory.* Cambridge, MA: Harvard University Press, 1951.

Paul, Sherman. *Emerson's Angle of Vision: Man and Nature in the American Experience.* Cambridge, MA: Harvard University Press, 1952.

Carpenter, Frederic Ives. *Emerson Handbook.* New York: Hendricks House, 1953.

Feidelson, Charles, Jr. *Symbolism in American Literature.* Chicago: University of Chicago Press, 1953.

Miller, Perry. "Emersonian Genius and the American Democracy." *New England Quarterly* 26 (1953): 27–44.

Whicher, Stephen. *Freedom and Fate: An Inner Life of Ralph Waldo Emerson.* Philadelphia: University of Pennsylvania Press, 1953.

Adams, Richard P. "Emerson and the Organic Metaphor." *PMLA* 69 (March 1954): 117–30.

Gross, Seymour. "Emerson and Poetry." *South Atlantic Quarterly* 54 (1955): 82–94.

Cameron, Kenneth Walter. "History and Biography in Emerson's Unpublished Sermons." *Proceedings of the American Antiquarian Society* n.s. 66 (1956): 103–18.

Whicher, Stephen. *Selections from Ralph Waldo Emerson: An Organic Anthology.* Boston: Houghton Mifflin Company, 1957.

Arvin, Newton. "The House of Pain and the Tragic Sense." *The Hudson Review* 12 (1959): 37–53.

Kleinfield, H. L. "The Structure of Emerson's Death." *Bulletin of the New York Public Library* 65 (January 1961): 47–64.

Nicoloff, Philip. *Emerson on Race and History: An Examination of English Traits.* New York: Columbia University Press, 1961.

Konvitz, Milton R. and Whicher, Stephen E. *Emerson: A Collection of Critical Essays.* Englewood Cliffs, NJ: Prentice Hall, 1962.

Spiller, Robert. "From Lecture to Essay: Emerson's Method of Composition." *The Literary Criterion* 5: 3 (1962): 28–38.

American Literary Scholarship. Durham, NC: Duke University Press, 1963–.

Baumgartner, A. M. "'The Lyceum is My Pulpit': Homiletics in Emerson's Early Lectures." *American Literature* 34 (1963): 477–86.

Bishop, Jonathan. *Emerson on the Soul.* Cambridge, MA: Harvard University Press, 1964.

Gonnaud, Maurice. *Individu et societe dans l'oeuvre de Ralph Waldo Emerson: Essai de biographie spirituelle.* Paris: Didier, 1964.

Hubbell, Jay. *South and Southwest: Literary Essays and Reminiscences.* Durham, NC: Duke University Press, 1965.

Porte, Joel. *Emerson and Thoreau: Transcendentalists in Conflict.* Middletown, CT: Wesleyan University Press, 1965.

Tanner, Tony. *The Reign of Wonder, Naivety and Reality in American Literature.* New York: Cambridge University Press, 1965.

Burke, Kenneth. "I, Eye, Ay: Emerson's Early Essay on Nature: Thoughts on the Machinery of Transcendence." *Sewanee Review* 74 (1966): 875–95.

Poirier, Richard. *A World Elsewhere: The Place of Style in American Literature.* New York: Oxford University Press, 1966.

Sowder, William J. *Emerson's Impact on the British Isles and Canada.* Charlottesville: University of Virginia Press, 1966.

Irie, Yukio. *Emerson and Quakerism.* Tokyo: Kenkyusha, 1967.

Pommer, Henry F. *Emerson's First Marriage.* Carbondale, IL: Southern Illinois University Press, 1967.

Sebouhian, George. "Emerson's 'Experience': An Approach to Contrast and Method." *ESQ: A Journal of the American Renaissance* 47 (1967): 75–78.

Strauch, Carl. "Emerson and the Doctrine of Sympathy." *Studies in Romanticism* 6 (1967): 152–74.

Bode, Carl. *Ralph Waldo Emerson: A Profile.* New York: Hill and Wang, 1968.

Conkin, Paul K. *Puritans and Pragmatists: Eight Eminent American Thinkers.* New York: Dodd, Mead, 1968.

Liebman, Sheldon W. "Emerson's Transformation in the 1820s." *American Literature* 40 (1968): 133–54.

Sowder, William. *Emerson's Reviewers and Commentators.* Hartford, CT: Transcendental Books, 1968.

Waggoner, Hyatt. *American Poets from the Puritans to the Present.* Boston: Houghton Mifflin, 1968.

Adams, Richard P. "The Basic Contradiction in Emerson." *ESQ: A Journal of the American Renaissance* 55 (1969): 106–10.

Strauch, Carl. "Emerson's Use of the Organic Method." *ESQ: A Journal of the American Renaissance* 55 (1969): 18–24.

Yoder, Ralph. "Emerson's Dialectic." *Criticism* 11 (1969): 313–28.

Sealts, Merton M., Jr. and Alfred R. Ferguson. *Emerson's Nature: Origin, Growth, Meaning.* New York: Dodd, Mead, 1969.

Bier, Jesse. "Weberism, Franklin, and the Transcendental Style." *New England Quarterly* 43 (1970): 179–92.

Mead, David, editor. *The American Scholar Today: Emerson's Essay and Some Critical Views.* New York: Dodd, Mead, 1970.

Neufeldt, Leonard. "The Severity of the Ideal: Emerson's 'Thoreau.'" *ESQ: A Journal Of The American Renaissance* 58: 77–84.

Sealts, Merton M., Jr. "Emerson on the Scholar, 1833–37." *PMLA* 85 (1970): 185–95.

Strauch, Carl. "The Mind's Voice: Emerson's Poetic Styles." *ESQ: A Journal Of The American Renaissance* 60 (1970): 43–59.

Anderson, John Q. *The Liberating Gods: Emerson on Poets and Poetry.* Coral Cables, FL: University of Miami Press, 1971.

Anderson, Quentin. *The Imperial Self: An Essay in American Literary and Cultural History.* New York: Knopf, 1971.

Barton, William B. "Emerson's Method as a Philosopher" in *Emerson's Relevance Today.* Eric W. Carlson and J. Lasley Dameron, editors. Hartford, CT: Transcendental Books, 1971: 20–28.

Bloom, Harold. *The Ringers in the Tower: Studies in the American Romantic Tradition.* Chicago: University of Chicago Press, 1971.

Carlson, Eric W. and J. Lasley Dameron, editors. *Emerson's Relevance Today.* Hartford, CT: Transcendental Books, 1971.

LaRosa, Ralph C. "Emerson's Search for Literary Form: The Early Journals." *Modern Prose* 69 (1971): 25–35.

Neufeldt, Leonard. "The Vital Mind: Emerson's Epistemology." *Philological Quarterly* 50 (1971): 253–70.

Buell, Lawrence. "Reading Emerson for the Structures: The Coherence of the Essays." *Quarterly Journal of Speech* 58 (1972): 58–69.

Cavell, Stanley. *The Senses of Walden.* New York: Viking Press, 1972.

Essays, First Series: Emerson's Strategies of Rhetoric. ESQ: A Journal Of The American Renaissance 18: 4 (1972).

Hubbell, Jay B. *Who Are the Major American Writers.* Durham, NC: Duke University Press, 1972.

Konvitz, Milton R. *The Recognition of Ralph Waldo Emerson: Selected Criticism Since 1837.* Ann Arbor: University of Michigan Press, 1972.

Rovit, Earl. "Emerson: A Contemporary Reconsideration." *American Scholar* 41 (1972): 429–38.

Wood, Ann Douglas. "Reconsiderations — Ralph Waldo Emerson." *New Republic* 1 & 8 (January 1972): 27–29.

Bloom, Harold. *The Anxiety of Influence: A Theory of Poetry.* New York: Oxford University Press, 1973.

Buell, Lawrence. *Literary Transcendentalism: Style and Vision in the American Renaissance.* Ithaca: Cornell University Press, 1973.

Cameron, Kenneth Walter, editor. *A Study of Emerson's Major Poems*. Hartford, CT: Transcendental Books, 1973 (articles by Charles Malloy, 1900–1905).

Duncan, Jeffrey L. *The Power and Form of Emerson's Thought*. Charlottesville: University of Virginia Press, 1973.

Neufeldt, Leonard, editor. *Ralph Waldo Emerson: New Appraisals: A Symposium*. Hartford, CT: Transcendental Books, 1973.

Rountree, Thomas, editor. *Critics on Emerson*. Coral Gables, Fl.: University of Miami Press, 1973.

Stapleton, Laurence. *The Elected Circle: Studies in the Art of Prose*. Princeton, NJ: Princeton University Press, 1973.

Waggoner, Hyatt H. *Emerson as Poet*. Princeton: Princeton University Press, 1974.

Allen, Gay Wilson. "A New Look at Emerson and Science" in *Literature and Ideas in America: Essays in Memory of Harry Hayden Clark*. Robert Falk, editor. Athens: Ohio University Press, 1975: 58–78.

Bercovitch, Sacvan. "Emerson the Prophet: Romanticism, Puritanism, and Auto-American-Biography" in *Emerson: Prophecy, Metamorphosis, and Influence*. David Levin, editor. New York: Columbia University Press, 1975: 1–28.

———. *The Puritan Origins of the American Self*. New Haven, CT: Yale University Press, 1975.

Bloom, Harold. "The Freshness of Transformation: Emerson's Dialectics of Influence" in *Emerson: Prophecy, Metamorphosis, and Influence*. David Levin, editor. New York: Columbia University Press, 1975: 129–48.

———. *A Map of Misreading*. New York: Oxford University Press, 1975.

Cole, Phyllis. "Emerson, England, and Fate" in *Emerson: Prophecy, Metamorphosis, and Influence*. David Levin, editor. New York: Columbia University Press, 1975: 83–106.

Cox, James. "R. W. Emerson: The Circles of the Eye" in *Emerson: Prophecy, Metamorphosis, and Influence*. David Levin, editor. New York: Columbia University Press, 1975: 57–82.

Gelpi, Albert. "Emerson: The Paradox of Organic Form" in *Emerson: Prophecy, Metamorphosis, and Influence*. David Levin, editor. New York: Columbia University Press, 1975: 149–70.

Gonnaud, Maurice. "Emerson and the Imperial Self: A European Critique" in *Emerson: Prophecy, Metamorphosis, and Influence*. David Levin, editor. New York: Columbia University Press, 1975: 107–28.

Levin, David, editor. *Emerson: Prophecy, Metamorphosis, and Influence*. New York: Columbia University Press, 1975.

Sealts, Merton M., Jr. "Emerson on the Scholar, 1838: A Study of 'Literary Ethics'" in *Literature and Ideas in America: Essays in Memory of Harry Hayden Clark*. Robert Falk, editor. Athens: Ohio University Press, 1975: 40–57.

Shea, Daniel B. "Emerson and the American Metamorphosis" in *Emerson: Prophecy, Metamorphosis, and Influence*. David Levin, editor. New York: Columbia University Press, 1975: 29–56.

Strauch, Carl, editor. *Characteristics of Emerson, Transcendental Poet: A Symposium*. Hartford, CT: Transcendental Books, 1975.

Bloom, Harold. *Figures of Capable Imagination*. New York: Seabury Press, 1976.

———. *Poetry and Repression: Revisionism from Blake to Stevens*. New Haven, CT: Yale University Press, 1976.

Leary, Lewis. "The Maneuverings of a Transcendental Mind: Emerson's *Essays* of 1841." *Prospects* 3 (1977): 499–520.

Neufeldt, Leonard. "The Science of Power: Emerson's Views on Science and Technology." *Journal of the History of Ideas* 38 (1977): 329–44.

Robinson, David. "Children of the Fire: Charles Ives on Emerson and Art." *American Literature* 48 (1977): 564–76.

Harris, Kenneth Marc. *Emerson and Carlyle: Their Long Debate*. Cambridge, MA: Harvard University Press, 1978.

Porter, David. *Emerson and Literary Change*. Cambridge, MA: Harvard University Press, 1978.

Richardson, Robert D. Jr. *Myth and Literature of the American Renaissance*. Bloomington: Indiana University Press, 1978.

Sheick, William J. *The Slender Human Word: Emerson's Artistry in Prose*. Knoxville: University of Tennessee Press, 1978.

Yoder, R. A. *Emerson and The Orphic Poet in America*. Berkeley: University of California Press, 1978.

Cavell, Stanley. "Thinking of Emerson." *New Literary History* 11: 1 (Autumn 1979): 167–76.

Gura, Philip. "Emerson in Our Time." *New England Quarterly* 52 (1979): 407–13.

Packer, Barbara. "The Instructed Eye: Emerson's Cosmogony in 'Prospects'" in *Emerson's "Nature" — Origin, Growth, Meaning*. Merton M. Sealts, Jr. and Alfred R. Ferguson, editors. Expanded Edition. Carbondale: University of Southern Illinois Press, 1979: 209–21.

Porte, Joel. *Representative Man: Ralph Waldo Emerson in His Time*. New York: Oxford University Press, 1979.

Ronda, Bruce. "Literary Grieving: Emerson and the Death of Waldo." *Centennial Review* 23 (1979): 91–104.

Sealts, Merton M., Jr. and Alfred R. Ferguson. *Emerson's Nature: Origin, Growth, Meaning.* Enlarged edition. Carbondale: Southern Illinois University Press, 1979.

Irwin, John T. *American Hieroglyphics: The Symbol of the Egyptian Hieroglyphic in the American Renaissance.* New Haven: Yale University Press, 1980.

Lowance, Mason I., Jr. *The Language of Canaan: Metaphor and Symbol in New England from the Puritans to the Transcendentalists.* Cambridge, MA: Harvard University Press, 1980.

Robinson, David. "Emerson's Natural Theology and the Paris Naturalists: Toward a Theory of Animated Nature." *Journal of the History of Ideas* 41 (1980): 69–88.

Allen, Gay Wilson. *Waldo Emerson.* New York: Penguin Books, 1981.

Cavell, Stanley. *The Senses of Walden: An Expanded Edition.* Includes "Thinking of Emerson" and "An Emerson Mood." San Francisco: North Point Press, 1981.

Cheyfitz, Eric. *The Trans-Parent: Sexual Politics in the Language of Emerson.* Baltimore, MD.: The Johns Hopkins University Press, 1981.

Giamatti, A. Bartlett. "Power, Politics and a Sense of History." Yale Baccalaureate Address, 1981 printed in *The University and the Public Interest.* New York: Atheneum, 1981: 166–79.

Gura, Philip F. *The Wisdom of Words: Language, Theology, and Literature in the New England Renaissance.* Middletown, CT: Wesleyan University Press, 1981.

Porter, Carolyn. *Seeing and Being: The Plight of the Participant Observer in Emerson, James, Adams and Faulkner.* Middletown, CT: Wesleyan University Press, 1981.

Tuerk, Richard. "Mythic Patterns of Reconciliation in Emerson's 'Threnody.'" *ESQ: A Journal Of The American Renaissance* 27 (1981): 181–88.

Bloom, Harold. *Agon: Towards a Theory of Romanticism.* New York: Oxford University Press, 1982.

———. *The Breaking of the Vessels.* Chicago: University of Chicago Press, 1982.

Burkholder, Robert E. "The Contemporary Reception of *English Traits*" in *Emerson Centenary Essays.* Joel Myerson, editor. Carbondale: Southern Illinois University Press, 1982: 156–72.

Cole, Phyllis. "The Advantage of Loneliness: Mary Moody Emerson's Almanacks, 1802–1855" in *Emerson: Prospect and Retrospect.* Joel Porte, editor. Cambridge, MA: Harvard University Press, 1982: 1–32.

Francis, Richard Lee. "The Poet and Experience: *Essays: Second Series*" in *Emerson Centenary Essays*. Joel Myerson, editor. Carbondale: Southern Illinois University Press, 1982: 93–106.

Gass, William. "Emerson and the Essay." *Yale Review* 71 (1982): 321–62.

Gilmore, Michael. "Emerson and the Persistence of the Commodity" in *Emerson: Prospect and Retrospect*. Joel Porte, editor. Cambridge, MA: Harvard University Press, 1982: 65–84.

Harris, Kenneth Marc. "Emerson's Second Nature" in *Emerson: Prospect and Retrospect*. Joel Porte, editor. Cambridge, MA: Harvard University Press, 1982: 33–48.

Hill, David. "Emerson's Eumenides: Textual Evidence and the Interpretation of 'Experience'" in *Emerson Centenary Essays*. Joel Myerson, editor. Carbondale: Southern Illinois University Press, 1982: 107–21.

Johnson, Glen M. "Emerson on 'Making' in Literature: His Problem of Professionalism, 1836–1841" in *Emerson Centenary Essays*. Joel Myerson, editor. Carbondale: Southern Illinois University Press, 1982: 65–73.

Jones, Joseph. "Thought's New-Found Path and the Wilderness: 'The Adirondacs'" in *Emerson: Prospect and Retrospect*. Joel Porte, editor. Cambridge, MA: Harvard University Press, 1982: 105–20.

Levine, Stuart. "Emerson and Modern Social Concepts" in *Emerson: Prospect and Retrospect*. Joel Porte, editor. Cambridge, MA: Harvard University Press, 1982: 155–78.

Loving, Jerome. *Emerson, Whitman and the American Muse*. Chapel Hill: University of North Carolina Press, 1982.

Marovitz, Sanford. "Emerson's Shakespeare: From Scorn to Apotheosis" in *Emerson Centenary Essays*. Joel Myerson, editor. Carbondale: Southern Illinois University Press, 1982: 122–55.

Myerson, Joel, editor. *Emerson Centenary Essays*. Carbondale: Southern Illinois University Press, 1982.

Neufeldt, Leonard. *The House of Emerson*. Lincoln: University of Nebraska Press, 1982.

Packer, B. L. *Emerson's Fall: A New Interpretation of the Major Essays*. New York: Continuum Publishing Company, 1982.

Porte, Joel, editor. *Emerson: Prospect and Retrospect*. Cambridge, MA.: Harvard University Press, 1982.

Richardson, Robert D., Jr. "Emerson on History" in *Emerson: Prospect and Retrospect*. Joel Porte, editor. Cambridge, MA: Harvard University Press, 1982: 49–64.

Robinson, David. *Apostle of Culture: Emerson as Preacher and Lecturer*. Philadelphia: University of Pennsylvania Press, 1982.

————. "'The Method of Nature' and Emerson's Period of Crisis" in *Emerson Centenary Essays*. Joel Myerson, editor. Carbondale: Southern Illinois University Press, 1982: 74–92.

Steele, Jeffrey. "Interpreting the Self: Emerson and the Unconscious" in *Emerson: Prospect and Retrospect*. Joel Porte, editor. Cambridge, MA: Harvard University Press, 1982: 85–104.

Sudol, Ronald. "'The Adirondacs' and Technology" in *Emerson Centenary Essays*. Joel Myerson, editor. Carbondale: Southern Illinois University Press, 1982: 173–79.

Alexander, Floyce. "Emerson and the Cherokee Removal." *ESQ: A Journal Of The American Renaissance* 29 (1983): 127–37.

Burkholder, Robert E. and Joel Myerson, editors. *Critical Essays on Ralph Waldo Emerson*. Boston: G. K. Hall, 1983.

Cavell, Stanley. "Genteel Responses to Kant? In Emerson's 'Fate' and Coleridge's *Biographia Literaria*." *Raritan* 3 (Fall 1983): 34–61.

Friedl, Herwig. "Mysticism and Thinking in Ralph Waldo Emerson." *American Studies* 28 (1983): 33–46.

Hagenbuchle, Roland. "Spontaneity and Form: Unresolved Tensions in American Transcendentalism." *American Studies* 28 (1983): 11–33.

Lang, Amy Schrager. "'The Age of the First Person Singular': Emerson and Antinomianism." ESQ*: A Journal of the American Renaissance* 29 (1983): 171–83.

Myerson, Joel. "An Emerson Celebration." *New England Quarterly* 56 (1983): 275–83.

Peacock, John. "Self-Reliance and Corporate Destiny: Emerson's Dialectic of Culture." *ESQ: A Journal Of The American Renaissance* 29 (1983): 59–72.

Simmons, Nancy Craig. "Arranging the Sibylline Leaves: James Elliot Cabot's Work as Emerson's Literary Executor." *Studies in the American Renaissance* (1983): 335–89.

Barish, Evelyn. "The Angel of Midnight: The Legacy of Mary Moody Emerson" in *Mothering the Mind: Twelve Studies of Writers and their Silent Partners*. New York: Holmes and Meier, 1984: 218–37.

Baym, Nina. *Novels, Readers and Reviewers: Responses to Fiction in Antebellum America*. Ithaca: Cornell University Press, 1984.

Buell, Lawrence. "The Emerson Industry in the 1980s: A Survey of Trends and Achievements." *ESQ: A Journal Of The American Renaissance* 30 (1984): 117–36.

Cascardi, A. J. "Emerson on Nature: Philosophy Beyond Kant." *ESQ: A Journal Of The American Renaissance* 30 (1984): 201–10.

Ellison, Julie. "Aggressive Allegory." *Raritan* 3 (1984): 100–115.

———. *Emerson's Romantic Style.* Princeton: Princeton University Press, 1984.

———. "The Laws of Ice: Emerson's Irony and 'The Comic.'" *ESQ: A Journal Of The American Renaissance* 30 (1984): 73–82.

Hughes, Gertrude Reif. *Emerson's Demanding Optimism.* Baton Rouge: Louisiana State University Press, 1984.

Loewenberg, Robert J. *An American Idol: Emerson and the "Jewish Idea".* Lanham, MD.: University Press of America, 1984.

McAleer, John. *Ralph Waldo Emerson: Days of Encounter.* Boston: Little, Brown, 1984.

Myerson, Joel, editor. *The Transcendentalists: A Review of Research and Criticism.* New York: Modern Language Association, 1984.

Smith, David L. "The End(s) of Scholarship." *Soundings* 67 (1984): 379–98.

Warren, Joyce. *The American Narcissus: Individualism and Women in Nineteenth-Century Fiction.* New Brunswick, NJ: Rutgers University Press, 1984.

Bloom, Harold, editor. *Ralph Waldo Emerson.* New York: Chelsea House, 1985.

Burkholder, Robert E. and Joel Myerson, editors. *Emerson : An Annotated Secondary Bibliography.* Pittsburgh: University of Pittsburgh Press, 1985.

Carton, Evan. *The Rhetoric of American Romance: Dialectic and Identity in Emerson, Dickinson, Poe and Hawthorne.* Baltimore: Johns Hopkins University Press, 1985.

Cascardi, A. J. "The Logic of Moods: An Essay on Emerson and Rousseau." *Studies in Romanticism* 24 (1985): 223–37.

Gilmore, Michael. *American Romanticism and the Marketplace.* Chicago: University of Chicago Press, 1985.

Greenberg, Robert M. "Shooting the Gulf: Emerson's Sense of Experience." *ESQ: A Journal Of The American Renaissance* 31 (1985): 211–29.

Grusin, Richard. "'Monadnoc': Emerson's Quotidian Apocalypse." *ESQ: A Journal Of The American Renaissance* 31 (1985): 149–63.

Patterson, Mark. "Emerson, Napoleon, and the Concept of the Representative." *ESQ: A Journal Of The American Renaissance* 31 (1985): 230–42.

Buell, Lawrence. *New England Literary Culture from Revolution through Renaissance.* New York: Cambridge University Press, 1986.

Cameron, Kenneth Walter. *The Emerson Tertiary Bibliography.* Hartford, CT: Transcendental Books, 1986.

Cameron, Sharon. "Representing Grief: Emerson's 'Experience.'" *Representations* 15 (Summer 1986): 15–41.

Carafiol, Peter. "Reading Emerson: Writing History." *Centennial Review* 30 (1986): 431–51.

Cavell, Stanley. "Being Odd, Getting Even: Threats to Individuality" in *Reconstructing Individualism: Autonomy, Individuality, and the Self in Western Thought*. Thomas C. Heller, editor. Stanford: Stanford University Press, 1986: 278–312.

Chmaj, Betty. "The Journey and the Mirror: Emerson and the American Arts." *Prospects* 10 (1986): 353–408.

Donadio, Stephen, Stephen Railton and Ormond Seavey, editors. *Emerson and His Legacy: Essays in Honor of Quentin Anderson*. Carbondale: Southern Illinois University Press, 1986.

Ellison, Julie. "The Edge of Urbanity: Emerson's *English Traits*." *ESQ: A Journal Of The American Renaissance* 32 (1986): 96–109.

Howe, Irving. *The American Newness: Culture and Politics in the Age of Emerson*. Cambridge, MA: Harvard University Press, 1986.

Packer, Barbara. "Origin and Authority: Emerson and the Higher Criticism" in *Reconstructing American Literary History*. Sacvan Bercovitch, editor. Cambridge, MA: Harvard University Press, 1986: 67–92.

Richardson, Robert. *Henry Thoreau: A Life of the Mind*. Berkeley: University of California Press, 1986.

Van Leer, David. *Emerson's Epistemology: The Argument of the Essays*. New York: Cambridge University Press, 1986.

Weisbuch, Robert. *Atlantic Double-Cross: American Literature and British Influence in the Age of Emerson*. Chicago: University of Chicago Press, 1986.

Chai, Leon. *The Romantic Foundations of the American Renaissance*. Ithaca: Cornell University Press, 1987.

Colacurcio, Michael. "The Corn and the Wine: Emerson and the Example of Herbert." *Nineteenth Century Literature* 42 (1987): 1–28.

Edmundson, Mark. "Emerson and the Work of Melancholia." *Raritan* 6 (1987): 120–36.

Friedl, Herwig. "Emerson and Nietzsche, 1862–1874." *Religion and Philosophy* 1 (1987): 267–88.

Gonnaud, Maurice. *An Uneasy Solitude: Individual and Society in the Work of Ralph Waldo Emerson*. Lawrence Rosenwald, translator. Princeton: Princeton University Press, 1987.

Goodman, Russell. "Freedom in the Philosophy of Ralph Waldo Emerson." *Tulane Studies in Philosophy* 35 (1987): 5–10.

Pease, Donald. *Visionary Compacts: American Renaissance Writings in Cultural Context*. Madison, WI: University of Wisconsin Press, 1987.

Milder, Robert. "Emerson's Two Conversions." *ESQ: A Journal Of The American Renaissance* 33 (1987): 20–34.

Poirier, Richard. *The Renewal of Literature: Emersonian Reflections.* New York: Random House, 1987.

Simmons, Nancy Craig. "Philosophical Biographer: James Elliott Cabot and *A Memoir of Ralph Waldo Emerson.*" *Studies in the American Renaissance,* 1987: 365–92.

Steele, Jeffrey. *The Representation of the Self in the American Renaissance.* Chapel Hill: University of North Carolina Press, 1987.

Toulouse, Teresa. *The Art of Prophesying: New England Sermons and the Shaping of Belief.* Athens: University of Georgia Press, 1987.

Bickman, Martin. "'The Turn of His Sentences': The Open Form of *Essays, First Series.*" *ESQ: A Journal Of The American Renaissance* 34: 1–2 (1988): 59–75.

Burkholder, Robert. "The Radical Emerson: Politics in 'The American Scholar.'" *ESQ: A Journal Of The American Renaissance* 34 (1988): 37–57.

Cady, Edwin and Louis J. Budd, editors. *On Emerson: The Best from American Literature.* Durham, NC: Duke University Press, 1988.

Cavell, Stanley. *In Quest of the Ordinary: Lines of Skepticism and Romanticism.* Chicago: University of Chicago Press, 1988.

Grusin, Richard. "'Put God in Your Debt': Emerson's Economy of Expenditure." *PMLA* 103 (1988): 35–44.

Lopez, Michael. "De-Transcendentalizing Emerson." *ESQ: A Journal Of The American Renaissance.* 34: 1–2 (1988): 77–139.

Marr, David. *American Worlds Since Emerson.* Amherst: University of Massachusetts Press, 1988.

Michael, John. *Emerson and Skepticism: The Cipher of the World.* Baltimore, MD.: The Johns Hopkins University Press, 1988.

Rosenwald, Lawrence. *Emerson and the Art of the Diary.* Oxford: Oxford University Press, 1988.

Wider, Sarah Ann. "What Did the Minister Mean: Emerson's Sermons and Their Audience." *ESQ: A Journal Of The American Renaissance.* 34: 1–2 (1988): 1–22.

Barish, Evelyn. *Emerson: The Roots of Prophecy.* Princeton: Princeton University Press, 1989.

Bosco, Ronald. "'Poetry for the World of Readers' and 'Poetry for the Bards Proper': Theory and Textual Integrity in Emerson's *Parnassus.*" *Studies in the American Renaissance* (1989): 257–312.

Cavell, Stanley. *This New Yet Unapproachable America: Lectures After Emerson After Wittgenstein.* Albuquerque: Living Batch Press, 1989.

Cayton, Mary Kupiec. *Emerson's Emergence: Self and Society in the Transformation of New England, 1800–1845.* Chapel Hill: University of North Carolina Press, 1989.

Dant, Elizabeth. "Composing the World: Emerson and the Cabinet of Natural History." *Nineteenth Century Literature* 44 (1989): 18–44.

Grusin, Richard. "Revisionism and the Structure of Emersonian Action." *American Literary History* 1 (1989): 404–31.

Hodder, Alan D. *Emerson's Rhetoric of Revelation.* University Park: The Pennsylvania State University Press, 1989.

Leverenz, David. *Manhood and the American Renaissance.* Ithaca: Cornell University Press, 1989.

Mott, Wesley T. *"The Strains of Eloquence": Emerson and His Sermons.* University Park: Pennsylvania State University Press, 1989.

Sebouhian, George. "A Dialogue with Death: An Examination of Emerson's 'Friendship.'" *Studies in the American Renaissance* (1989): 219–39.

West, Cornel. *The American Evasion of Philosophy: A Genealogy of Pragmatism.* Madison, WI: University of Wisconsin Press, 1989.

Bercovitch, Sacvan. "Emerson, Individualism and the Ambiguities of Dissent." *Southern Atlantic Quarterly* 89: 3 (1990): 623–62.

Cavell, Stanley. *Conditions Handsome and Unhandsome: The Constitution of Emersonian Perfectionism.* Chicago: University of Chicago Press, 1990.

Dimock, Wai-chee. "Scarcity, Subjectivity and Emerson." *Boundary 2: An International Journal of Literature and Culture.* 17: 1 (Spring 1990): 83–99.

Goodman, Russell B. *American Philosophy and the Romantic Tradition.* New York: Cambridge University Press, 1990.

———. "East-West Philosophy in Nineteenth-Century America: Emerson and Hinduism." *Journal of the History of Ideas* 51 (1990): 625–45.

Gougeon, Len. *Virtue's Hero: Emerson, Antislavery and Reform.* Athens: University of Georgia Press, 1990.

Hansen, Olaf. *Aesthetic Individualism and Practical Intellect: American Allegory in Emerson, Thoreau, Adams, and James.* Princeton: Princeton University Press, 1990.

Reynolds, Larry J. *European Revolutions and the American Literary Renaissance.* New Haven, CT: Yale University Press, 1990.

Van Cromphout, Gustaaf. *Emerson's Modernity and the Example of Goethe.* Columbia: University of Missouri Press, 1990.

Cavell, Stanley. "Aversive Thinking: Emersonian Representations in Heidegger and Nietzsche." *New Literary History* 22 (Winter 1991): 129–60.

Colacurcio, Michael J. "'Pleasing God': The Lucid Strife of Emerson's 'Address.'" *ESQ: A Journal Of The American Renaissance* 37 (1991): 141–212.

Grusin, Richard. *Transcendental Hermeneutics: Institutional Authority and the Higher Criticism of the Bible.* Durham, NC: Duke University Press, 1991.

Hodder, Alan C. "'After a High Negative Way': Emerson's 'Self-Reliance' and the Rhetoric of Conversion." *Harvard Theological Review* 84 (1991): 423–46.

Johnson, Linck C. "Reforming the Reformers: Emerson, Thoreau and the Sunday Lectures at Amory Hall, Boston." *ESQ: A Journal of the American Renaissance* 37 (1991): 235–89.

Lasch, Christopher. *The True and Only Heaven: Progess and its Critics.* New York: Norton, 1991.

Burkholder, Robert. "History's Mad Pranks: Some Recent Emerson Studies." *ESQ: A Journal Of The American Renaissance* 38 (1992): 231–63.

Coltharp, Duane. "Landscapes of Commodity: Nature as Economy in Emerson's Poems." *ESQ: A Journal Of The American Renaissance* 38 (1992): 265–91.

Elbert, Monika. "From Merlin to Faust: Emerson's Democratization of the 'Heroic Mind'" in *Merlin versus Faust: Contending Archetypes in Western Culture.* Charlotte Spivack, editor. Lewiston: E. Mellen Press, 1992.

Gustafson, Thomas. *Representative Words: Politics, Literature and the American Language, 1775–1865:* New York: Cambridge University Press, 1992.

Kateb, George. *The Inner Ocean: Individualism and Democratic Culture.* Ithaca: Cornell University Press, 1992.

Myerson, Joel. *Emerson and Thoreau: The Contemporary Reviews.* New York: Cambridge University Press, 1992.

Poirier, Richard. *Poetry and Pragmatism.* Cambridge, MA: Harvard University Press, 1992.

Robinson, David M. "Fields of Investigation: Emerson and Natural History" in *American Literature and Science.* Robert Schlock, editor. Lexington: University of Kentucky Press, 1992: 94–109.

———. "The Road Not Taken: From Edwards, Through Chauncy, to Emerson." *American Quarterly* 48: 1 (1992): 45–61.

Sealts, Merton M., Jr. *Emerson on the Scholar.* Columbia: University of Missouri Press, 1992.

———. "Emerson Then and Now." *Wisconsin Academy Review* 38 (1992): 29–32.

Stack, George. *Nietzsche and Emerson: An Elective Affinity.* Athens: Ohio University Press, 1992.

Wright, Frank Lloyd. *Collected Writings* 5 vols. Bruce Brooks Pfeiffer, editor. New York: Rizzoli, 1992–95.

Bercovitch, Sacvan. *The Rites of Assent: Transformations in the Symbolic Construction of America*. New York: Routledge, 1993.

Brantley, Richard E. *Coordinates of Anglo-American Romanticism: Wesley, Edwards, Carlyle and Emerson*. Gainsville: University Press of Florida, 1993.

Bremen, Brian A. "Du Bois, Emerson, and the 'Fate' of Black Folk." *American Literary Review* 24: 3 (1993): 80–88.

Buell, Lawrence, editor. *Ralph Waldo Emerson: A Collection of Critical Essays*. Englewood Cliffs, NJ: Prentice Hall, 1993.

Greenberg, Robert M. *Splintered Worlds: Fragmentation and the Ideal of Diversity in the Work of Emerson, Melville, Whitman and Dickinson*. Boston: Northeastern University Press, 1993.

Hertz, David Michael. *Angels of Reality: Emersonian Unfoldings in Wright, Stevens and Ives*. Carbondale: Southern Illinois University Press, 1993.

Jacobson, David. *Emerson's Pragmatic Vision: The Dance of the Eye*. University Park: Pennsylvania State University Press, 1993.

Loving, Jerome. *Lost in the Customhouse: Authorship in the American Renaissance*. Iowa City: University of Iowa Press, 1993.

Robinson, David. *Emerson and the Conduct of Life: Pragmatism and Ethical Purpose in the Later Work*. New York: Cambridge University Press, 1993.

Shklar, Judith N. "Emerson and the Inhibitions of Democracy" in *Pursuits of Reason: Essays in Honor of Stanley Cavell*. Ted Cohen and Paul Guyer, editors. Lubbock: Texas Tech University Press, 1993.

Simmons, Nancy Craig, editor. *The Selected Letters of Mary Moody Emerson*. Athens: University of Georgia Press, 1993.

Versluis, Arthur. *American Transcendentalism and Asian Religions*. New York: Oxford University Press, 1993.

Wolfe, Cary. *The Limits of American Literary Ideology in Emerson and Pound*. New York: Cambridge University Press, 1993.

Bosco, Ronald. "'What Poems Are Many Private Lives': Emerson Writing the American Plutarch." *Studies in Literary Interpretation* 27: 1 (1994): 103–29.

Burkholder, Robert and Joel Myerson, editors. *Ralph Waldo Emerson: An Annotated Bibliography of Criticism, 1980–1991*. Westport, CT: Greenwood, 1994.

Cavell, Stanley. "What is an Emersonian Event? A Comment on Kateb's Emerson." *New Literary History* 25 (1994): 951–58.

Clark, William Bedford. "In the Shadow of His Smile: Warren's Quarrel with Emerson." *SR* 102 (1994): 550–69.

Dauber, Kenneth. "On Not Being Able to Read Emerson, or 'Representative Man.'" *Boundary II* 21: 2 (1994): 220–42.

Gougeon, Len. "Holmes's Emerson and the Conservative Critique of Realism." *Southern Atlantic Review* 59: 1 (1994): 107–25.

Patell, Cyrus R. K. "Emersonian Strategies: Negative Liberty, Self-Reliance, and Democratic Individuality." *Nineteenth Century Literature* 48 (1994): 440–79.

Ryan, Barbara. "Emerson's 'Domestic and Social Experiments': Service, Slavery and the Unhired Man." *American Literature* 66 (1994): 485–508.

Von Frank, Albert J. *An Emerson Chronology.* G. K. Hall, 1994.

Wolfe, Cary. "Alone in America: Cavell, Emerson, and the Politics of Individualism." *New Literary History* 25 (1994): 137–57.

Albrecht, James. "'Living Property': Emerson's Ethics." *ESQ: A Journal Of The American Renaissance* 41 (1995): 177–217.

Cavell, Stanley. *Philosophical Passages: Wittgenstein, Emerson, Austin, Derrida.* Cambridge, MA: Blackwell, 1995.

Kateb, George. *Emerson and Self-Reliance.* Modernity and Public Thought, vol. 8. Thousand Oaks, CA: Sage Publishing, 1995.

O'Keefe, Richard. *Mythic Archetypes in Ralph Waldo Emerson: A Blakean Reading.* Kent, Ohio: Kent State University Press, 1995.

Packer, Barbara. "The Transcendentalists" in *The Cambridge History of American Literature, 1820–1865*, vol. 2. Sacvan Bercovitch, editor. New York: Cambridge University Press, 1995: 329–604.

Richardson, Robert D., Jr. *Emerson: The Mind on Fire.* Berkeley: University of California Press, 1995.

Roberson, Susan R. *Emerson in His Sermons: A Man-Made Self.* Columbia: University of Missouri Press, 1995.

Teichgraeber, Richard F. *Sublime Thoughts/Penny Wisdom: Situating Emerson and Thoreau in the American Market.* Baltimore, MD.: The Johns Hopkins University Press, 1995.

Thomas, David Wayne. "Godel's Theorem and Postmodern Theory." *PMLA* 110 (1995): 248–61.

Zwarg, Christina. *Feminist Conversations: Fuller, Emerson, and the Play of Reading.* Ithaca: Cornell University Press, 1995.

Baker, Carlos. *Emerson Among the Eccentrics: A Group Portrait.* New York: Viking Press, 1996.

Lopez, Michael. *Emerson and Power: Creative Antagonism in the Nineteenth Century.* DeKalb: Northern Illinois University Press, 1996.

Mott, Wesley, editor. *Biographical Dictionary of Transcendentalism*. Westport, CT: Greenwood, 1996.

————. *Encyclopedia of Transcendentalism*. Westport, CT: Greenwood, 1996.

Newfield, Christopher. *The Emerson Effect: Individualism and Submission in America*. Chicago: University of Chicago Press, 1996.

Packer, Barbara. "Turning to Emerson." *Common Knowledge* 5 (1996): 51–60.

Von Frank, Albert J. "The Composition of *Nature*: Writing and the Self in the Launching of a Career" in *Biographies of Books: The Compositional Histories of Notable American Writings*. James Barbour and Tom Quirk, editors. Columbia: University of Missouri Press, 1996.

Addison, Elizabeth. "Obedience and Algebra: From Listening to Language in Emerson's Response to Mary Rotch." *ESQ: A Journal Of The American Renaissance* 42 (1996): 153–94.

Albrecht, James. "'The Sun Were Insipid, If the Universe Were Not Opaque': The Ethics of Action, Power, and Belief in Emerson, Nietzsche, and James." *ESQ: A Journal Of The American Renaissance* 43 (1997): 113–58.

Bauer, Ralph. "Against the European Grain: The Emerson-Nietzsche Connection in Europe, 1920–1990." *ESQ: A Journal Of The American Renaissance* 1997: 69–94.

Bosco, Ronald. "His Lectures Were Poetry, His Teaching the Music of the Spheres: Annie Adams Fields and Francis Greenwood Peabody on Emerson's 'Natural History of the Intellect.'" Harvard Library Bulletin n.s. 8 (1997): 1–79.

————. "The 'Somewhat Spheral and Infinite' in Every Man: Emerson's Theory of Biography" in *Emersonian Circles: Essays in Honor of Joel Myerson*. Wesley T. Mott and Robert E. Burkholder, editors. Rochester: University of Rochester Press, 1997: 67–104.

Brown, Lee Rust. *The Emerson Museum: Practical Romanticism and the Pursuit of the Whole*. Cambridge, MA: Harvard University Press, 1997.

Buell, Lawrence. "Emerson's Fate" in *Emersonian Circles: Essays in Honor of Joel Myerson*. Wesley T. Mott and Robert E. Burkholder, editors. Rochester: University of Rochester Press, 1997: 11–28.

Cadava, Eduardo. *Emerson and the Climates of History*. Stanford: Stanford University Press, 1997.

Carlson, Larry A. "Emerson, Friendship, and the Problem of Alcott's Psyche" in *Emersonian Circles: Essays in Honor of Joel Myerson*. Wesley T. Mott and Robert E. Burkholder, editors. Rochester: University of Rochester Press, 1997: 115–26.

Colacurcio, Michael J. *Doctrine and Difference: Essays in the Literature of New England*. New York: Routledge, 1997.

Cole, Phyllis. "'Men and Women Conversing': The Emersons in 1837" in *Emersonian Circles: Essays in Honor of Joel Myerson*. Wesley T. Mott and Robert E. Burkholder, editors. Rochester: University of Rochester Press, 1997: 127–59.

Collison, Gary. "Toward Democratic Vistas: Theodore Parker, Friendship, and Transcendentalism" in *Emersonian Circles: Essays in Honor of Joel Myerson*. Wesley T. Mott and Robert E. Burkholder, editors. Rochester: University of Rochester Press, 1997: 161–80.

Conant, James. "Emerson as Educator." *ESQ: A Journal Of The American Renaissance* 43 (1997): 181–206.

Deese, Helen. "'A Liberal Education': Caroline Healey Dall and Emerson" in *Emersonian Circles: Essays in Honor of Joel Myerson*. Wesley T. Mott and Robert E. Burkholder, editors. Rochester: University of Rochester Press, 1997: 237–60.

Engstrom, Sallee Fox. *The Infinitude of the Private Man: Emerson's Presence in Western New York, 1851–1861*. New York: Peter Lang, 1997.

Friedl, Herwig. "Fate, Power, and History in Emerson and Nietzsche." *ESQ: A Journal Of The American Renaissance* 43 (1997): 267–94.

Goodman, Russell. "Moral Perfectionism and Democracy: Emerson, Nietzsche, Cavell." *ESQ: A Journal Of The American Renaissance* 43 (1997): 159–80.

Gougeon, Len. "Emerson's Circle and the Crisis of the Civil War" in *Emersonian Circles: Essays in Honor of Joel Myerson*. Wesley T. Mott and Robert E. Burkholder, editors. Rochester: University of Rochester Press, 1997: 29–52.

Grey, Robin. *The Complicity of Imagination: The American Renaissance, Contests of Authority, and Seventeenth-Century English Culture*. New York: Cambridge University Press, 1997.

Gura, Philip F. "The Widening Gyre: Out from Emerson" in *Emersonian Circles: Essays in Honor of Joel Myerson*. Wesley T. Mott and Robert E. Burkholder, editors. Rochester: University of Rochester Press, 1997: 261–70.

Kronick, Joseph. "Repetition and Mimesis from Nietzsche to Emerson; or, How the World Became a Fable." *ESQ: A Journal Of The American Renaissance* 43 (1997): 241–66.

Lopez, Michael, editor. *Emerson/Nietzsche. ESQ: A Journal Of The American Renaissance* 43 (1997).

Lundquist, Kent P. "'Valdemar' and the 'Frogpondians': The Aftermath of Poe's Boston Lyceum Appearance" in *Emersonian Circles: Essays in Honor of Joel Myerson*. Wesley T. Mott and Robert E. Burkholder, editors. Rochester: University of Rochester Press, 1997: 181–206.

Mitchell, Charles. *Individualism and Its Discontents: Appropriations of Emerson, 1880–1950.* Amherst: University of Massachusetts Press, 1997.

Morris, Saundra. "The Threshold Poem, Emerson, and 'The Sphinx.'" *American Literature* 69 (1997): 547–70.

Mott, Wesley T. and Robert E. Burkholder, editors. *Emersonian Circles: Essays in Honor of Joel Myerson.* Rochester: University of Rochester Press, 1997.

Parkes, Graham. "'Floods of Life' around 'Granite of Fate': Emerson and Nietzsche as Thinkers of Nature." *ESQ: A Journal Of The American Renaissance* 43 (1997): 207–40.

Patterson, Anita Haya. *From Emerson to King: Democracy, Race,, and the Politics of Protest.* New York: Oxford University Press, 1997.

Richardson, Joan. "Emerson's Sound Effects." *Raritan* 16 (1997): 83–101.

Richardson, Robert D., Jr. "Emerson as Editor" in *Emersonian Circles: Essays in Honor of Joel Myerson.* Wesley T. Mott and Robert E. Burkholder, editors. Rochester: University of Rochester Press, 1997: 105–14.

———. "Liberal Platonism and Transcendentalism: Shaftesbury, Schleiermacher, Emerson." *Symbiosis* 1 (1997): 1–20.

Robinson, David. "Thoreau's 'Ktaadn' and the Quest for Experience" in *Emersonian Circles: Essays in Honor of Joel Myerson.* Wesley T. Mott and Robert E. Burkholder, editors. Rochester: University of Rochester Press, 1997: 261–70.

Rowe, John Carlos. *At Emerson's Tomb: The Politics of Classic American Literature.* New York: Columbia University Press, 1997.

Shealy, Daniel. "Singing Mignon's Song: The Friendship of Ralph Waldo Emerson and Louisa May Alcott" in *Emersonian Circles: Essays in Honor of Joel Myerson.* Wesley T. Mott and Robert E. Burkholder, editors. Rochester: University of Rochester Press, 1997: 225–36.

Stack, George. "Nietzsche and Emerson: The Return of the Repressed." *ESQ: A Journal Of The American Renaissance* 43 (1997): 37–68.

Van Cromphout, Gustaaf. "Areteic Ethics: Emerson and Nietzsche on Pity, Friendship, and Love." *ESQ: A Journal Of The American Renaissance* 43 (1997): 95–112.

Von Frank, Albert J. "'Build Therefore Your Own World': Emerson's Constructions of the 'Intimate Sphere'" in *Emersonian Circles: Essays in Honor of Joel Myerson.* Wesley T. Mott and Robert E. Burkholder, editors. Rochester: University of Rochester Press, 1997: 1–10.

Walls, Laura Dassow. "The Anatomy of Truth: Emerson's Poetic Science." *Configurations* 5: 3 (1997): 425–62.

Wilson, Eric. "From Metaphysical Poverty to Practical Power: Emerson's Embrace of the Physical World." *ESQ: A Journal of the American Renaissance* 43 (1997): 295–321.

Cole, Phyllis. *Mary Moody Emerson and the Origins of Transcendentalism.* New York: Oxford University Press, 1998.

Decker, William Merrill. *Epistolary Practices: Letter Writing in America before Telecommunications.* Chapel Hill: University of North Carolina Press, 1998.

Gougeon, Len. "Emerson and the Woman Question: The Evolution of His Thought." *New England Quarterly* 71 (1998): 570–92.

Malachuk, Daniel. "The Republican Philosophy of Emerson's Early Lectures." *New England Quarterly* 71 (1998): 404–28.

Mueller-Vollmer, Kurt. "Translating Transcendentalism in New England: The Genesis of a Literary Discourse" in *Translating Literatures, Translating Cultures: New Vistas and New Approaches in Literary Study.* Kurt Mueller-Vollmer and Michael Irmsher, editors. Stanford: Stanford University Press, 1998.

Von Frank, Albert. *The Trials of Anthony Burns: Freedom and Slavery in Emerson's Boston.* Cambridge, MA: Harvard University Press, 1998.

Cole, Phyllis. "Ralph Waldo Emerson in his Family" in *The Cambridge Companion to Ralph Waldo Emerson.* Joel Porte and Saundra Morris, editors. New York: Cambridge University Press, 1999: 30–48.

Ellison, Julie. "Tears for Emerson: *Essays, Second Series*" in *The Cambridge Companion to Ralph Waldo Emerson.* Joel Porte and Saundra Morris, editors. New York: Cambridge University Press, 1999: 140–62.

Lopez, Michael. "*The Conduct of Life*: Emerson's Anatomy of Power" in *The Cambridge Companion to Ralph Waldo Emerson.* Joel Porte and Saundra Morris, editors. New York: Cambridge University Press, 1999: 243–66.

Milder, Robert. "The Radical Emerson?" in *The Cambridge Companion to Ralph Waldo Emerson.* Joel Porte and Saundra Morris, editors. New York: Cambridge University Press, 1999: 49–75.

Morris, Saundra. "Metre-Making Arguments: Emerson's Poems" in *The Cambridge Companion to Ralph Waldo Emerson.* Joel Porte and Saundra Morris, editors. New York: Cambridge University Press, 1999: 218–42.

Porte, Joel. "Representing America — The Emerson Legacy" in *The Cambridge Companion to Ralph Waldo Emerson.* Joel Porte and Saundra Morris, editors. New York: Cambridge University Press, 1999: 1–12.

Porte, Joel and Saundra Morris, editors. *The Cambridge Companion to Ralph Waldo Emerson.* New York: Cambridge University Press, 1999.

Richardson, Robert D., Jr. "Emerson and Nature" in *The Cambridge Companion to Ralph Waldo Emerson*. Joel Porte and Saundra Morris, editors. New York: Cambridge University Press, 1999: 97–105.

Robinson, David. "Transcendentalism and Its Times" in *The Cambridge Companion to Ralph Waldo Emerson*. Joel Porte and Saundra Morris, editors. New York: Cambridge University Press, 1999: 13–29.

Steele, Jeffrey. "Transcendental Friendship: Emerson Fuller, Thoreau" in *The Cambridge Companion to Ralph Waldo Emerson*. Joel Porte and Saundra Morris, editors. New York: Cambridge University Press, 1999: 121–39.

Tufariello, Catherine. "'The Remembering Wine': Emerson's Influence on Whitman and Dickinson" in *The Cambridge Companion to Ralph Waldo Emerson*. Joel Porte and Saundra Morris, editors. New York: Cambridge University Press, 1999: 162–91.

Van Cromphout, Gustaaf. *Emerson's Ethics*. Columbia: University of Missouri Press, 1999.

Von Frank, Albert. *Essays: First Series* (1841) in *The Cambridge Companion to Ralph Waldo Emerson*. Joel Porte and Saundra Morris, editors. New York: Cambridge University Press, 1999: 106–21.

Weisbuch, Robert. "Post-Colonial Emerson and the Erasure of Europe" in *The Cambridge Companion to Ralph Waldo Emerson*. Joel Porte and Saundra Morris, editors. New York: Cambridge University Press, 1999: 192–217.

Wilson, Eric. *Emerson's Sublime Science*. New York: St. Martin's Press, 1999.

Wilson, R. Jackson. "Emerson as Lecturer: Man Thinking, Man Saying" in *The Cambridge Companion to Ralph Waldo Emerson*. Joel Porte and Saundra Morris, editors. New York: Cambridge University Press, 1999: 76–96.

Myerson, Joel, editor. *A Historical Guide to Ralph Waldo Emerson*. New York: Oxford University Press, 2000.

Garvey, T. Gregory, editor. *The Emerson Dilemma: Essays on Emerson and Social Reform*. Athens: University of Georgia Press, forthcoming, 2001.

Index